Snail Eggs
and Samphire

Snail Eggs and Samphire

Dispatches from the Food Front

DEREK COOPER

MACMILLAN

First published 2000 by Macmillan
an imprint of Macmillan Publishers Ltd
25 Eccleston Place, London SW1W 9NF
Basingstoke and Oxford
Associated companies throughout the world
www.macmillan.com

ISBN 0 333 78306 9

1 3 5 7 9 8 6 4 2

A CIP catalogue record for this book is available from
the British Library.

Typeset by SetSystems Ltd, Saffron Walden, Essex
Printed and bound in Great Britain by
Mackays of Chatham plc, Chatham, Kent

Contents

v

Contents

Contents

Contents

Contents

Contents

Introduction

Perhaps the title of this book needs some explanation. Snails have been eaten since ancient times; Shakespeare in *King Lear* wrote about the dread trade of those who gathered samphire from the sea cliffs. But what about the dispatches? That sprang from an entry in a US publication called *Contemporary Authors*. For a period I wrote a regular column for the *Observer* about wine. One fine summer day I was sitting at my writing table in the Isle of Skye gazing across the loch at the grape-blue peaks of the Cuillin hills when the phone rang. It was my son Nicholas.

'Enjoying your R&R?' he asked.

'R&R?'

'Rest and recreation,' he said, 'what the American troops in Vietnam used to go to Thailand for.' He then revealed that *Contemporary Authors* had me listed as the *Observer*'s food and *war* correspondent.

It became a family joke. From then on my articles were referred to as dispatches and from time to time the children would ask how the battle was going. I began to notice how the vocabulary of strife was beginning to dominate the food debate. Those who questioned the excessive use of chemicals and drugs in farming or the poor nutrition afforded by cheapened food were often referred to as the enemy.

Things reached a hysterical peak when a Tory MP summoned a platoon of food industry executives to the House of Commons for a battle briefing. They must marshal their forces, she said, and fight the left-wing activists and the food fascists. An equally militant line was taken by the Chairman of Food From Britain, a body set up to promote the interests of our food and drink producers. Speaking at a lunch organized by the Farmers Club he claimed that the enemies of our country were 'holding the floor by default'. Lapsing into military jargon he admonished his audience somewhat windily 'to occupy the high ground in the debate on food and the nation's health and attack the assailants whose self-seeking objectives capitalize on public ignorance and public concern'.

Those who drew attention to the high levels of saturated fats, sugar and salt in processed food or the dangers of feeding farm animals on contaminated protein were made to feel unpatriotic if not subversive. Food campaigners were likely to find themselves dismissed as the 'food police'. A wag dubbed them Marxist-Lentillists.

Those who use the metaphors of war when they talk about food are often more accurate than they would care to admit. A body like War on Want is in no doubt that it is engaged not in a skirmish but in a major battle against poverty and hunger. The richer countries, enforcing their historic rights to the raw materials of the Third World, have become increasingly belligerent. Trade wars which may seem bloodless are often only one step removed from full-scale economic aggression. As resources become scarcer conflict escalates. Food has become politicized; it is no longer possible to write about food without questioning the status quo and that could be construed as a political act. The Brazilian archbishop Dom Helder Camara phrased the dilemma eloquently: 'When I give food to the poor', he wrote, 'they call me a saint. When I ask why the poor have no food they call me a communist.'

So how did I get caught up in the food wars? It happened purely by chance. In the 1960s after ten years as a broadcaster in South East Asia I returned to London and began working for ITN as a producer. It was only a matter of months before it became clear that as a television producer I was a total failure. I began writing and presenting current affairs programmes for BBC Schools. I narrated the first series of *World in Action*, started working for *Tomorrow's World* and Radio 4's *Today* programme.

On 1 September 1965 I did a piece for *Today* on the British attitude to food and the effect it had on the tourist industry. The following week the *Listener* reprinted the talk under the headline 'the bad food guide'. On the 23 September Colin Franklin, a director of Routledge and Kegan Paul, wrote and asked me if I thought it would make a bestseller. I had no idea what made a bestseller, so I wrote back saying I was sure it would make a wonderful bestseller. *The Bad Food Guide* was published on 20 April 1967 and it did become a bestseller. In September that year I joined the *Guardian* as a food columnist. I wrote not about cooking – I'm pretty hopeless at that – but about the social aspect of food and its politics. I became a campaigner for good food and in the following years I wrote on a regular basis for newspapers and magazines as different from each other as the *Listener, World Medicine, Catering Times,* the *Observer* magazine, the Scottish *Sunday Standard, Scotland on Sunday* and *Saga Magazine.* In 1979 I began writing and presenting *The Food Programme* for BBC Radio 4 and in recent years I've worked with great pleasure on *Scotland's Larder* originally commissioned by Grampian TV.

My food journalism has been fuelled by curiosity, a delight in people and places and dismay at the injustices and inequalities which create poverty and hunger. In 1974 the United Nations held its first World Food Conference. There was good food to eat, lots of drink and even more rhetoric. 'Today', Henry Kissinger told the delegates, 'we must proclaim a bold objective that within a decade no child will go to bed hungry, that no family will fear for its next day's bread, and that no human being's future and capacities will be stunted by malnutrition.' Very little happened. Estimates of the number of chronically and severely malnourished people in the world today range from the FAO's 500 million to the World Bank's one billion. It has been estimated that every day 35,000 mothers see one of their children die from lack of food. You could say that the bold objective failed. I prefer to think that it has still to be achieved. These dispatches were written in a spirit of optimism not despair.

In 1953 I was lucky enough to marry a woman who came from an extended farming family in the East Riding. Janet Feaster turned out to be a natural cook and she brought the rich heritage of traditional Yorkshire food to our kitchen. Without her informed contribution this book would not have happened. She has given our children Penny and Nick and our grandchildren Alice and Iona an enlightened sense of the cultural role that the dining room plays in family life. She gave me the time and the inspiration to write.

The French have a word – *affineur* – for which there is no equivalent in English. It describes the way an enthusiast can improve a product. Janet has been my constant *affineuse* and my companion on many a food jaunt. This book is dedicated to her with my love and affection.

My special thanks go to Sam Boyce who found a publisher for this book and to George Morley, my editor at Macmillan, who spent a great deal of talented time knocking these essays into a logical shape.

Part One

∗

FRUITS OF THE EARTH

1. Quick-brek with UHT

Stormbound on the Hebridean island of Barra a few weeks ago, I wandered round the Castlebay shops seeing what the locals were likely to eat that day. When it came to vegetables it wasn't going to be much. The best display was a mound of onions, a handful of mould-ravaged carrots and two time-expired cabbages, limp after their hundred-mile lorry ride from the Glasgow market to Oban and the six-hour boat journey across the Minch.

Dr Bickle, who looks after the health of the 1,519 islanders, may well worry about the state of their nutrition. The shelves of the Co-op were packed with biscuits, sweets, cakes, pudding mixes and instant preparations, much of it the blatantly non-nutritious packets and sachets which the manufacturers inaccurately refer to in their offguard moments as 'fun' food.

All these expensive products have taken the place of a simpler and, many doctors would say, a healthier diet based on what the sea and the impoverished soil would yield. A hundred years ago, each family had a cow to provide fresh milk, butter, crowdie and cream. Potatoes would have come from seaweed-fertilized lazybeds, not from Cyprus. There would have been a high natural intake of fibre from oatcakes and porridge. There was herring in abundance.

A great part of this traditional diet has been replaced by expensive value-added convenience foods bristling with additives and beguiling TV-advertised offers. I met a party of visitors from Shrewsbury whose first meal on Barra had been Heinz spaghetti in tomato sauce, instant mashed potato, tinned peas and a foamy junk pudding sprayed with Dream Topping. The following morning there was UHT milk on the Quick-brek.

It was Dr Frank Fraser Darling who, in his *West Highland Survey* published in 1955, drew attention to the specious benefits conferred by improved communications on isolated communities. 'We can think of a sea loch in the north-west Highlands where there is a road on one side and a track on the other. Those on the road side served by vans are able to buy Glasgow bread and expensive packeted goods of all kinds. I have even seen tinned porridge. On the other side of the loch more cows are kept, the men fish more and the standard of husbandry is higher.'

If the sapping of self-reliance and self-sufficiency had been compensated by an improved and better-balanced diet, then hooray for roads and vans. But roll-on ferries and refrigerator trucks have brought only small quantities of fresh food. Quick profits lie not in perishables but in over-refined raw materials processed into an easy-to-eat, easy-to-serve snack – something bland to fork down while watching *Coronation Street*.

Paradoxically, although hundreds of new products are launched every year, they don't present a widening of choice. One packet of soup is very much like another; whatever the label, bread made by the Chorleywood process has the same taste of flannelized felt.

In 1883, when the Royal Horticultural Society held an exhibition at Chiswick, they were able to put 1,500 varieties of apple on display. This month the RHS held a centenary exhibition and showed a mere 200 apples. Although they have 670 different varieties in their Wisley orchards, the choice in supermarkets doesn't reflect this potential abundance. Centralized bulk-buying dictates a consistent, uniform apple which will travel well, have a long shelf-life and look good.

The Apple and Pear Development Council only advertise four apples these days; the government only gives grants to farmers if they plant one of three approved varieties. Any colour, said Henry Ford, as long as it's black. Any apple, says the Ministry of Food, as long as it's Cox, Spartan or Bramley.

When it comes to expensive air-freighted exotica, there's

never been so much variety. Strawberries and asparagus all the year round; passion fruit, rambutan and mango if you want them. But what about simple things – like apples, pears or carrots?

Do not despair. I foresee a satisfying role in the future for the small independent farmer interested in quality, not quantity. Those fed up with the ubiquitous Golden Delicious might well be happy to drive out into the country to pick up a few pounds of Allington Pippin, Lord Derby or Tydeman's Early. Varieties rendered commercially unsound by the bulk-buying demands of the supermarkets might – who knows? – command a premium price in time to come. It happened with beer; why not with food?

2. A Vintage Year for Painting in Oils

Even in January you can understand why Renoir, Matisse, Bonnard and Cézanne went south to Provence to paint. The light is special and the landscapes dramatic. In high summer the fields are purple with lavender and yellow with sunflowers; the air is aromatic with the scent of wild thyme, marjoram and rosemary. In the small hilltop villages market stalls are piled with the perfumed melons of Cavaillon, giant unshapely tomatoes, artichokes, figs, peaches and apricots.

But at this time of the year it is the olive groves which command the eye. Aldous Huxley called the olive the painter's tree; ubiquitous but almost impossible to capture on canvas. For Van Gogh cypresses and almond blossom could be dashed off at a canter but not the shimmering apparition of an olive tree with a breeze playing in its branches. 'I struggle to capture this,' he wrote, 'it is silver, a while ago more blue, on the whole green, whitish bronze, against the yellow, rose, purplish-blue, orange ochre-red earth.'

Gnarled rows of olives, fields of wheat, and old stone farmhouses conjure up the soft-focus films based on the novels of Marcel Pagnol. *Jean de Florette* and *Manon des Sources* filled the cinemas; Peter Mayle's whimsical stories of the Provençal peasantry are breaking paperback records. The Beautiful People who in the 1950s invaded fishing villages from St Tropez to Cannes are now renovating chateaux around the Fuji-like peak of Mont Ventoux. Inland Provence has become expensive and immensely chic.

But it's still rural and it still produces some of the most

superb olive oil in the Mediterranean. Olive trees were planted in southern France more than 3,000 years ago and their fruit, in the words of Lawrence Durrell, yields 'a taste older than meat, older than wine. A taste as old as cold water.'

The olive is an integral part of the culinary culture of Provence. It provides green and black fruits for the table; olives for stuffing into artichokes and pounding into a paste with herbs and capers to make the salty tapenade, and for finishing off soups and stews. But above all in the form of oil for making *aioli* (the garlic version of mayonnaise), vinaigrettes and for frying, marinading and trickling over everything from grilled fish to lamb chops.

I was in Provence recently for the harvesting of the new season's olives. Picking will go on until the end of next month; already old men are prophesying that the 1991–92 vintage will be the best of the century.

There are 500 million olive trees planted in EC countries and they are almost all picked by hand. I was shown a prototype mechanical picker at a farm called Mas de la Dame which is supposed to grab the trunk of the tree and shake it like a dog with a rabbit so that the olives fall into a net on the ground. All the machine succeeded in doing was break a big branch. 'Back to the drawing board,' shouted a wag in French.

In the Provence area, it is north Africans who do the picking, combing the branches with flails like back scratchers. In a good year such as this one each tree will produce up to fifty kilos of olives. They are green when unripe and then mature through the colours of rose and red to a dark brown or damson black when fully ripe. I'm told it takes twenty years before a tree reaches its full maturity and then it can go on bearing fruit through the centuries.

Like vines, olives have good and bad years. The sun, the climate and soil, the way in which the groves are husbanded, all determine what the winter crop will be like. Where fine wines need years to mature fully, olive oil should be used as soon as possible.

French production is minute compared with the output of Spain, Italy and Greece – those three countries produce 1.5 million tonnes compared with the annual 2,000 tonnes of France.

Experts claim that the finest oil of all is produced in Maussane, which lies at the foot of Les Alpilles, a limestone range carved into tortured crags by the razor-sharp *mistral* as it funnels down the Rhone valley. Here in La Vallée des Baux they press the fragrant oils which are then sold in shops such as Fauchon in Paris and used by chefs Roger Vergé, Joel Robuchon, Michel Guérard and the Frères Troisgros.

The mill dates from the beginning of the seventeeth century. It's powered by electricity now but the way in which the oil is squeezed from the olives hasn't changed at all in the last 400 years. Crushed by giant millstones, the olives are reduced to a paste, spread on mats which are piled one on top of the other like pancakes and put in a hydraulic press which slowly compresses them while the dark green oil drips down to a collecting tank.

The first pressing retaining all the natural flavours is the best – five kilos of olives make one perfect litre of oil as thick and green as motor oil. This is the equivalent of a first growth claret, almost handmade and, understandably, fairly expensive.

The following day I went to the medieval town of Nyons, which lies at the foot of the Alps on the river Aigues. Nyons is to olives what the Médoc is to grapes or Arbroath to smokies. It was in Nyons that they invented the brotherhood of the Chevaliers de l'Olivier to promote the olive and all its goodness, and it was the growers of Nyons who, in 1968, became the first in France to receive an Appellation d'Origine for their oil.

Christian Teulade, who runs the co-operative which processes the fruit brought in from 450 farms in the surrounding countryside, told me that the *appellation* was awarded largely because of Nyons' ideal micro-climate. 'There are sixty-one communes entitled to the *appellation*. When they came the

Commissioners looked at our soil, the hours of sunshine, all these things and it was only then that we received the classification. It is unique – there are only two other *appellations* and they are in Spain.'

There are scores of different varieties of olives grown in the Mediterranean countries. They have names such as *cellina, barese, frantoio, blanqueta, cuquillo, coroneiki, picholine, grossane*, and *salenenque*.

At Nyons the main species is *La Tanche*, of which 70 per cent is converted into oil, the rest is prepared for the table and kitchen. Nyons is the biggest producer of virgin oil in France.

Recently the civil servants in Brussels, with their enthusiasm for standardization, have been trying to lay down a code of practice to regulate the industry. It's not going to be easy; olive groves cover six million hectares and it's reckoned that about a million families depend on olives for all or part of their income.

What the new regulations will not necessarily tell you is where the oil in the bottle originates. Greece, for instance, exports 90 per cent of its oil to Italy, where it's used for blending. So an Italian oil may say 'produce of Italy' or 'bottled in Lucca' but it could well contain a high proportion of oils from other countries.

Connoisseurs go for unfiltered, estate-bottled oils from small farms or co-operatives where the owners might be expected to take more pride in their produce than some giant company producing refined oil for the mass market. The best Provençal oils are sweet, smooth, rounded, strong and distinctive in flavour. Italian oils are delicate with a good fruity flavour and very often a peppery finish. Spanish oils vary from region to region – they can be sweet and mild while Greek oils are perhaps the 'fattest' of all.

At Nyons I tasted six different oils of different vintages and from different areas. There was a notable range of flavours considering they were all from Provence. I used to think that the greener an oil was the better it would taste. Untrue. The green is chlorophyll and has little effect on the bouquet or flavour, which is why the professionals taste from blue glass bowls so the colour is masked and won't influence their judgement.

What tasters are marking is the sweetness, sourness, saltiness and fruitiness of an oil. In recent years the EC has been standardizing techniques of tasting in an effort to achieve some kind of uniformity. Judy Ridgway, who is working on what will be the definitive book on the olive industry, tells me that recently the same oil was tasted by two different panels, one in Italy and one in Spain. Their assessment differed by only a decimal point.

Thirty years ago in Britain you only found olive oil in the kitchens of Spanish and Italian restaurants. This year we will spend £16 million on olive oil. Its image as a healthy food high in monounsaturated fats which can reduce cholesterol and inhibit coronary heart disease has a lot to do with its growing sales.

The theory is that a diet rich in monounsaturated fats helps reduce the presence of low density lipo-proteins which encourage cholesterol to fur up your arteries, and at the same time maintains the presence of high density lipo-proteins which are thought to reduce cholesterol levels in the blood.

It has been observed that people living in the olive-growing areas of the Mediterranean have some of the lowest rates of cardiovascular disease in the world – whether that's to do with their low consumption of dairy fats and high consumption of olive oil is open to debate.

What is not open to debate is the versatility of olive oil in the kitchen. If you remain unconverted to its joys can I suggest you try this simple snack? It takes only a few moments to prepare and it appears in different guises all over the Mediterranean – it's as common there as bread and butter is here.

It's found in its most elemental form in Italy where it's known as *bruschetta* or *fett'unta*. Take a few slices of baker's good crusty white bread and grill them on both sides until they are crisp and golden brown. Then rub the toast with a generous-sized clove of garlic until it vanishes into the bread. Dribble thick virgin oil over it and sprinkle salt and pepper on top and eat it hot.

When you've tasted that you'll realize why the kings and queens of Europe had themselves anointed with olive oil at their coronations and blessed with it as they lay on their death beds. And if that doesn't convince you, turn to Exodus Chapter 30, verse 24.

3. A Decadent Fragrance

Of all my gastronomic memories, none was more unexpected, bizarre and successful than a visit to a wood of beech trees in East Lothian. It was a wet and miserable morning in November. The rain was relentless as we drove down the A1 from Edinburgh. I had a rendezvous at 11 with an amateur mycologist called Peter Christopher who has a gift for divining the most expensive fungus in the world.

When I met him Peter was armed only with a basket, a soft-tined garden rake and a ten-inch meat skewer. Strangely mundane instruments, I thought, with which to hunt for what the famous French connoisseur of good hot dinners, Anthelme Brillat-Savarin, described as 'the diamond of cookery'.

It was the truffle we were seeking, that little globule of black gold which Alexandre Dumas had apostrophized as 'the ambrosia of the gods, the *sacrum sacrorum* of gastronomies'. It is the heady scent, the decadent fragrance of the truffle that commends itself to cooks. Where money is no object, truffles are poached in Champagne and devoured whole, but they reach their apotheosis embedded in *foie gras*.

'I'd rather,' said Peter, 'you didn't tell anyone where you've been today. Truffle-hunting leaves salmon-poaching standing as a money-spinner and if people got to know where truffles could be found they'd just be out with spades ruining the whole ecology of a place like this.'

By now we had entered a big stand of beeches which Peter reckoned might well have been there for centuries. Interspersed among the giant trees were smaller clumps of beeches which he was eyeing expectantly. A graduate in botany from Dundee

University, he explained the symbiosis which yokes the tuber to its host tree.

The botany of the truffle is so complicated that the ancients couldn't make head nor tail of it. Pliny thought them wondrous, so magical that they combusted into living without a root; Plutarch believed that they sprang into being when lightning struck the ground.

The truth is to my mind even stranger. The truffle plants, which grow entirely underground, throw out a tangled web of filaments which interact with the roots of trees, especially the beech and the oak, in what botanists call a mycorrhizal partnership. The filaments enable the tree to extract the minerals it needs from the soil and the truffle grows strong on the nourishment it draws from the tree roots.

Of the three main species of truffle, the one we find in Britain, *tuber aestivum*, the summer truffle, is not the tastiest. To find the finest truffles you need to go to France and in particular Périgord, where the *tuber melanosporum* is traditionally detected by pigs and dogs. 'The aroma', Peter tells me, 'is not dissimilar to the male pheronome and sows get quite excited when they find one. It's sometimes quite tricky to separate them from a truffle. All sorts of animals go for them. In this wood they'll be taken by deer and voles so maybe we won't find any.'

The tell-tale signs of the truffle are often the disturbed bits of ground where an animal has had a stroke of luck, but you need to be on limestone soil. Where the truffle grows nothing else will, so if you see a barren patch round the trunk of a tree, that may be a likely place to start searching.

What we were looking for was a dark globose object, perhaps the size of a golf ball, sometimes bigger, covered with warts. The British truffle is neither black like the French one nor white like the Italian *tuber magnatum*. Its interior is a marbled grey-brown the colour of wholemeal flour.

Peter homes in on a likely patch of ground. 'These seven or eight young trees are promising. If you see a protruberance it may be a truffle or it may be a bulb; you don't know until you dig down.' 'Down' is not very far, as the tubers lie about three or four inches below the surface. For about half an hour the search is fruitless. Peter clears the ground of leaves with his rake and then painstakingly explores with his skewer. 'After a time you know exactly when you've hit on a truffle. It's spongy, quite resistant and – I think I've got one!'

And he had – a beauty the size of a pullet's egg. It had the unmistakable truffle smell: meaty, sweet, sexual, nutty, slightly depraved, heavily scented, corrupt – no vocabulary is satisfactory to suggest the intimacies of a really ripe truffle. In his *Memorials of Gourmandising*, Thackeray captured the anticipation that attends the entry of a really fine specimen: 'Presently we were aware of an odour gradually coming towards us, something musky, fiery, savoury, mysterious – a hot, drowsy smell, that lulls the senses and yet enflames them – the truffles were coming.'

On the day that Peter found this truffle, the French variety were selling in a London food hall for £16 per ounce! Fortunately you don't need more than a slice or two to perfume a dish. Later David Wilson of the Peat Inn showed how a minute amount of truffle can lift a dish to unexpected heights. When it's food for free that's all very well, but at £260 a pound it has to remain the ambrosia of the gods.

My advice if you want to enjoy the *tuber aestivum* is to equip yourself with a skewer, seek out a likely wood and start probing. The best time is late summer to early autumn.

4. A Bird in the Boot . . .

Have you noticed when out in the country how game birds assume noticeably different postures depending on what time of the year it is? During the open season you hardly ever see them; presumably they're skulking in copses, one ear cocked for the distant sound of sporting rifles. When the guns are put away they strut about fearlessly and rashly in the open. Last year I drove in the month of June, when it's illegal to shoot grouse, over the high moors on my way from Alford to Ballater. If I saw one bird I must have seen fifty, pecking away at the young heather bells and no doubt fully aware that they had until 11 August to fatten themselves in safety.

In April this year I was in the Borders and here again the birds were conspicuous at every turn winging lazily over hedges and standing carelessly by the roadside, particularly the cock pheasants resplendent in their metallic green and coppery plumage.

It is forbidden to shoot pheasants from February until the end of September but accidents can happen. Driving up a lonely track on my way to meet a local food historian I unforgivably despatched a foolish pheasant which hurled itself suicidally against the bumper of my car.

What to do? Death it seemed had been merciful and instantaneous. Should I carry it to the side of the lane and cover it respectfully with leaves or should I perhaps place it reverently in the boot of my hired car? I decided that the poor bird should not ever be said to have died in vain. That night the staff at the welcoming and comfortable Dolphinton House Hotel kindly plucked and drew it for me and I flew back with the carefully trussed corpse to London.

On the way from the airport the highly knowledgeable cab driver listened to this tale of pheasantry with interest and then he told me that I had actually broken the law. 'It's not illegal to kill a bird accidentally as you did,' he said, 'but it is an offence to *take* it.' Putting it into the car made me liable to prosecution, he said.

Now, if that's true I never knew it. Plea: not guilty through abysmal ignorance of the Game Laws, m'lord. Even as you read this I expect phones are ringing in the Procurator Fiscal's office in Peebles. Writs of attachment are being scrivened to bring me in chains before the Sheriff Clerk.

If so I shall ask for a previous and no doubt equally heinous offence to be taken into consideration. It, too, occurred in Scotland one November morning as I was speeding from Aviemore to lunch with George Grant and his son John at their Glenfarclas distillery. At the wheel was my old friend Michael Fraser, editor, at the time, of a monthly journal to do with stalking, fishing and shooting. As we belted down the road towards Ballindalloch where Glenfarclas has stood since 1836 our thoughts were on lunch and the welcoming dram that was no doubt already being prepared by the hospitable Grants.

The distillery sits at the foot of Ben Rinnes from whose springs it draws the crystal clear ice-cold water which makes one of the finest of all the Spey malts; a smoky, sherried whisky full of complex and gently unwreathing flavours.

Anyway, we were not more than a few miles from our destination when ahead in the middle of the road I sighted the recumbent body of a fine cock pheasant arranged as in death. Before we knew it we had passed over the defunct bird, fortunately not even disarranging its feathers.

Stop, I cried and Michael, who had not noticed this trophy, pulled the car to the side of the road. When we walked back we found the pheasant was still alive having no doubt been concussed by a car that had just passed that way. I suggested that as the editor of a sporting magazine Michael should put the bird out of its misery. That was not his scene, he said.

Although in the editorial chair, he was not personally a practising shootist. So I wrung the neck of this golden bird with compassion and put it in the boot of the car. Three days later, roasted and served with game chips, forcemeat balls, slices of bacon, bread sauce and a thick gravy compounded from the innards, it ate very well indeed.

That's twice I've infringed the ancient laws which surround the taking of game. In Victorian times I would no doubt have been considered a suitable candidate for transportation – that horrendous punishment for the taking of game illicitly only ended in 1868 when the last remaining penal colony in Western Australia received its last convicted poacher.

If I talk of pheasants, when they are so out of season (June after all is for asparagus, salmon and strawberries) it is only to remind you of autumn joys to come. Pheasants have been remarkably cheap in recent years and will no doubt be so this winter – they are always in plentiful supply and their relative lack of appeal keeps the price down.

They can be roasted and eaten hot and later cold; they can be braised, put into a game pie, turned into a luscious soup, pot-roasted, devilled, sautéed, prepared with apples, calvados and cream, grilled and even boiled.

But they must not be put in the boot of your car if you happen to see one lying around. They should be celebrated as Alexander Pope did and mourned in the moment of their death:

> See! from the brake the whirring pheasant springs,
> And mounts exulting on triumphant wings.
> Short is his joy: he feels the fiery wound,
> Flutters in blood, and panting beats the ground.
> Ah! what avails his glossy, varying dyes,
> His purple crest and scarlet-circled eyes,
> The vivid green his shining plumes unfold,
> His painted wings, and breast that flames with gold?

5. Watercress and Weeds

Bishop's Sutton in Hampshire lies in the heart of watercress country. A friend who lives there has, over the years, made a collection of watercress recipes. Being a gifted amateur cook she has created a repertoire of soups, sauces, bakery, mousses, salads and stuffing based on the peppery leaves of watercress.

A steam railway runs through the countryside; the Watercress Line, as it's known, is popular, particularly in the summer. It reminds us that in the days when almost everything went by train, a daily cargo of fresh-picked watercress went from Alton to London every afternoon. In those days you could get a big bunch of cress for a penny. Now we're into polythene bags of 'mixed leaves' and watercress isn't easy to come by. Which is a pity because cress is an excellent source of vitamin C and beta-carotene. Dr Nicholas Culpepper in his *Compleat Herbal* first drew attention to the health-giving properties of watercress in 1653. 'Water-cress pottage', he wrote, 'is a good remedy to cleanse the blood in the spring and help headaches and consume the gross humours winter has left behind; those that would live in health may use it if they please, if they will not, I cannot help it.'

Almost 200 years later that inspired observer of the labouring classes Henry Mayhew described how: 'the first coster-cry heard of a morning in the London streets is that of "Fresh wo-orter cresses"!' At the main entrance to Farringdon market, the watercress sellers used to assemble with their hampers packed with bright green cresses. In those days the poor rose before dawn: 'Even by the time the cress market is over, it is yet so early that the maids are beating the mats in the road and mechanics with their tool baskets slung over their shoulders are still hurrying to their work.'

It may be my imagination but in the days before the Second World War we seemed to eat more watercress than we do now. I remember going to the Regent Park Zoo and having afternoon tea. Just inside the door of the café was a blackboard with the specialities of the day chalked in a big confident hand. At the bottom it said: Watercress Ad Lib. What was that, I asked my father? 'It means you can eat as much as you like.' Although watercress is now grown all the year we only eat a mere 4½ ounces a year in the UK. What's surprising about that figure is that watercress can be eaten stalks and all, so there's no waste.

Country folk believed that watercress cured hiccups, headaches and migraine. It was considered to be a great help in easing the discomfort of rheumatism and there is recent research which suggests that along with other cruciferous vegetables like Brussels sprouts, broccoli, cabbage and cauliflower it may help to reduce the risk of cancer.

With spring coming up over the horizon, is anyone thinking of pale green nettle tops as a source of health and pleasure? Cooked like spinach they lose their sting and are highly regarded by herbalists. Nettles have been a part of the country culinary heritage for centuries in Europe. Combined with sorrel and watercress they make a stunning soup.

And while we're on the subject of forgotten foods, how many families in the north of England will be making dock pudding this spring? Docks which grow in the same ground that suits the nettle were reputed to flush the system after a long winter of stodgy foods and a special day was set aside for their collection. And how about the diuretic dandelion which the French call *pissenlit*. When did you last eat those slightly bitter leaves?

Country enthusiasts are still making dandelion wine but, like many another wild plant they lack commercial value. When the Industrial Revolution divorced us from the countryside it did more than tear up our roots. Within a few generations we had lost our traditional dependence on wild foods. We diminished docks and dandelions to the status of weeds and did ourselves a great disfavour.

6. The Stinking Rose

I spent some of the summer on the trail of good fresh food all over Britain. My journey took me to Scotland and Wales but I began just about as far south as you can get at Langbridge Farm near Newchurch on the Isle of Wight, where Colin Boswell grows a pungent crop of garlic.

I don't know about you but I didn't hear about garlic when I was young. It wasn't the sort of thing you saw in the greengrocer's. The funny thing about garlic is that although it grows wild in Britain and has been used for hundreds of years as a rural remedy, until recently it just wasn't considered socially acceptable.

The Elizabethans used it lavishly in cooking but it died a culinary death in polite society towards the end of the eighteenth century. The thing about this egregious member of the onion family is that it does leave more than a trace of its presence on the breath. It wasn't christened 'the stinking rose' for nothing!

Then, suddenly, the package tour was invented and we discovered the delights of garlic in Spain, Italy and the south of France. Today you can buy garlic in the remotest village shop. We stuff it into chicken, press it on salad leaves, chop it into stews. Recent medical research seems to confirm that it's good for the heart and the blood pressure, so sales are buoyant.

Colin grows about a hundred tons of *ail rosé*, that's the pink garlic, every year, and he imports another thousand tons for selling on to supermarkets and processing into garlic purée. What he has proved dramatically, as the English wine growers also have, is that if you can find the right microclimate you can grow almost anything in England despite the unpredictable weather.

When I went in July to the pea fields of East Anglia they were hoping for a bit more rain. It had been a dry summer and peas thrive on moisture. The size of the harvest in those parts is prodigious. Birdseye alone pick enough peas to fill 144 Olympic-sized swimming pools. The pods are gathered into a harvester at the front end and peas come out of the back – within a few hours they have been blanched and blast-frozen. That means when you open them in your kitchen they are probably much fresher than fresh peas.

But I have reservations. The pea they grow in the fields is a hybrid developed for mechanical harvesting. It looks beautifully green, it's soft and tender, but does it taste of much? Another thing, when I was young we looked forward to the summer peas. The season only lasted six weeks and a plate of peas and new potatoes was a treat. Now we can have them all the year round the pleasure of expectation is missing.

I feel the same way with raspberries – they are something to look forward to, not a fruit to keep in the deep freezer. The best raspberries of all, I believe, are grown in the Carse of Gowrie; the sandy soil is good to them and the long days give them plenty of time to ripen. I went towards the end of July to Flocklones Farm to watch raspberries being picked for the supermarkets. Because shelf-life is important the berries are picked before they are ripe. Grower Andrew Bain who with his wife Anne runs Flocklones agreed that raspberries are at their best when picked perfectly ripe so if you want them that way I suppose you either have to grow them yourself or go to a Pick-Your-Own farm.

Three years ago the Scottish raspberry industry was almost on the verge of collapse. Prices had dropped from £650 a ton to £400 – less than the cost of production. Then the growers, realizing that unless they did something about cheap imports from Eastern Europe they would be put out of business, formed themselves into a co-operative. The EC gave them support and today the 150 growers have set up their own processing plant and do their own negotiating with the jam-makers. The raspberry fields of Scotland have been saved!

Belatedly we are beginning to realize that there is a lot worth preserving in the British countryside. Importing massive quantities of food from abroad may seem like a smart thing to do but it puts our own agriculture at risk.

★

The market-driven youngsters who buy food for the super-markets are interested mainly in low prices. If a truck-load of asparagus can be bought more cheaply in Spain than in Norfolk then it's to Spain they turn. If apples are cheaper in Belgium than in Kent then the Belgian apple growers get the order.

I wonder if these young buyers realize that if they continue to source their salads, tomatoes, strawberries, carrots and cher-ries from abroad it's only a matter of time before market gardeners and growers in this country will be driven out of business. There were plenty of cherries in the supermarkets this summer but how many of those were English? Hardly any. The protection of our native horticulture seems to have been largely abandoned.

But all is not lost. There are still scores of enthusiastic men and women all over the country producing good fresh food, not to make a fortune but to satisfy an inner quest for perfection. I went in June to Wales to meet a couple who care deeply about the integrity and quality of their dairy produce.

Rachel and Gareth Rowlands run an organic farm a few miles from the coast near Aberystwyth. Besides their famous yoghurt they make modest amounts of unpasteurized cream and butter from the milk of eighty-five brown and white Guernsey cows which graze on pastures unpolluted by chemicals.

Rachel showed me her old-fashioned stone-walled dairy and the wooden churn in which she makes her butter. Rich and creamy, it has a wonderful flavour you just don't find in mass-produced butter. Mind you, it isn't cheap; hand-made in small quantities it commands a premium price. But it is well worth the extra pennies.

When you meet food producers who refuse to compromise it restores your faith in our culinary heritage. It reminds you that there's still a healthy living food culture in Britain not obsessed with shelf-life, profit margins, packaging and commercial hype. When that food is produced with concern for the environment, sound husbandry and a respect for animal life then the pleasure of eating it is boundless.

7. *An Inspired Marriage*

I took part the other day in a discussion that didn't really get anywhere in which we were invited to nominate the All-Time Great Dishes of the World. Soups, stews, roasts, pâtés, puddings and pies all came in for appraisal. It wasn't until later that I kicked myself for not proposing bacon and eggs which in terms of aroma, taste and flavour is a meal that has few rivals. Sadly there is no historical record of the genius who first put a few sizzling rashers on the same plate as a couple of fried eggs. The earliest mention I can find in any of my books is a recipe first printed in 1615 for a prototype collation of meat and eggs which may well have been the inspiration for what came later.

The bringing together of eggs and bacon was an inspired moment in gastronomic lore; far more significant, may I suggest, than the marriage of steak and kidney, sausage and mash or even fish and chips. In its fundamental simplicity and its ease of preparation, bacon and eggs remains the pre-eminent dish of these islands and one that has conquered the world from Australia and New Zealand to the States, where they do strange things like dishing it up with waffles and maple syrup.

The apotheosis of eggs and bacon came in the Railway Age when the dining car breakfast, a banquet on wheels, became a national ritual. Crisp rashers, fried bread, eggs ('one or two sir?') tomatoes, sausages and sauté potatoes set you up for the rest of the day. Ironically, the bacon that British Rail rests its reputation on is imported unpatriotically from abroad – best Dutch back rashers, smoked and specially packed for BR.

When, immediately after the war, I made my first visit to Ireland I found that the dish which I had assumed to be an invention of the mainland had assumed an all-day ascendancy in the Emerald Isle. Wherever we went from sunrise to sunset we were offered only two choices. 'What will it be then?' the little waitresses in their black dresses asked, 'meat and salad or rashers and eggs?' We had come from a frugal land where eggs were rationed to one a week and bacon was a luxury. Fuelled by unlimited rashers and often three eggs on the same plate we freewheeled from Cork to Killarney and on to Limerick and Leenane feeling well fed for the first time in years.

In my childhood traditional Irish, Welsh and Scottish bacon all had their distinctive flavours. Some claim that the finest bacon of all comes from Wiltshire where juniper berries, black treacle and beer were added to the salt brine to create a mild and delicious texture. I still think that bacon from Ayrshire pigs fed on potatoes and milk was unmatchable. The pork was boned and rubbed with salt, saltpetre and moist brown sugar, left to pickle for a month and then rolled up tightly, tied with string and hung up to dry. Ayrshire roll is still to be had in Scotland if you search it out.

It is the smell of frying bacon, pervading a kitchen on a summer morning, the audible spluttering of the eggs as they are dropped into the hot fat, that sets the saliva running in a way few other dishes achieve. Sadly, these days the eggs may come from batteries and the bacon, impregnated mechanically with polyphosphates, is often slimy when you slit open the vacuum pack and will go on to give off excessive amounts of water in the pan.

Oh, for the taste of the past. When did you last see a capable grocer boning out a side of bacon and lifting the meat on to the slicer ready to be cut to the width of your choice? These were men knowledgeable about the virtues of different styles of bacon and ham and they always had on offer smoked bacon with its brown rind and the 'green' unsmoked pale bacon with its less assertive taste. They could talk to you about forehock, top streaky, prime streaky, thin streaky, flank, gammon slipper, gammon hock, corner gammon, long and short back, oyster, top back and prime collar. Bacon is far too interesting a commodity to be packed anonymously in polythene pouches. Bring back the slicer!

Bacon and egg has been a victim of the current passion for a healthy start to the day. Displaced by muesli, oak flakes, bran and prunes it didn't stand a chance. All that fat and all that cholesterol. Bacon curers have been fighting back with leaner cuts but as we connoisseurs know it is the crisp, curling fat that imparts the flavour.

We grill our bacon these days as a desperate compromise and often scramble the egg so that it will not be tainted by the dreaded dripping but it's not the same. Nothing, I reassure myself, that tastes as glorious as a plate of bacon and eggs can be bad for you. Too much bacon and eggs yes – but in moderation what a continuing joy. And yes, I will have some fried bread, mushrooms and a sausage and a strong pot of tea, if it's going.

8. Glorious Spuds,
Warts and All

In terms of versatility in the kitchen, taste, flavour and general delight, the potato is our outstanding vegetable and yet we seem to know very little about it. How many of us know which are the best tatties for boiling, which for roasting, baking, frying or mashing? It makes a great difference. None of us would dream of going into a shop and asking for 'fish', we're specific about choosing our cod, haddock, plaice, skate or lemon sole. So why are we content just to pick up a bag of potatoes not knowing half the time what they are, what they're called or where they've come from?

Fortunately for our culinary heritage there have been some remarkable friends of the potato who have waged a battle to preserve it in all its splendour and glory. None was more influential than the late Donald MacLean who on his family farm at Crieff grew 370 different potatoes, the largest private collection in the world. Some were so rare and special that he despatched them for on-growing not by the kilo but by the single tuber. His annual list of those he was prepared to sell was eagerly awaited by gardeners all over the country and his death in 1988 was a great loss to the cause of this historic and irreplaceable plant.

Many years ago I suggested that we ought to have some kind of society for the preservation of the potato; a pressure group that would make it commercially worthwhile for farmers to grow a wider range of potatoes. Nothing wrong with the popular maincrop King Edward but why couldn't we put our hands on some of the equally tasty varieties which were no longer being planted?

Another enthusiast who has campaigned most effectively for the survival of the potato in all its diversity is Lawrence Hills of the Henry Doubleday Research Association. His first success was in the 1970s when he was instrumental in having a ban lifted on the cultivation of potatoes which were susceptible to wart disease, a fungus which first appeared in Cheshire in 1902. The Wart Disease Order of 1973 made it illegal to grow a whole range of potatoes including King Edward, Duke of York, Epicure, Arran Chief and Royal Kidney because they were susceptible to the fungus. Lawrence marshalled public resistance against this dotty order and the regulations were quietly dropped. So, thanks to him, if you want to plant Eclipse, Epicure or British Queen in your garden or allotment you can still go out and buy the seed potatoes.

There have been other setbacks. One of them is a confusing piece of legislation called the Seeds (National Lists of Varieties) Act which became law of the land in 1973. Without going into complicated bureaucratic details it means that every country in the EC now has a National List of vegetable seeds (and this includes seed potatoes). If a plant is not on that list and a seedsman puts it in his catalogue or attempts to sell it he can be fined up to £1,000.

When the Lists were compiled many old strains were dropped. To reinstate a seed on the List is expensive. First you have to prove that it is unique, uniform and stable and then pay to keep it there. The only advantage in having a seed on the List is that you can claim royalties on sales. As Lawrence Hills points out the money involved is an enormous sum to pay for the right to produce seed of a fine old potato if you're only going to sell it in small quantities to a handful of amateur gardeners.

Although there are 4,000 different clones at the International Potato Centre in Peru fewer than thirty are commercially grown in Britain and half of those, high in yield but not necessarily in flavour, go exclusively for processing. So if you're lucky you might find fifteen varieties in the average green-grocer's in the course of a year.

Recently the supermarkets have been vying with each other to present a wider range of British-grown potatoes in their flagship superstores. This year, at various times, Safeway for instance, will have twenty-two different potatoes on sale, some of which have been difficult in the past to grow commercially.

Potatoes which have impressed me at two recent cook-ins have been:

Kerr's Pink bred by a Banff farmer in 1907. A cross between Fortyfold and Smith's Early; round, pink with dry floury creamy flesh, it is ideal for baking and for frying. Has a tendency to discolour and disintegrate if boiled.

Catriona produced in 1920. A long oval, purple tuber with white, floury flesh it has a buttery taste. Ideal for chipping and roasting.

Pink Fir Apple dates from the 1850s, has a yellow, waxy flesh which remains firm when diced, making it ideal for salads. A delicious, sweet spud, it has a pink knobbly skin that turns brown when cooked. Also excellent for boiling and sautéeing.

Cara, an oval, pink potato with floury white flesh. Excellent for baking in the jacket; a good alternative to King Edward and available all the year round.

Other potatoes to watch out for which are good for boiling and steaming are **Carlingford** (developed in 1982), **Maris Bard** and **Maris Peer, Premier, Desiree, Estima, Jersey Royal** and **La Ratte**.

For baking in their skins try **Catriona, Golden Wonder, Pentland Squire** and **Estima**. Floury varieties for roasting include **Cara, Desiree, King Edward, Maris Piper, Pentland Dell** and **Record**.

9. Tales from a Sussex Orchard

In 1953 David Atkins chucked in his career as a chartered accountant and took up farming in the Weald of Sussex. Forty years later he is a wiser and in some ways a sadder man. 'When I started there were about 3,000 apple growers in England, now there's only about 800 of us left and maybe by the end of the century there will only be a handful.' And that's a grim prospect, for English apples are the finest in the world. The competition from abroad is almost overwhelming with Golden Delicious pouring into the UK from France by every boat.

David, who is chairman of the largest apple co-operative in the country, says the French have an unfair edge on the English farmers. 'This year our growers putting apples into intervention will get £90 a ton; the French get that *plus* a £60 subsidy which is denied but it exists.'

And there's another marketing advantage of the tasteless, insipid Golden Delicious. 'It's cheaper to produce for a start. It takes 123 days for a Cox to mature, only 90 days for a Golden Delicious. The Cox is difficult to pollinate and only produces four tons an acre while the Golden Delicious produces twenty tons.'

I asked David what he thought of the influence of super-markets on the apple trade and that unleashed some tough comments. 'When I took over these orchards Britain had the best wholesale market in Europe for fresh produce. I used to pick my Worcesters in the morning, grade them in the after-noon, have them in Covent Garden by ten-thirty at night and most of them would be eaten by the following evening. Now it probably takes a week to get an apple into a supermarket trolley.'

As a grower, David feels the power of the supermarkets is being exploited ruthlessly. 'They dictate everything. If the fruit has to be bar-coded you have to buy the machinery. If it has to be pre-packed you have to pay for the packing and the machine to do it.' The day I went to see him David had learnt that in future he would have to stick a label on every unwrapped apple so that the checkout girls would know how much to charge. 'That's going to add a penny a pound which the growers will have to finance. Who wants a sticky label on an apple? If the supermarkets want it they should pay for it themselves.'

The most profitable sector of supermarketing is fruit and vegetables, representing only 18 per cent of total turnover but accounting for 37 per cent of gross profits. Last year the Atkins made only one per cent profit on their investment in apple growing; they are hanging on by their finger tips. As an environmentalist David is disturbed by the unnecessary waste of home-grown apples.

'You see, they don't accept any fruit unless it's 100 per cent perfect. They've found that shoppers don't want blemished fruit, but that's rubbish. I've got two farm shops and last year I sold 3,000 boxes of damaged apples at 10p a pound. People came from as far as fifty miles away just to buy them. They tasted as good as perfect fruit and people were more than happy to eat them.'

The dictatorial power of the Big Six supermarkets is often exercised in ways which infuriate growers and it doesn't seem to make sense to someone outside the trade like myself. 'One of the things that's happened is that to increase selling space the supermarkets have cut back on storage space. That means we have to deliver apples, pallet by pallet, every day. Although they know they are going to use five pallets that week they won't take a week's supply because it takes up too much room. On top of that, they impose rigid conditions on when you can deliver. If they say they'll accept your apples between 9 and 9.30; if you miss your slot you have to go away and come back tomorrow. As the grower is paying for the lorry he has to bear the cost.'

This pursuit of profit, David believes, has been the ruin of many a small grower and in the long run has limited choice on the shelves. 'One of the things the supermarkets have done, having knocked out all the old varieties of English apple, is to realize what they've done and they're now desperately hunting for old varieties. There are very few left because they've been grubbed up. I've pulled out all my Fortune, all my George Cave, most of my Lord Lambourne's because for years the supermarkets would only buy Cox and Bramley. Sainsbury's say they sell forty-seven varieties of English apples. That's misleading – they may sell ten boxes of something obscure but the bulk of what they've got for sale comes down to Cox and Golden Delicious.'

As we walked through his orchard I suggested to David that if only he grew the old favourites people would seek them out. He shook his head. 'A few might. At one time I started The Apple Shop in Knightsbridge but it wasn't a commercial success, people wouldn't pay enough for them.'

And there's no getting away from it, the old apples often have all sorts of inbuilt obstacles to success. 'The Tydemans Late Orange has a beautiful flavour but it's too small to sell well; Fortune has a lovely taste but falls off the tree too early; Scarlet Pimpernel becomes smothered in mildew; George Cave cracks on the tree; Blenheim Orange doesn't crop for ten years; the Egremont Russet is on the tree one day and on the ground the next.'

For the Atkins it's been a fascinating and more often than not an anxious forty years of hail and gales, crop failures and unwanted gluts. In the quiet nights of winter David wrote two books about his experiences in the army. 'They were turned down by all the publishers – they said there were too many old buffers wanting their memoirs published. So I published them myself.'

★

They were so well received, *The Reluctant Major* and *The Forgotten Major*, that David, now seventy-six, went on to write a third book about his Sussex apple-growing adventures. The title is taken from a line in Shakespeare's Henry IV: 'He was but as the cuckoo is in June, heard, not regarded.' The day I went to see David he'd just had two cheery letters. One from a leading Fleet Street reviewer who said that *The Cuckoo in June* had done for Sussex what Peter Mayle had done for Provence – but more wittily and more entertainingly. The second was from BBC Radio 4 announcing plans to serialise the book this coming September.

If you want to enjoy these tales of a Sussex orchard before that, you can buy a copy direct from author, publisher and apple grower extraordinary David Atkins at the Toat Press, Pulborough, West Sussex. It's a wonderful read and it records a golden age which we may, alas, never see again.

10. Let's Hear it for the Rabbits

Staying with some old friends one weekend, all of us in our sixties and still rushing about, we fell to talking about foods that seem to have fallen out of favour. We agreed that one delicacy the younger generation were missing out on was rabbit.

In medieval times the aristocracy and the princes of the church all had their private warrens run by skilled warreners and rabbits were always on the menu at the King's Christmas feast. Like many another child in the days before the Second World War, when chicken was a luxury, I was brought up on rabbit. Stewed with pork and served with mashed potatoes, I can taste the gravy yet.

Even in the early 1950s, we were still eating four times as much rabbit as poultry in Britain. Then myxomatosis was, deliberately or by accident, released into the rabbit kingdom. That was just about the same time that entrepreneurs began to discover how cheaply chickens could be reared for the table in batteries. The taste for rabbit and the number of wild rabbits available plummeted. Today we eat 600,000 tons of poultry a year and only 10,000 tons of rabbit. Indeed, so desperate are we for supplies of rabbit that we've been importing most of it from China. Rabbit at around £1.20 a pound, if not more, is these days something of a luxury but extremely good for you. It has more protein than beef or pork and is low in fat and cholesterol.

The French, who seem to eat anything that moves, get through sixteen times as many rabbits as we do and they prepare them in a variety of ways; you can do with a rabbit exactly the same sort of things that you can with a chicken. I remember a court case in the Thirties when a famous West

End hotel had to pay substantial damages to a diner who got a small piece of 'chicken' bone lodged in her throat. When it was removed the doctor said: 'I see you have been eating rabbit, madam!' Are we likely to see a revival of rabbit eating here? Probably not, for rearing rabbits in captivity is a difficult business and not many people seem to want to take the financial risk. Farmers are emotionally opposed to the whole business anyway.

In the early fifties there were estimated to be 100 million rabbits rushing around eating everything they set eyes on from allotment cabbages to fields of wheat. Within a few years 99 per cent of them had been wiped out by myxomatosis and the farmers breathed again. But rabbits, as anyone who has read *Watership Down* will know, are resilient and splendid animals. They have built up an immunity to that dreadful disease and now some 20 million of them are doing about £100 million worth of damage to Britain's crops every year. And that's not a state of affairs that is likely to be tolerated.

The Ministry of Agriculture is exploring all sorts of options from electrified fences to birth control pills and, of course, they are bearing in mind that the rabbit is not a lone animal living in a vacuum but an integral part of the ecological chain.

It was noticed that when myxomatosis spread, the buzzard population declined, and in some cases, almost disappeared. Rabbits are vital in other ways to the eco-system and exterminating them on a large scale seems to be a very selfish act on our part.

Meanwhile there are still rabbits to be had in the shops; they make a tasty terrine and an even tastier stew. If you can get a wild rabbit then so much the better. The flesh has more character: a young wild rabbit has the white flesh of a chicken, adult rabbits have darker flesh.

I found in Dorothy Hartley's nostalgic *Food in England* a Victorian recipe for a tough old pensioned-off rabbit which sounds delicious. You could try it with some pieces of super-market rabbit and imagine yourself back in the past: 'Clean, skin and fill the bellies with parsley and onions whole and stew them till the meat falls off the bones (which pick out). Chop up the meat, onions and parsley and meanwhile thicken the gravy in the pot with flour and butter and season with pepper, spice and cider. Return the chopped meat and onions into this thick sauce to reheat and serve on snippets of fried toast.' You could add vegetables but, whatever you do, be sure there's plenty of sauce.

11. Nuts about Walnuts

I had a letter from a reader recently who wondered if I had ever done any research into taste preferences. 'Why', she wrote, 'do I dote on beetroots and my children detest them and why have I inherited my mother's fondness for leeks? If ever she comes to stay and there are leeks about we have an orgy.'

Somewhere at some time someone must have done a doctoral thesis on this subject but I haven't seen it. The letter set me thinking about our own family. I vividly remember my maternal grandmother sitting in her long black dress in front of the blazing grate in her Kentish home with a bowl of walnuts on her lap and a heavy glass cellar of salt to hand. I recall her giving me one as a child and I spat it out.

But when I grew up I discovered that some mysterious gene had transmitted the passion down to me. Kentish cobnuts and walnuts straight off the tree were irresistible. Don't confuse these with the shrivelled kiln-dried nuts you get at Christmas – they're not the same thing at all. The fresh green nuts demand to be dipped in salt, that's half the pleasure.

My wife can take walnuts or leave them; my son is indifferent. But my daughter and I find them so tempting that we can knock back a pound in no time at all. Is there some particular chemical in walnuts that attracts us both; does our metabolism crave for whatever the walnut has to offer or do we just have the same palatal spectrum? I must find out.

If you like the taste of nuts but like me find them dull and unrewarding when dried you might tempt yourself with some of the nut oils which you can now find in up-market delicatessens and even on supermarket shelves. They are ideal for dressing salads, for flavouring stir-fry dishes or for tossing vegetables in.

My favourites are walnut oil and hazelnut oil. In the eighteenth century walnut oil was made into varnishes and used by crafstmen like Stradivarius to impart a deep, rich colour to the wood of violins. Now we have a much better use for it.

As with so many gastronomic delights the French are considered to grow the finest walnuts in the world and the best of all come from the Dordogne. I was in Grenoble a few years ago on my way to visit the monks who make the deep green Chartreuse and I found the shops full of fresh walnuts. France presses about 350 tonnes of walnut oil a year. Like all oils there are different qualities – the most expensive is called *Blanc Extra* and the second best is Arlequin. There are many different species and connoisseurs hunt for nuts from their favourite trees.

The walnuts I saw in Grenoble came from a variety of tree called La Franquette and the harvesting begins in the first week of October. Descendants of these trees have been grown in California since the 1870s. Around Sarlat and Souillac where many Brits have bought holiday homes La Grandjean is the favoured tree; it produces a superb nut with a white skin.

Today the world's largest producer of walnuts is the United States followed by Turkey and Romania. If you are lucky enough to have a walnut tree in your garden then treasure it because they take a long time to get into their stride. A new oil which came on the market for the first time in 1978 is even more delicate in flavour than the walnut. Hazelnut oil has an unmistakable smell and a few drops in a salad bowl can transform it remarkably. Just as well it's so powerful because it's not cheap – it takes 2½ kilos of hazels to produce one litre of oil.

Almond oil is another novelty. The French introduced it in 1980 and most of the almonds they use come from Spain.

Almond oil goes particularly well with fish and it is of course the perfect oil in which to fry salted almonds. Pistachio oil was marketed for the first time last year. It's dark green in colour, high in iodine and like most of these other nut oils is low in saturated fatty acids and high in monounsaturated fatty acids; the ones we're now told that do us a power of good.

These are what you might call 'niche' oils. Only small quantities are available and they command a high price.

Compared with the 15 million tonnes of soya oil produced in various parts of the world these oils hardly make a blip in commercial statistics – but what a difference they make in the kitchen.

I'm indebted to a fascinating little pocket book just published by Mitchell Beazley called *Oils, Vinegars and Seasonings* for awakening my awareness of just how important all these things are in the culinary repertoire. Its authors Mark Lake and Judy Ridgway combine history, production and nutritional analysis with recipes to provide the best compact rundown on these vital essentials I've yet seen.

Here are all the old favourites – horseradish, cayenne pepper, vanilla, cloves, chives, raspberry vinegar and nutmegs. Alongside them the exotica which have enlivened our cooking in recent years – pesto, aioli, anchoiade, garam masala.

As the authors point out a careful use of good flavourings can add disproportionately to the interest and subtlety of any dish.

It's worth finding out what are the precise differences between French and English mustard, between roasted and unroasted sesame oil and between the enormous range of oils made from the olive.

All too often these days the flavourings and fragrances in our food come from the chemist's palette. Maybe we have to put up with these often unsavoury substitutes in commercially processed food but in the kingdom of our own kitchens we have the privilege of using the best ingredients we can find and afford. Sea salt or rock salt instead of the packet variety induced to flow freely with added magnesium carbonate; a good wine vinegar (perhaps sherry) and not the vile concoction of acetic acid and caramel which is the common condiment of fish and chip shops.

12. Holy Grail with Bubbles

'When we saw Appletise we thought this could be the Holy Grail – in the soft drinks business the Holy Grail is an *adult* soft drink.' The speaker was Don Knight of Crayton, Lodge and Knight, one of the most successful firms of marketing consultants in Europe. He explained the problem: 'For people who may be driving, for people who just don't want alcohol, all you've got are rather sickly sweet drinks or something like Perrier, and in a pub 60p is an awful lot to give for a glass of water. There are a lot of drinks which *half* fulfil the role but none of them is entirely satisfactory. The latest thing is a non-alcoholic gin and tonic, which is such an incredible paradox that it just doesn't work. We wanted an adults' drink, but the danger is that even if you put it in a sophisticated package, people would just say, "That's a kid's drink tarted up." But Appletise has got a lot of things going for it. It's pure juice, it's got a very clean sharp flavour with the smell of real apples, it's quite expensive and it has very healthy associations. That seemed to us to be a very credible starting-point.'

When Don Knight was approached to mastermind the launch of this new apple drink in Britain he was aware that it was already doing remarkably well in other parts of the world. 'Overseas it's called Appletiser, but of course we've got Tizer here, so we dropped the last letter. The trouble is that if you put something in front of people and say "Here is a sparkling apple juice", their first reaction will be to construe it incorrectly. They'll say it's appleade, or cider, or Cydrax, or Schloer. So what we had to do was create something which people treated as *sui generis* and not as something they already knew.'

The pack had to be unlike anything ever seen before, and

Don knew that it had to have a masculine image. 'We wanted it to be drunk by men and women so it couldn't have feminine associations: to put it simply, women don't mind wearing trousers but men don't like wearing dresses. The pack is unequivocally masculine and slightly alcohol-looking to maintain that masculine imagery.'

In 1978 we drank only 247 million litres of fruit juice. It rose to 667 million litres in 1983, an increase of 170 per cent, which created a market worth £370 million. By then, 47 per cent of adult fruit-juice drinkers were men. Although orange is still the most popular flavour, apple and pineapple have increased their share of the market at the expense of grapefruit and tomato.

These trends were well known to Don Knight and his researchers, and they did their job well. 'We designed the pack, we were able to estimate the market positioning, we helped them negotiate with Schweppes, who were going to distribute the drink, and we helped them appoint an advertising agency, which was Young and Rubicam.'

The achievement Don Knight was most proud of was the scenario for the future which he was able to present to the agency. 'I described it as the Road To Maturity, and I said that eventually Appletise will sell well in pubs because in a grocery context at 27p it'll look expensive, but in a pub it'll be half the price of a glass of wine. People are much more prepared to experiment in pubs because there's a pressure to have a drink anyway. When people have sampled it in pubs, they will start looking for it in grocers' shops, and in doing so will introduce it to the rest of the family.

'The moment it moved from the pubs you had to change the packet size, so you put it in a big bottle or a multi-pack. Ultimately the experience of having it in the home would introduce men to it and they'd start ordering it in pubs. Then it would move into newsagents and sweetshops for children, and at that stage it might be appropriate to put it in a can.'

The point Knight was making was that the whole campaign

to sell Appletise could have collapsed if the marketing had not been minutely researched. 'It would have been disastrous to launch it in a can in the first instance because that would make it appear like a lemonade. You only put it in a can when everyone knows what it is and the initial packaging is no longer a relevant communicator.'

So successful has Appletise been that it is set to sell 30 million bottles this year, and its popularity with all members of the family is high. The marketing was brilliant: as Don Knight modestly put it, 'The most important thing about the launch pack is that it told you what the product *wasn't!*'

An identical sales path has been taken by Bulmer's new sparkling apple juice Kiri which also, in deference to the health lobby, contains no preservatives, no artificial colourings or flavourings, and no added sugar. It too is packaged in a sophisticated bottle. According to the consultancy handling the account, 'Bulmer's market research showed that adults were looking for soft drinks . . . which men in particular would be prepared to ask for in a pub as an alternative to alcohol.' Like Appletise, Kiri now comes in two bottle sizes and as a four-pack. Analysts are predicting that the fruit-juice market will grow by 10 per cent this year. There will be an esurient rush to hunt the sparkling new Holy Grail; the temptations of the apple cannot be resisted.

13. Discrete Meat

I've always been a fan of Marks & Spencer; their reputation for good value, high standards and scrupulous regard for quality is well deserved. Their wines are almost invariably well chosen. I recall talking to a *négociant* near Nantes who told me how the St Michael buyers demanded the best. 'If they find a dirty bottling line,' he said, 'they just get back in their cars.' I heard, too, that at their food plants there was a special area set aside where operatives were encouraged to go if they needed to sneeze. And I remember being told by a canner with an international reputation for excellence that the specification the M&S buying team set for the soup he made them was more demanding than his own. It all adds up to an image of probity and concern for the consumer.

As a result, I have always felt safe in a Marks & Spencer store, even though you have to pay for the privilege. You'll find that half a pound of well-matured Cheddar in Marks is about the same price it is in Harrods. It's not cut-price bargains that people go for, but high quality. This July, heading home to Skye from the Black Isle, we parked in the new shopping mall in Inverness, of which the glittering showpiece is Marks & Spencer's most northern store. My wife said she'd get something for supper; I went off to buy a typewriter ribbon. When we met back in the car park, my wife said she'd bought a nice joint of gammon and added, 'Well, it ought to be nice – it was nearly £4.'

We boiled the joint with carrots and onions, but when we came to carve it, somehow it didn't look like a piece of bacon at all. We peered with mounting misgiving and diminishing appetite at this cosmetically pink lump of something on the carving board which had the consistency of the foam backing on cheap carpets. Under the knife it bounced and flexed like rubber. Could it really be a gammon joint?

I went out to the dustbin and retrieved the polythene wrapper bag from among the tea leaves and potato peelings. 'GAMMON JOINT' claimed the label in large unequivocal letters. Smaller letters contained the additional information that it was 'unsmoked Danish topside with added bacon fat'. To me, a joint of meat is a joint of meat – what the *OED* defines as 'one of the portions into which a carcass is divided by the butcher'. This was no ordinary joint.

We tried eating it. It had the texture of abalone and left a bland presence in the mouth; there was little or no taste of either pork or ham. The water content was relatively high – indeed water was the second most prominent ingredient on the label (pork, water, pork fat, salt, sodium polyphosphate . . .)

'I've been swindled,' said my wife. I corrected her. She hadn't been swindled; she had just mistakenly bought a re-formed meat product thinking she was buying a real joint of meat. 'Then why doesn't it say "pork with added water" instead of "pork with added fat"? It would be more accurate.'

To that there was no answer. 'I shall write to Lord Sieff,' my wife said, 'and tell him the thing is an imposture.' And she did. The lord, or one of his servants, passed her letter to Mr P. G. McCracken, Technical Executive, Meat Group. He admitted that the meat was not perhaps what *she* regarded as a joint, but *they* considered it was a joint 'since it is made from entire and discrete muscles taken from a recognized part of the pork leg'. He went on to admit that what she had bought was actually bits of meat pressed and formed into an oval shape 'dressed with a thin slice of loin fat to give the product succulence during roasting'.

Although Mr McCracken did not dispute that the second most important ingredient in the 'joint' was water, he claimed: 'The amount of water used is carefully controlled and it is not our policy to seek to increase yields by adding excess water.'

Marks & Spencer, he said, have had many discussions with the Danes who make this product for them, with Trading Standards officers and with the Bacon and Meat Manufacturing Association. 'It is generally recognized', said Mr McCracken, 'that the description "joint" is widely used and accepted in the high street and trade for this type of product.' They had, he wrote, been selling similarly re-formed products for more than twenty years and describing them without challenge as joints.

Time, I feel, that the regulations were changed. If meat has been processed to resemble a natural joint of bacon or meat, it should be made amply clear to the consumer that this is what has been done. There is a precedent for this. Beef which has been chopped and shaped to look like a steak is called a steaklette. Perhaps Marks might call their product 'bacon roll' or 'bacon jointlette'. Normally, when meat is processed in this way, it is done to provide a cheaper product for what is known in these hard times as budget shoppers. But in the week in which Marks & Spencer were charging £2.25 per pound for their re-formed 'joints', Sainsbury were selling traditional joints – that is, a piece of bacon cut off a carcass – at substantially lower prices. They had a wide variety of real bacon joints in all their stores, ranging from corners at £1.20 per pound to prime-quality gammon at £1.84 per pound – 41p per pound cheaper than Marks's 'gammon joint'. It pays when you are in the high street to shop around.

14. Ova the Odds

In 1985 *The Food Programme* recorded the strangest interview of the year. It took place in the foothills of the Pyrenees, whither for some time now emissaries of the great chefs of Europe have been wending their way to persuade a former palmist called Alain Chatillon to part with small amounts of what has become the hottest gastronomic ingredient of the decade.

In Rennes-le-Château, the numinous village where in 1885 the fabulous treasure of the Knights Templar was discovered, Alain has set up a picayune enterprise which has shaken the world of *haute cuisine*. Foodies thumb eagerly through their copies of *A La Carte, Taste, Gourmet* and *Gluttony* for the latest sightings of the new treasure of Rennes, and chefs vie with each other to perfect culinary creations for their display.

The story begins, as many good stories have done, in distant Tibet, an unlikely Shangri-La, you may think, for the discovery of anything more *recherché* than curdled yak's milk. But it was here five years ago in a remote lamasery that M. Chatillon, with a mind tuned to the perception of the previously unperceived, watched as villagers deposited their offerings in the lap of a gilded Buddha. Among the oblations was a bowl of what looked like pinky-beige opalescent pearls. When no one was looking, M. Chatillon put a finger in the bowl and conveyed two of the small globules to his mouth.

'I ate them,' Alain told us, 'and I think immediately zees is *fantastique*. It is a revelation!' And thus was the secret of snail eggs brought back from the land of eternal snows. Or something like that. Back in Rennes, Alain spent five years experimenting until he found the perfect gastropod, the indigenous *petit gris*. Now he has over 300,000 worker snails in twelve farms in different parts of France. The annual production of one snail, he claims, is only a hundred eggs, which makes them as expensive as the finest Beluga caviar. And they have to go through a secret process for at least a month before they are edible. Detractors say that this includes brining the eggs in almond essence and pepper to impart a smidgen of taste to the otherwise tasteless.

When Alain produced his first batch, nobody was interested. Alain went to the three-star L'Oasis at La Napoule-Plage to beard the famous Louis Outhier. Louis, in the imperious manner of the superstar chef, kept him waiting at the kitchen door for a week, and then, according to Alain, he instantly became converted: 'He ate zem on toast with butter and he thinks, effectively, zees product is *sensationelle*. It's something crazy. Something unimaginable. "OK, I put zees things immediately in my menu!"'

M. Outhier is currently dividing his time between L'Oasis in the south of France and London W1, where he is supervising the cuisine at the Grosvenor's crack restaurant, Ninety Park Lane. It was here that last week he prepared a small dinner based on the dainty *morceaux*. His snailathon, which I was privileged to attend, began with the little eggs, no larger than peppercorns, scattered among almonds on a tossed salad. 'I'm getting almonds,' said the foodie opposite me. I found the eggs moist and unusual, but I was getting nothing.

The salad plates were whisked away and replaced with a canapé of quail eggs coated with red wine sauce and adorned with more of the glistening ova. I was getting the taste of quail eggs all right, but from the snail eggs – well, the quintessential taste was still elusory. Round three was a *paupiette* of turbot and scallops with – brilliant touch – diced snails and yet more eggs. It was delicious. I bit through a few eggs and found them far from unpalatable. Perhaps I was working too hard at it.

I did better with the next course, a *granité Rennes-le-Château* created by M. Outhier to honour the birthplace of the new delicacy. For those not cognisant with such matters, a *granité* is more of a sherbet than a sorbet. This one was lemon and laced generously with vodka. Among the chopped parsley and what looked like frozen hailstones was another small dispensation of the treasure of *Helix aspersa*. In their gelid state they were more enticing – or perhaps it was the vodka.

For the *pièce de résistance*, M. Outhier himself swept into the dining room in his tall white *toque* to unveil thin slices of chicken breast encarnadined in beetroot sauce and peppered with . . . snail eggs. By now I was getting quite fond of the little fellows and I was rather thrown when at the end of the banquet I found there weren't any at all in *la caravane des desserts*.

Already five restaurants in France and seven in Brussels feature *les oeufs d'escargot*. They are on sale at £32.50 for a two-gram jar in Harrods and Fortnum & Mason, a price based more, I feel, on their scarcity than on their intrinsic virtue. Roy Groves, director of the Snail Centre in Colwyn Bay, which produces 400,000 edible snails a year, thinks Alain must be pulling someone's leg. 'We keep careful records here,' he tells me, 'and on average our snails produce in the order of 1,500 eggs a year.' That's fifteen times more than the gallant little hermaphrodites of Rennes. But the chefs can't get enough of them.

Meanwhile M. Chatillon is well on his way to making his first million. There is no truth in the malicious rumour put about by the envious that he is now investigating the possibility of bottling edible moonbeams.

15. Clearing the Decks for a Cargolade

'Come,' said the voice on the phone, 'to a cargolade.' It was Charles Eve, wine development director of Peter Dominic. To say that I dropped everything, packed my bag and left for the airport immediately would be an unnecessary exaggeration. But I certainly cleared the decks for action.

You don't get invited to a cargolade every day of the week – indeed, cargolades do not occur every day of the week, even in the South of France; they are special events which require a great deal of preparation, like a kirk bazaar or a Burns supper.

I had only attended one such event before, but the memory was vivid. It took place in May in a small village in Roussillon. The mistral was blowing, or rather the *tramontane* as they call it in those parts. An abrasive, dust-making, relentless wind funnelling down the Rhône Valley, rustling the vines and raising rural tempers. The best cargolades occur in the open, but this one had been celebrated inside a hangar-like winery; it was far too draughty out of doors.

June, though, was an ideal time for this alfresco feast. Not baking hot, but predictably warm enough to make it enjoyable. When I arrived in Perpignan, one-time capital of the kings of Majorca, it was 81 in the shade and there wasn't much of that around. Perpignan is just about the last airport before you hit the Pyrenees. There they lay shimmering in the noonday heat, snow-capped still and somewhere on the other side miles and miles of the Costa Brava, paella and chips and high tea and high rise hotels.

This part of France has a pre-Spain feel. They call the auto route that runs to the frontier La Catalane and for centuries this fertile landscape rich in vines, olives, fruit trees and corn was in feoff to the Catalonians. If Belgium was the cockpit of Europe, Roussillon was its royal chessboard, fought over by the kings of France, Aragon and Spain.

The cargolade on this peaceful midsummer day was to occur in the rolling countryside north of Montalba, a half-hour drive from Perpignan.

The mayor intimates that we have arrived. A cheer goes up. Welcome to the cargolade. Already assembled are about a dozen weather-beaten villagers. They wear berets, smoke pungent gauloises and are knocking back tumblers of something that looks like Ribena but patently isn't.

Glasses are poured. This is the preferred aperitif of the South of France. Rivesaltes is a fortified sweet wine which is not to my taste, especially before a meal, and it is not a wine exported to this country. Its alcoholic strength, a minimum of 15 per cent by volume, puts it in the sherry range for the purposes of duty and having neither the elegance of sherry nor the distinction of port, I doubt if it would ever catch on. But it's catching on here all right and the mayor, M. Henri Sire, is toasting everyone in sight.

Underneath the green umbrella of an ancient spreading oak tree there's a large marble table which looks as if it might have been part of a floor once upon a time. The clearing is surrounded by a natural garden of white dog roses and the yellow profusion of wild broom stretches as far as the eye can see. There isn't a sound but the occasional pulling of a cork and the crackle of the wood-fire on which the food is going to be barbecued. The aroma of vine shoots, the smell of the roses, the occasional waft of wild thyme and the warmth of the sun. That's all, but it's more than enough.

The minute centrepieces of this meal have already been prepared. A thousand snails carefully arranged on iron grids. Each one has been primed with a few drops of hot pork fat and at this stage those of vegetarian inclination may well wish to pass on to something less demanding – like, the sports pages.

You see, a cargolade is a conspicuous consumption of what the French call *escargots* – hence *cargolade*. This is not *Helix aspersa* of the British back garden but *Helix pomatia*, the Roman snail inside whose curious shell is the small winkle-like body in which the French delight.

Tending the fire is Pierre Fillols, who owns ten hectares of vines and is the undisputed king of the cargolade. It is he who will judge when the fire is hot enough to partially bake the tiny gasteropods. Helpers are spreading the marble slab with pages from old copies of *Midi Libre*. There's a great cutting of crusty fresh-baked bread and stirring of *aioli*, the mayonnaise heavily flavoured with crushed garlic, which is as indispensable an accompaniment to snails as neeps are to haggis.

At a signal from Pierre the embers are spread, the heavy iron trivets are carried across to the heat of the fire and there's a sizzling and a licking of lips. It only takes a few minutes to seal the fate of a snail. Small two-pronged winkling forks have been distributed and as the hot snails come to the table everyone falls to.

If I have to be honest, as far as I'm concerned, eating snails is a rubbery experience. There are many viands I prefer, but here they are, a thousand of them, and down they go oiled with the eye-watering *aioli*, so strong in garlic that a naked flame passed near the lips might result in a spontaneous and unwelcome combustion.

The cargolade follows its ritual course. After the snails there are highly spiced sausages and tender grilled lamb chops, lots of wine, a feeling of holiday.

16. Double Glazing

I've been dipping into a riveting report by David Walker, who works as a food inspector for Shropshire County Council. In 1982 he was given a research scholarship by the Institute of Trading Standards Administration to look at new developments in food technology and he turned his attention to fish processing. One of the first things he looked at was cod, 65 per cent of which has to be imported. It arrives in frozen skinless, boneless blocks which can be sawn, chopped or sliced into convenient sizes for further processing.

The majority of these blocks contain water deliberately added in the form of polyphosphate solution; water, it is claimed, enhances the product. This does not seem to be an entirely supportable proposition; all it enhances are the profits. Seven years ago, the Food Standards Committee recommended that added polyphosphates should be declared on the label, but nothing has been done. Mr Walker comments dryly: 'The industry has commissioned research which is said to demonstrate that consumers have expressed a clear preference for fish fingers made from polyphosphated blocks. That being so, the reluctance of the industry to declare the presence of the solution . . . is a little hard to understand.'

Since the early 1970s nearly all fish fingers have contained fish mince, retrieved by passing skeletons and trimmings through bone-separating machines. The mince added to fish fingers can vary from 10 per cent to 100 per cent. The give-away often comes in the use of the words 'Economy', 'Value' or 'Super Value' for fingers with the most mince. Current research, refuted by the trade, suggests that the proportion of fish to batter and crumbs on a fish finger has dropped from 80 per cent in the 1960s to an average level today of 56 per cent – the meanest finger dissected for inspection yielded only 33.7 per cent fish. The industry maintains that it aims for a 60:40 fish-to-coating ratio but even on this unlikely ambition Mr Walker suggests that annually some 2,400 tonnes of added water goes into our fish fingers, replacing fish to the tune of £6 million.

Scampi are big business too. Machines have been introduced which mould and re-form the meat into scampi-shaped pieces. Some firms whirl scampi and polyphosphates in a dough mixer and mince it all together. The mince is then extruded and moulded under pressure into tail-shaped pieces. The polyphosphate factor is all important. Although two minutes' immersion in the solution is considered adequate to impart any technological benefit, Mr Walker alleges that some companies allow their scampi to soak for twenty-four hours. One firm who anticipated an uptake of excess water of 10 per cent to 13 per cent expressed the view that some of his rivals were adding 50 per cent!

When you buy cod or prawns coated in batter and breadcrumbs you presumably expect the fish content to be a variable feast, but you may be surprised to know that water is also added to frozen fillets of fish like whiting, haddock and cod. The industry claim that, apart from increasing the weight, phosphates lend the fish a nice glossy blue-white colour and, says David Walker, 'dipping may sufficiently mask some of the symptoms of deterioration to give a slightly false impression about the quality of the end product'.

Glazing frozen fish or coating it with a layer of ice is another equally enterprising activity. Some companies just spray the fish, others give it a bath in polyphosphates as well – the technique is, fortunately, not visible to the naked eye. 'Any system', says Walker, 'which enables a layer of iced water to be applied to any product leaves itself open to abuse.' He reckons that some 2,100 tons of undeclared ice is 'being sold as filleted fish every year, with a retail value of around £4.8 million.'

The marketing of prawns presents even greater temptations. Here, claims Walker, 'there is clear evidence of abuse, bordering in some instances almost on the fraudulent'. Prawns are not cheap; buy a 1lb bag for £2.89 and you may find that £1.04 of that is added ice, because some prawns have up to 35 per cent ice on them – an effect achieved in this country by importing prawns already glazed with a layer of ice and then spraying them with more water and freezing that as well. 'The practice', says Walker, 'has given a whole new meaning to the term "double glazing".' Some firms claim that if it weren't for glazing, the prawns would cost more; others reckon that they can adjust the price to suit the market by varying the amount of glazing – Britain is one of the few countries in the world which still allows fish to be sold at a weight which includes ice glaze.

And the future? New technology now makes it possible to create fish analogues with great ease; already Japan has replaced between 10 per cent and 20 per cent of the fish she uses with soya protein. The 'crab' sticks currently being sold in fishmongers here come from Japan and are fabricated from minced fish, salt, sugar, polyphosphates and starch; they are given a crab flavouring and then dyed red on the outside to resemble a piece of crab meat. Although they have trade names like 'Ocean Stick', there is no doubt that many people buy them in the belief that they are re-formed shellfish.

17. A Taste of Honey

A couple of weeks ago, the pick of Britain's amateur bee-keepers and commercial bee farmers gathered in London for the 56th National Honey Show. Like the little workers they look after, bee enthusiasts are a resilient breed. Despite all the climatic setbacks of the last few years – this summer was the third bad one in a row for nectar gatherers – there are still 40,000 beekeepers coping as best they can without any financial help from the Government. They point out that support for sugar-beet farmers is costing £1 million a day, while they get nothing. Commercially produced honey has fallen from 4,000 tonnes in 1972 to a British harvest this year, if we're lucky, of about 1,250 tonnes. The winter before last was particularly devastating; the prolonged frosts killed up to half of the native bee population. The recent storms have destroyed hundreds of hives. Bee farmers could, if they wished, argue that, if it's sugar you need, then the healthiest source of that form of energy comes without doubt from the labour of bees.

Nectar, from which 900 bees can make a pound of honey in a day, is composed of sugars, minerals, vitamins and enzymes, which the bees transform in their bodies into honey. Where fruit and vegetables begin to lose their vitamin content as soon as they are picked, honey retains all its inherent properties indefinitely. The natural occurrence of more than two dozen trace elements essential to health in honey has given it over the years a prominent place in folklore, and latterly on the shelves of health-food shops.

But beware: some commercial honeys may well be less nutritious than others. In order to liquefy crystallized honey from the comb to the clear, runny product that most people seem to prefer, heat has to be applied. If the process is not done with due care and attention, taste and flavour can be lost, along with the very things that give honey its edge on other sugar products.

Books have been devoted to the cosmetic and medicinal powers of honey. At the very least, honey, high in pre-digested sugars, affords a quick and easily assimilated boost of energy, but the presence of its wide spectrum of micro-nutrients has given it a reputation for alleviating, if not curing, everything from constipation to the common cold.

Intensive chemical farming and the proliferation of vast prairies devoted to cereal growing has made it more and more difficult for the industrious bee to keep up its traditional production levels. One part of the landscape which hasn't been drastically affected is the uncultivable heather moor, which produces a highly sought-after honey.

Archie Ferguson keeps bees both for the pleasure of their company and the enjoyment of their labours. I went to Dumfriesshire to ask him what makes heather such a fine source of nectar, but he destroyed quite a few illusions.

First of all, he said, there was no such thing as 'pure' heather honey. 'It's very rare that you get absolutely pure honey of any kind. The trouble is that if you take bees from home, where they've been working willow-herb, say, or clover, and you take them to the heather, there are still some of these other honeys in the hive and these will get mixed with the heather honey. You've also got to remember that there's nothing to prevent the bees from working other plants on the moors besides the ling heather.'

Archie's favourite honey is not heather at all, but hawthorn: 'I've only had it once in my life but it was absolutely delicious. It had a beautiful aroma and a slightly nutty almond flavour.' I wondered if bees had preferences, too, when they were at work? Yes, said Archie, they invariably went for the honeys with the highest concentration of sugars: 'In times of dearth, though, they'll work anything; I've seen them working the common daisy.'

Bees seem to be natural connoisseurs. 'If there's a very choice species they may well fly to that, even if it's a couple of miles away. Raspberries, for instance, have a very high sugar content, so when they are in flower they'll look at nothing else.'

The most remarkable thing about honey is that where other foods ferment, decay and become toxic with the passage of time, raw honey is the only food known to man which has built-in immortality. No wonder people who have hives tend to talk about bees with both wonder and admiration. After all, bees were making honey long before mankind appeared on earth, and it's more than likely that they'll be here long after we're gone. According to Henryk Ostach, head of the Polish beekeepers' association, local bees had so great a sense of survival that when they sensed contamination from the Chernobyl explosion they hid immediately in their hives; that was well before humans were being laboriously alerted to the disaster.

18. A Distaste for Game

We were discussing the inter-relation of class and diet in *The Food Programme* recently and I thought we'd explored most aspects of what, in this costively class-structured country, is a rich and eccentric field for investigation. But the following weekend, Patrick Stevenson added a new dimension to the debate. He and his wife Sonia live in game-rich Devon, where they have provided good food at the Horn of Plenty for the last two decades.

Being in deer country, one of the first dishes they put on the menu when they opened was venison. None of the locals would eat it. 'I'm convinced', said Patrick, 'that their repugnance to deer meat was nothing to do with what it tasted like but with what it represented. You see, for centuries it was the reserve of landowners, and if you were found in possession of game you really were in trouble.'

I mulled over this and found it a bit of a contradictory theory; if the peasantry didn't like game, why did they engage so enthusiastically in poaching? Was it perhaps an activity designed less to fill the pot than to assert their independence? But perhaps there is something in Patrick Stevenson's basic assumption that game is still regarded as something only upper-class people eat. Although pheasant, at £3 a head this winter, has been one of the cheapest meats on the market, it appeals only to a minority. Hare and rabbit figure on the menus of fashionable restaurants but are seldom cooked in ordinary homes; most of our venison goes to the Continent, where all classes enjoy it equally; grouse is still regarded as something only the nobs eat.

Old eating habits die hard. And old fears too. In country

districts, folk memories flow back through the generations as clear as a stream to the days when you could be removed to the colonies for seven years for snaring a rabbit.

I wasn't aware of how wide the social divide was between those who were entitled to game and those who weren't until I began reading Harry Hopkins' engrossing and horrifying account of what he calls 'the poaching wars'. *The Long Affray* explains in vivid detail how game came to be regarded by the landowning classes not only as a social marker but as a symbol of power and authority. Eating it was merely incidental to serving it and, paradoxically, slaughtering it on a scale unprecedented anywhere else in the world.

By the end of the nineteenth century, an army of 17,000 gamekeepers had been recruited to protect the sport of kings, brewing barons and assorted trigger-happy *arrivistes*. The fight had been long and bloody, involving mantraps lightly covered with moss and leaves and spring-guns whose trip-wires laid low the guilty and the innocent. The horror of these engines of maiming and destruction was not perceived by the gentry, who almost to a man felt they were waging a just war on the lower classes. Harry Hopkins quotes Colonel George Hanger who included poachers among the many forms of vermin which threatened his pheasants. In his battle manual, *To All Sportsmen*, he suggested that if spring-guns weren't a strong enough deterrent, six-pounder cannon should be set up in pheasant-haunted woods.

The preservation of game reached such competitive proportions in Edwardian times that the Prince of Wales was forced to build a larder at Sandringham which could take 7,000 birds at a time, and his trigger-happy cronies began listing their insatiable lust for the shoot in *Who's Who*. Lord Walsingham recorded with vulgar precision: '1,070 grouse to his own pair of guns, in 14 hours, 18 minutes.'

Is it too fanciful to conclude that the methods used to preserve game for the few constituted a powerful aversion therapy for the masses? The emotional hatred of the game laws may well have carried over a residual distaste to the table. France has had no such problem. As Harry Hopkins reminds us, Thomas Carlyle was convinced that the Revolution was made by the poachers of France. One of the first acts of the revolutionaries was to dismantle the game laws. To what extent that altered rural cuisine is debatable, but to this day all kind of game from the rabbit to the partridge is far more widely eaten in France than it is here. *The Long Affray* is an essential read for anyone attempting to explore food and class. I shall never enjoy rabbit again without remembering that labourers were, not all that long ago, murdered, transported and hanged for wanting to eat them.

19. Fresh as a Turkey

It was a long time coming, and it is quite appropriate that it arrived in 1984. I am referring to a semantic leap forward in food marketing that has released us, in a poetic and creative burst of imagination, from the tyranny of words.

The Fresh Style Frozen Turkey!

A brilliant concept, when you come to think of it. It offends not against the Trade Description Act, neither does it not roll effortlessly off the tongue . . . fresh-style frozen! What a rewarding thought.

Anything that isn't stale must be fresh, and if it is well within its date-stamp limit it must be very fresh indeed. Why bother with the word 'style' at all? What's wrong with 'fresh-frozen'?

But what style is fresh, and what does 'fresh' mean? When applied to cream, it presumably means it isn't sour; but how fresh is fresh? Fresh eggs may well be new-laid, or they may be described as fresh to distinguish them from spray-dried.

Fresh-style. Does that mean that we are talking about a turkey reared intensively and fed with granules, which may well be confused with the kind of turkey that used to strut round Norfolk farms picking at worms? Or does it mean that it tastes better than the normal frozen cardboard-and-lint turkey?

I'm only asking because, if you can have a fresh-style frozen turkey, then you can have a fresh-style apricot fruit pie made of flour, sugar, apricot, animal and vegetable fat, dextrose, modified starch, sorbitol syrup, glucose syrup, salt, citric acid, potassium sorbate, polyglycerol esters of fatty acids, ethyl-methylcellulose, tartrazine, sunset-yellow FCF, mono- and diglycerides of fatty acids, flavouring and whey powders.

And if it is fresh-style, why can't it be country-fresh, or perhaps farmhouse-fresh? 'Farmhouse' may be difficult because nobody, however visually disadvantaged, could mistake a food-processing factory for a farmhouse, even if the factory had a thatched roof.

But, supposing you were only verbally disadvantaged, maybe you might assume that something frozen solid as a board was fresh? After all, millions of Cornish choc-ices are sold every year and nobody seems bothered by the fact that they are not made in Cornwall, aren't covered with chocolate and aren't made from cream.

And supposing you put the word 'naturally' in front of the word 'fresh'. How about a Naturally Fresh Style Frozen Turkey or a Naturally British Fresh Style Frozen Turkey? And, to take the fantasy a stage further, supposing the unit where the turkeys were reared was in the heart of the countryside, then couldn't we legitimately have a Naturally British Country Fresh Style Frozen Turkey?

And, as the turkey would indisputably be not a plastic model of a turkey, then might it not qualify for the ultimate accolade of being a 'real' turkey, as in Real Ale? It could also be a 'guaranteed' bird, a 'genuine' bird, a 'quality-tested' bird, or almost anything you wanted to call it if you were so minded.

The other day I had the opportunity to taste a really real, truly fresh, country-reared Norfolk black turkey. Its flesh was succulent and moist, it had – dare I use the word? – *real* flavour, and I suppose this rare and vanishing breed of turkey must have been not unlike the ones which they drove in their thousands in the eighteenth and nineteenth centuries from East Anglia to Smithfield market.

It was a delight, and it didn't need any advertising to turn it into something it wasn't. I have a feeling that 1985 may well be the year in which the food industry, triggered by the growing public demand for less highly processed food and more evidence of the natural and the fresh, may attempt to achieve by words what it cannot accomplish by deeds.

20. Tempeh – 'the greatest food since yoghurt'

Soya is one of those words that doesn't hold out much hope of joy. I was not surprised to learn that during the Second World War the German High Command put *edelsoja* in every soldier's knapsack. They used soya flour in soups, bread, pastry and pasta, having found out that 1lb of the stuff yields 2,000 calories and is equal in protein content to 2lb of lean meat, 30 eggs or a gallon of milk.

Soya has always bulked large in those cardboard packets of vegetarian food you used to see in health food shops. It looked like sawdust, and when you stirred water in and shaped it into a cutlet it tasted like sawdust too. Then in the 1970s, through the magic of new technology, soya was set to become the wonder food that would give you all the nourishment of meat without the cost. Textured Vegetable Protein, it was called, and it could be got up with artificial flavourings to taste like chicken or veal or mince. But it never caught on. Soya was left with a second-rate image. And that's a pity because, in the Orient, soya has been eaten and enjoyed for more than 2,000 years. The Chinese discovered that for flavour, nutrition and cheapness, soybeans were unrivalled.

The Japanese developed all sorts of salty soya-bean pastes, which they called *miso*, and their *tofu*, soya-bean curd, is infinitely adaptable. Made from soy milk and coagulated like cottage cheese, tofu can be steamed, boiled, grilled, deep-fried, freeze-dried and used in everything from soups to grills. The Chinese for soya is *doufu*; in Korea it becomes *doopoo* and in Indonesia *tahu*. Currently in the United States, the cult food among bean-freaks and counter-culture groups is not tahu but tempeh, a chewy manifestation of the soya bean which is peculiar to Java.

Tempeh, unlike tofu, has a residual natural dietary fibre. It is very low in saturated fats, contains absolutely no cholesterol, has all the eight essential amino-acids and many other desirable nutrients. It was seized upon with cries of delight in the mid-1970s by a spiritual community of 1,400 souls living in Tennessee who call themselves The Farm. In 1977, *Mother Earth News* published a testimonial from them which described tempeh as 'the greatest food since yoghurt'. In the US there are some fifty shops and firms making tempeh, and at the Soyfood Center in Lafayette, California, William Shurtleff and his wife Akiko Aoyagi have become the leading gurus of the tempeh movement. They see it as one of the soya foods which could be a vibrant force for what they call 'planetary renaissance'.

In Wimbledon Village, at Mustika Rasa, the Indonesian and South-East Asian food shop, Roger and Sri Owen in their own small way are equally enthusiastic about tempeh. Roger encountered tempeh when he was working for the British Council in Indonesia; Sri started eating tempeh as a child in Central Java and they are now making and selling this delicate and nutritious stuff which looks, in its uncooked form, rather like Brie.

Tempeh owes much of its flavour, its chewiness and its dietary value to fermentation. Although soybeans are a potentially rich source of nutrition, they are extremely indigestible, which is why they are normally processed into sauce or paste or curd. Tempeh is fermented with a mould called *Rhizopus oligosporus*. The Owens get this starter or inoculum not from Java but from America. Making tempeh in SW19 is slightly more difficult than in Java where some 41,000 families produce about 169,000 tons of tempeh a year. In the equatorial humidity of Java the beans, once they have been soaked, steamed, dehusked and split, incubate happily in temperatures which are way up in the eighties. In March in London you need to provide the warmth artificially.

Easier, perhaps, to buy the tempeh, but if you are going to make it yourself it costs very little – a 20p 1lb bag of soya beans will produce 2½lbs. Once you have your tempeh it's amazing what you can do with the traditional addition of garlic, chilli powder, turmeric, onions, paprika, cumin, coriander and ginger.

Sri Owen has several recipes for tempeh in her excellent *Indonesian Food and Cookery*. This July, nutritionists from all over the world will be converging on Java for a teach-in on the scientific and culinary aspects of tempeh, organized by the United Nations University. There are Americans who devoutly believe that one day the tempeh burger will oust the beefburger in the fast-food charts. America already grows more soya than any other country in the world – much of it goes to fatten animals. Converted into tempeh, it could be a healthier wholefood alternative, and far cheaper than any form of meat.

21. Talking Rhubarb

There's a major thesis to be written on the creation and destruction of food choices by the onward march of transport. Take that close relative of wild dock and sorrel which came originally from Siberia and the wastes of Tartary. The Greeks got theirs from beyond the Volga, which they called *Rha*; it was a gift from the barbarians and they gave it the name *rhabarbarum*.

We welcomed it, as we did many herbs and plants, for its medicinal properties, and from its generic name *Rheum* eventually came our word 'rhubarb'. As a mild purgative, *rheum ponticum* was as useful as senna and manna, but its popularity in the kitchen stemmed from its early ripening powers – it was the first arrival of spring, the harbinger of the soft fruit season.

It is no coincidence that the National Rhubarb Collection, totalling some eighty cultivars, is housed not in the south of England but in the cold north, where poor soil and grimy air proved a bonus. The Director of the Northern Horticultural Society, Philip Swindells, told *The Food Programme* recently how the eighteen square miles round Leeds and Wakefield became the rhubarb capital of the world.

'In very depressed times,' he explained, 'it was a plant which families could derive some income from – industrial pollution was so bad there was very early leaf fall. The winters were harder than in the south and this stimulated the plants for good forcing. It meant that northern growers could produce a crop far earlier than in the south – even if the southern growers cut all the leaves off and exposed the roots to frost, they couldn't achieve what happened quite naturally in the north.'

And then the great Victorian railway system made the

distribution of early rhubarb up and down the country quick and cheap. In the heyday of our national passion for rhubarb tart there used to be a train that left the West Riding every night from Monday to Friday laden with rhubarb. The Cartilidge family of Tingley dominated the trade. Alec Cartilidge recalled his father's forty forcing sheds. 'Each shed would produce about a ton; end to end they would have stretched about a mile and a half!'

But we have lost our pre-war passion for stewed fruit and custard. Just as the age of the train made rhubarb commonplace in every part of the country, so the jet age has eclipsed the long red stems. Who wants tart sticks of rhubarb when they can have strawberries, kiwi fruit, mangoes and melons all the year round? 'You go into a greengrocer's shop now,' says Alec Cartilidge sadly, 'and there's a choice of fifty to a hundred different fruits and vegetables flown in from all over the world.'

In the days of poverty there were plenty of hands to work in the sheds, but today 80 per cent of those sheds have fallen into disuse. Lifting two-year-old crowns in the winter is back-breaking work; heating the sheds is expensive. It has made rhubarb into a high-cost crop, and the two-foot-long sticks weren't the kind of product that lent themselves to supermarket packaging.

John Whitwell, director of Stockbridge House, the government-funded research station just outside Wakefield, and his staff are concentrating on species that can be presented attractively in supermarket packs. 'Shorter sticks look better; it's a matter of presentation.'

As a staunch defender of the National Rhubarb Collection, Philip Swindells is in no doubt that when a market is in decline you've got to attract people to buy the product by any means you can. But he's not all that happy about the new strains. 'Shorter sticks are probably more attractive, certainly brighter colours are, but they don't necessarily taste better. If the public are given the option of red sticks or green sticks they'll go for the red ones, but we have proved from our own experience of eating these things that many of the green-stick varieties are equal if not superior to the red-sticked ones. I always think the forced rhubarbs are not as sweet as the outdoor ones.'

The staff of the National Rhubarb Collection are all agreed on their outright winner for taste and flavour. 'We all test them at home and we believe that German Wine is absolutely superb. You wouldn't be able to buy it in the shops; you're restricted probably to three major varieties.'

The fate that has already overtaken apples and plums – commercial concentration on a few strains to make production and distribution more profitable – has now rationalized the diminished supply of rhubarb. 'If you grow rhubarb yourself,' says Philip Swindells, 'for example an old Yorkshire variety called Cherry, which is very sweetly flavoured, it bears no resemblance to what you find in the greengrocer's. If you're keen on rhubarb, then plant a really first-class variety, not the cast-offs of commerce.'

It is a damning indictment of the cosmetic approach to food – as long as the plants can be grown easily, as long as the sticks are small and pack well, as long as they have a nice colour, why bother about the taste? And so the pride of Yorkshire is bred not for the palate but for the mini-pack.

22. Chicklettes, not Chickens

I was interested to see a TV commercial the other night for cod in parsley sauce. 'The menu,' said the voice-over, 'created to make time for the way you want to live your life.' The visuals showed a glamorous and expensively dressed model, full of frozen fish, moving across the screen to gaze ecstatically at a pot of tomato plants.

Was she raising the tomatoes for soup? Or was there perhaps in her larder a 25-portion catering pack of McDougalls smooth, rich tomato soup ('Always a wintertime favourite, especially when served with a swirl of cream and a sprinkling of chopped parsley')?

With over three million unemployed, the preoccupation among food manufacturers with saving the nation's time seems a bit perverse. Reading the pages of the catering press is to be transported into a bleak economy where time is of the essence, where skilled staff are non-existent and all food preparation must be accomplished only with cold water and a mixing-bowl, or the benefits of microwave.

'Just add water and mix . . . whisked in a trice . . . seconds only from packet to plate . . . heat 'n' eat.'

Did you know that the reconstituted crisps market sector is now worth £22 million? Golden Wonder, a brand leader in quik-snax marketing, is spending the national equivalent of £1 million on television advertising on Harlech, bringing the attention of the deprived to the newest bagged-snack wonder – Worcester sauce-flavoured square crisps.

Would you believe that six out of every ten people questioned in a recent independent survey carried out for Carnation Food Service preferred Coffee-mate for creaminess to coffee whitened with milk? And here's even more good news: 'Coffee-mate can actually save the caterer around 50 per cent of the cost involved when milk or cream are used.'

Hey! Have you heard about Lucas Ingredients Ltd of Bristol? The firm began in 1926 with two employees; it has succeeded in altering the taste of Britain unrecognizably. What they don't know about seasonings, coatings, flavours and protein processing is scarcely worth knowing.

'Crumbs!' you may cry. And well you might. It was Lucas who perfected the crumbs that coated the first fish finger. They have just invested £1 million in a new rusk process for a product which can bulk out everything from traditional bangers to Christmas puddings. Lucas are deeply committed to soya, an excellent emulsifier for comminuted meat, and they produce it in a range of grades, colours and flavours.

They also have their highly technological fingers into pies, pâtés, hams, soups, sauces, pot snacks, pizzas, meat pastes, crisps and roasted nuts. Lucas believe in the synergistic approach. Synergism in theological terms is the doctrine that the human will co-operates with Divine grace in the work of regeneration. In crumb and rusk language it means slightly less. Lucas claim that they have adopted the 'synergistic approach to help our customers achieve their goals ... we combine our multi-technological expertise in extrusion, spray drying, mixing, baking and other areas with an appreciation of trends in market requirement to devise innovative ingredients for successful food products.'

Trends. That's what it's all about. And innovation. 'Ocean Sticks' that look like pieces of lobster but patently aren't have become the fastest-selling seafood items since fish fingers were introduced. They come from Japan along with Ocean Claws, each covered with a coating of Oriental Pandora Crumb. I like that ... 'Pandora Crumb', it rolls round the mouth. This, as far as food is concerned, is of course the age of the analogue. Burgers, not beef; 'dream', not cream; chick-lettes, not chickens.

Even the Ministry of Agriculture is being forced to compromise on the meaning of words. They published some proposals last year about the role of meat in the burger. Any food described as a burger, they suggested, should have a meat content of no less than 80 per cent. It then turned out that 15 per cent of that didn't have to be meat at all; it could be fat. And what you and I know as meat is now deemed to include, as well as fat, such accessories as gristle, sinew, skin and rind.

The failure rate in the world of innovation is high. The most hotly contested area is value-added chicken products. Chicken itself is a static market – jazzing it up gives extra profit, and a judicious use of flavourings and seasonings can impart induced taste to a basically tasteless product. Crispy chicken fries, thigh meat marinated with Gruyère cheese, chickenburgers, even re-formed chicken on a stick like a lollipop, have all been tried. According to John Petter of Webbs Poultry and Meat Group, 'Out of every ten products you try out, perhaps only one will win through, but that's something you've got to live with.'

How about going back to the farmyard and rearing chickens that taste so good they won't need comminuting, mincing, marinating, injecting and assorted rubbishing? Or is it too late to turn back the technological clock?

23. The Champagne of Fermented Milks

At its best, Kefir has what the French describe as *pètillance* when it appears in wine. Indeed, Kefir has been described by enthusiasts as the champagne of fermented milks – effervescent, refreshing and probably good for you. Although it is found all over the Middle East and in other originally nomadic cultures, Kefir is thought to have originated in the Caucasus where people feel cheated if they don't clock up a reasonable amount of injury time beyond their allotted span of five score years. In Russia, millions still swallow a glass of Kefir to start the day.

When *The Food Programme* was investigating Kefir, along with other fermented food and drinks, we found it impossible to buy any commercially. Eventually the managing director of the Danish Dairy Board, who happened to be flying to London, brought some samples in his briefcase. Kefir is more drinkable than yoghurt, it is delectably fizzy and lively in the mouth. Would it catch on here? Not according to Carol Duncan, who carried out a study of Kefir in Europe and the USA in 1986.

Carol, who produces the yoghurt and cream on a farm in North Devon with her husband Peter, was given a grant by the Nuffield Farming Scholarships Trust to find out how Kefir is produced and whether there might be a future for it in British chilled cabinets. What she found on her travels is that Kefir is as varied as cheese; during its life it changes and matures just as Brie and Stilton do, and that makes it an unpredictable product with none of the uniformity and consistency which supermarkets insist on.

Kefir forms from white and gelatinous grains built by

bacteria which feed on milk. They look rather like cauliflower-florets and they need constant care and attention. Although grains from which to make Kefir are not easy to acquire, once you have them, like a vinegar mother or sourdough yeast, they last indefinitely.

It takes a lot of milk to build the grains, and the two kilos which the Duncans treasure in their dairy are worth about £350. Although the microflora of Kefir has been examined in some detail, it remains a mystery. Attempts to create the grains synthetically in a laboratory have not been successful. The magic of these living organisms obviously captivates Carol Duncan: 'I have looked through an electron microscope and seen fat yeast budding and chains of lactobacilli playing in the milk.' They work together to form the grain, she observes, much as the coral organism builds slowly into a reef.

According to Carol, the best Kefir she found was in Finland, where the mother grain is large and vigorous and resembles a huge white slug. It came originally from Estonia and is fed on skimmed milk. Consumption of Kefir, which is in competition with other fermented milks, has slumped in Finland from 11.4 million litres in 1975 to 1.5 million in 1985.

Because Kefir is a living thing, it tends to bulge in its carton and upon opening it, you never quite know what mood it will be in. Young Finnish consumers have reacted against this temperamental lactic elixir and prefer the comparatively static yoghurt, or something called Viili, a soured milk which Carol Duncan describes as being a bit like wallpaper paste adulterated with spaghetti.

In Sweden too, sales of Kefir are falling. The production of Kefir in Denmark has been cut by 40 per cent in the last three years. In Germany, despite an upbeat and sexually oriented TV commercial, Kefir is losing out to other living milk products. In Switzerland, the Kefir is so solid that sticking a spoon in the tub leaves an excavation behind. 'I was bitterly disappointed,' Carol records. 'The German product had been something of a let-down, but even though it was too thick, it did move at least.' Californian Kefir also failed to come up to Carol's expectations – it tasted like yoghurt and did not appear to be leading a life of its own as the traditional product should.

Like other fermented milks, Kefir contains lactobacilli and streptococci which medical opinion suggests may reduce serum cholesterol, improve calcium absorption, combat food-borne pathogens, cure disorders of the stomach, liver and intestines and keep the immune system on its toes.

In her report, published in August 1987, Carol Duncan admits that Kefir's impact appears to be declining worldwide but believes that a good advertising agency could give it a profitable niche in the British market. She calls for a greater initiative on the part of the dairy industry in this country to take advantage of the growing health food market. Already, she claims, the Japanese are funding and carrying out research into new milk cultures which could make them world leaders in this field. Carol Duncan reckons that until Dairy Crest learns to produce a soft-cultured yoghurt which 'does not look and taste as if it is flavoured with beetroot', we shall continue to be net importers of fermented milk products which could easily be made in Britain.

24. Singing the Herring

I am deeply suspicious of national campaigns to get people to consume more. The Tea Council keeps nagging us to drink more tea, there was the Great British Banger campaign, the French importune us with 'Le Crunch' and there are all those hoardings hyping 'Naughty But Nice' double cream. For all I know the Breakfast Advisory Bureau are even now hatching a plan to treble the sale of Super Sugar Frosties and the Packet Soup Authority are about to spend a fortune promoting the pleasures of pouring lukewarm water over a sachet of chemicals.

A current campaign which does deserve every support comes from the Sea Fish Industry Authority. All summer they have been singing the virtues of that greatly neglected fish the herring. Quite rightly, they point to its nutritional features – low in carbohydrates, high in proteins and minerals and poly-unsaturated fats – and its long and valuable history as a British staple food.

The herring is patently an intelligent fish. Where a haddock or a cod will take a hook, herrings have to be netted, and the fact that they conveniently swim in shoals has always made that easy. Herring dominated the economy of the northern waters to such an extent that when in the 1830s they forsook the sea lochs of the west coast, many families became destitute. It has been estimated that in 1845 there were almost 10,000 High-landers employed as porters, packers and gutters at the port of Wick, the busiest herring centre in Scotland. Export of herrings to Russia and the Baltic kept thousands of women working from six in the morning until light failed, packing herring into barrels ready for salting.

Even in the nineteenth century there were fears that over-fishing might destroy stocks altogether. In 1838 an unprece-dentedly large shoal of herrings entered Loch Fyne. Two Tarbert fishing-boats came upon this thrashing mass of silver fish and, unable to take them with the traditional drift-nets, had the bright idea of encircling the fish with the biggest net they could find. It worked: the ring-net had been invented. So effective was the new net that it was outlawed, but the law was difficult to enforce and it was finally repealed in 1860.

The drift-nets, long lines of nets hung just below the surface like a curtain, were so constructed that they trapped only mature fish, and although the herring came and went in an unpredictable manner, overfishing was never a problem. The ring-net was much more lethal. In the period after the First World War, ring-netting displaced drift-nets, and the purse-seiner which was introduced in the mid-1960s virtually ended trawling for herring.

The overfishing of the grounds in the last few decades led to a ban on herring fishing in the North Sea in 1977. The following year the west of Scotland was closed to herring fishermen for three years. The North Sea was reopened in 1983, but catches are far smaller than they were in the past.

In his excellent book *North Atlantic Seafood*, Alan Davidson points out that supplies of herring have fluctuated in a bewil-dering fashion for as far back as any records exist, but the general picture, he writes, 'is one of dwindling stocks being pursued by fewer and fewer boats with more and more sophisticated equipment'.

It is depressing these days to go to an island like Barra, where in the nineteenth century scores of curing stations worked round the clock from early May to the end of June, and find not a herring to be had. In Castlebay, you can see the remains of the herring jetties sticking out of the water, and old men will tell you that you could walk across the bay on the decks of the fishing boats, so big was the herring fleet.

Early photographs show a sea of masts, the quay full of

barrels and the herring girls at work with lightning fingers. They could gut sixty or seventy herring a minute. The last time I was in Barra, John Allan Macneil, who operates the ferry to Vatersay, told me that his father remembered when there were still forty-two curing stations lining the shore in Castlebay. His theory for the decline in herring catches is the way in which the Dutch have been taking herring outside the 12-mile limit. Whether it's the Dutch or ourselves who are to blame is difficult to pinpoint. The good news is that we haven't in our folly completely wiped the herring out. In an effort to promote sales, the Sea Fish people have prepared all sorts of recipes involving coconut, yogurt and raspberry sauce. But the best way to take the king of fish is the simplest – coat them in coarse oatmeal and fry them.

And now the bad news. I'm told that as most people will only eat fish when it's shaped like a bar of nougat and covered with breadcrumbs, the herring folk are busy at the drawing-board fabricating their ultimate sales weapon . . . the herring finger! If they have to go to those lengths, maybe they will at least enrobe it in oatmeal.

25. Sugar Caned

Nitza Vaillapol has been presenting a weekly programme on Cuban TV for the past thirty-four years. In pre-Castro days she had to build her recipes around commercials for processed American foods; since 1959 she has had complete freedom to expound the virtues of a healthy diet. Although Cuba still has rationing, nutritionally vital foods are sold at controlled prices, guaranteeing that everyone gets a fair share.

But, since the revolution, there has also been an increase in heart disease and obesity; people are eating more and the traditional dependence on sugar in this island of sugar cane, far from diminishing, is now being officially subsidized – every man, woman and child is entitled to a ration of 5lb of sugar a month, double what we buy in Britain. In Batista's day, when malnourishment was endemic, it was a cheap source of energy, and the taste has become compulsive.

Just indeed as it has in Britain. We gave sugar cane to the Caribbean through our prosecution of the slave trade, but we also gave ourselves a cheap supply of sugar which radically altered our cookery. Before cane sugar became accessible even to the poorest, honey and dried fruits were used for sweetening, and herbs and spices added interest to almost all our dishes. The new cheap sugar made tasteless foods more palatable and sweetened bitter ones. Expensive spices fell out of fashion and we became a sugar-addicted nation.

Although we are now buying less sugar over the counter, our overall consumption is not declining – more and more sugar is being consumed in manufactured foods. Apart from obviously sweet things, like puddings, cakes, biscuits and con-fectionery, sugar is increasingly being added to savoury foods, and sugar in one of its various forms finds its way into the most unlikely products – corned beef, frozen chips, salt-and-vinegar-flavoured crisps and packet soup. The processor's rule of thumb seems to be 'if in doubt add sugar'.

The health lobby are increasingly concerned about our growing compulsion to eat over-sugared food and the way in which the labelling regulations fudge the facts for the uninitiated. Sugar also appears as fructose, sucrose, glucose, dextrose and maltose, which enables manufacturers to ring the changes happily. A bottle of baby food marketed, less than carefully, by Mothercare claims in bold print on the front of the label 'No Added Sugar (sucrose)' but in minute print on the back label one of the ingredients turns out to be dextrose. A current added confusion is the fallacy, fostered particularly by health-food shops, that in some magic way 'brown' sugar is nutritionally more valuable than white sugar.

Almost all our information about the virtues of sugar comes from the Sugar Bureau, funded largely by the two firms who control over 95 per cent of the sugar industry, Tate & Lyle and British Sugar. Its director-general, a keen lobbyist for sugar, is the Tory MP for Uxbridge, Michael Shersby. He and his bureau have just published a free brochure claiming, with carefully selected quotes from medical papers, that sugar cannot be associated with disease and if it is, then it's not the only cause.

The message is comforting, reassuring and an open invitation to disregard the alarmist wing of the dental and medical profession. 'There is no proven link between sugar and coronary heart disease,' the copy runs. 'Sugar is not the single cause of dental disease . . . Sugar by itself does not make you fat . . . There is no evidence to support a direct relationship between sugar consumption and diabetes . . . Sugar does not cause behavioural changes.'

Confident in the purity of the product, British Sugar, who market Silver Spoon, the brand leader, are currently spending two million pounds to highlight the taste enjoyment of sugar in the biggest ever campaign mounted by a sugar manufacturer. Despite the fact that the retail market (not including much larger amounts of sugar used by the food manufacturers) is in excess of 800,000 tonnes a year and worth £430 million, Silver Spoon's marketing director, Peter Gibbs, thinks we could do better. 'Sugar is not achieving its potential,' he said. 'We aim to put that right!'

Saatchi & Saatchi, who are in charge of the campaign, have devised special recipes to be handed to cookery writers, and with an eye on the future, have devised films, videos, filmstrips, wallcharts and booklets 'telling the fascinating story of sugar production in Britain' for free distribution in primary and middle schools. Because it is women who buy sugar, the Sugar Bureau has invested £200,000 in promoting women's sports. And so the pressures to increase consumption of sugar mount.

If you feel like an alternative dentist, Richard Cook and his wife Elizabeth have produced their guide to sugar-free living, *Sugar Off*. It contains cogent arguments against excessive consumption of sugar and a variety of recipes which don't use sugar at all. Contrary to the propaganda of the Sugar Bureau, food and drink actually taste better unmasked by sugar – but there's no profit in paying Saatchi & Saatchi to tell you that.

26. Hard to Swallow

Here's a fairly inflammatory bit of information. Did you know that Nittedal, the crack Norwegian cycling team, are on drugs? They owe their pedal power to GX2500 Premier Korean Ginseng, which enhances the level of oxygen absorption in their blood by a staggering 6ml per kilo of body weight. Last year the Korean wonder-root gave them no fewer than five international victories and they are going for gold at the 1992 Olympic Games in Barcelona.

I derived this fascinating fact from a deluge of bumf and free samples which have been billowing through the letter-box since I inadvertently ticked a questionnaire requesting details of products on offer at a recent health exhibition called Helfex.

As I tap this piece out I am sucking a small lozenge of Miracle CQ10 which, according to Dr Emile Bliznakov (a moniker straight from the pages of Perelman), can, according to the evidence of double-blind trials, reverse my periodontal dilemma – that's the one where your gums recede and your teeth fall out. Birch extract, silica and thyme, those are the restorative specifics which are going to redress decades of neglect and decay.

I'm also rather keen on something called Aloe Vera which Cleopatra used constantly to help her dry and itchy scalp. Aloe Vera, according to the firm who sell it, is mentioned in the Bible, although my own tattered Concordance does not exactly confirm this. Nefertiti, that lesser serpent of old Nile, bathed in the stuff, which is packed with useful things like steroids, antibiotic substances, trace sugars, eighteen amino acids and the efficacious xylose. Apart from tightening facial tissues, alleviating gout and regenerating dead skin, it's also very useful for arthritis, sunburn, cramps and constipation. On top of all that, it has the power to aid the heart's rhythms. At around £7 for 480ml, it's a therapeutic snip.

I'm also anxious to try a sample of Rangus Massage Oil, which was perfected by a witch doctor of that name from Lapland. Although the original reindeer fat has been replaced by vegetable oil (a wise precaution considering the appallingly high post-Chernobyl levels of caesium in the far north), it still has magic properties which arrest growing pains in infancy and counter numbness in the joints.

Helfex was not entirely devoted to medicines and ointments for sick humans. Elderly cats and dogs have been offered new hope by the launch in the UK of McFarlane DF4, a nostrum based on the anti-inflammatory powers of *Perna canaliculus*, better known in gastronomic circles as the New Zealand green-lipped mussel. Grateful pet owners countrywide are endorsing the dramatic effects achieved by this natural marine product, which not only relieves arthritis but promotes a noticeable improvement in the animal's coat.

I'm also watching out in my local health store for the remarkable Blueberry C tablets, as used by pilots of Air France 'because of their ability to take off gas, to give appetite and to soothe'. And that's not all. Blueberry C expedites the formation of something referred to as 'eye purple', which helps one to see in the dark.

These products come from all over the world and none are more wondrous than those from Switzerland. It was the Swiss who gave you Bio-Strath, made by feeding yeast with over ninety medicinal herbs and adding germinated barley, honey and the juice from biologically grown apples – muesli on speed, so to speak. Despite the Consumer Association's unkind verdict on Bio-Strath ('It all depends whether you think there are fairies at the bottom of the bottle'), the Swiss elixir still sells something approaching three-quarters of a million bottles a year in Britain alone.

Using modern scientific techniques, Swiss researchers have

now perfected a millet-based capsule to prevent falling hair. Robert Golaz, whose ancestors went prematurely bald and who is pretty bald himself, found that millet had been associated with hair growth for centuries. Using only the finest golden millet from Argentina, the Laboratoire Golaz have created 'Pil-Food', containing amino acids well known for their contribution to the biosynthesis of nature's own essential hair-building block, keratin.

There's no doubt that the health-through-pills market is booming in food-scared Britain. In publishing circles, the high ground in the health-through-food market has been brilliantly secured by the Wellingborough-based firm of Thorsons. Their list of dietary books for those with problems has a guaranteed readership; they estimate that at least one in twenty people are affected by food and chemical allergies and millions more could achieve greatly improved health by feeding themselves more wisely.

Their latest title in the Special Diets series, *Hyperactive Child: Special Diet Cookbook* by Janet Ash and Dulcie Roberts, was originally published as *Happiness is Junk-Free Food* and its uncranky list of 'Do's and Don'ts' for buying and preparing food and making simple, healthy meals could improve the nutritional balance of every household. I certainly wasn't aware that most frozen vegetables are treated with a chemical to help preserve their colour. The list of foods to be avoided by those who don't want a chemical cocktail on their plate grows longer by the day.

Do you get headaches, stomach pains, aching joints? Do you wake sweating and are you permanently exhausted, moody and depressed? The answer may well be to throw away your pills and drugs and buy a Thorsons guide to healthier eating.

27. Eggs from the Garden

To the north-east of Bury St Edmunds lies the ancient village of Troston isolated now among the grain prairies. Opposite the church, with its fifteenth-century screen, is a timeless cottage in which Francine Raymond lives with her husband Jean-François. He is an industrial designer and inventor; Francine, in a former life, was a highly successful fashion designer working in Milan.

In 1996 she decided to combine her favourite pastimes – cooking, gardening, keeping hens and running a shop – into a full-time occupation. In July, when I went to Troston, the garden of Church Cottage was a riot of flowers, fruit and vegetables. Francine had been out in the sweet-smelling herb garden and the salad beds snipping away at rocket, basil, coriander, garlic chives and sorrel for a lunch-time bowl of summer leaves. 'Each day's salad is different, each meal is delicious. Because I don't spray my produce the leaves don't need washing, just a dressing of good olive oil and vinegar.'

Francine is particularly proud of her small flock of hens, and their attendant cockerel, who form a vital part of the garden's ecosystem. They follow her around as she digs and delves and harvests her produce. Besides being decorative, hens are excellent pest controllers; as well as eggs, they provide manure and are voracious devourers of kitchen scraps. In her stylish booklet, *Keeping A Few Hens in Your Garden*, Francine suggests a simple way of providing yourself and your family with fresh eggs nearly all year round.

'The egg', she writes, 'is a perfect natural food – unrefined, unprocessed, unenriched – and free-range eggs definitely taste better. Depending on the breed, you can get brown, tinted, white, speckled or even turquoise blue eggs.' All domestic chickens are descended from the jungle fowl of Asia and today there are some 160 domestic birds to choose from. The traditional Rhode Island Red and the English Light Sussex are relatively cheap; pure breeds tend to be more colourful and expensive. Francine's favourite is the Orpington; large, docile and available in several colours. At the end of its life it makes a very good table bird but eating your Orpington would be, as Francine says, rather like eating the family Labrador.

What I didn't know was that unless you register your flock, and have the whole operation inspected, you can't sell eggs even to your neighbours. Francine stressed the importance of checking the rules and regulations about hen-keeping with the local Environmental Health Officer, and telling the neighbours what you're up to, especially if you're going to keep a noisy cockerel. I asked Francine what role the cockerel played apart from fathering chicks. 'He's surprisingly useful. He keeps an eye on the hens. If he finds anything to eat he always offers it to them first. He's very keen on finding them new places to lay and he's very protective.'

With a little luck all your birds will live long, happy and productive lives. 'I've got a nine-year-old who lays about forty eggs a year. In commercial breeding they'd probably kill them in their second year.' Watching and listening to the hens as they strutted and foraged in the garden conjured up an age when salmonella was not a threat to health. 'People of my generation', said Francine, 'can remember hearing hens when they were children. During the war most country people kept hens but no longer.'

For lunch there were hard boiled eggs to go with the salad and egg mayonnaise to dip artichoke leaves into. I had a bit of a struggle peeling my boiled egg, a lot of the white clung to the shell. It was a sign of their freshness. 'People forget how nice fresh food is,' said Jean-François. 'It's nice to be able to go into the garden and find the salad and pick up eggs laid that morning; we enjoy that very much.' And so did I. Sad, as we approach the end of the twentieth century, to have to face the fact that you can only have a really fresh egg if you keep your own hens. Sad, too, to have been reminded that the government is still advising that mass-produced eggs intended for infants, pregnant women and the elderly should be thoroughly cooked.

28. *Olive Oil – not just for Medicinal Purposes*

At the Bertolli olive oil plant in Lucca last week I was comforted to see them filtering their finer oils through cotton wool. It was a comforting childhood association which brought back memories of golden oil warmed in a spoon, poured into an aching ear and dammed with a twist of cotton wool. It was a long time before I found out that olive oil was more exciting when applied internally down the throat. I still haven't got used to the idea of drinking it, though.

'I have devoted by life to olive oil,' said Dottore Pier-Vincenzo Mazzoni, passing a sample of extra virgin over his sensitive tastebuds. We were standing in a nineteenth-century olive mill on the outskirts of Lucca. The millstones the size of lorry tyres were still there. In their time they had reduced a hundred harvests of olives to a paste which was then pressed to a liquid in the wooden structure, like a giant windlass, which stood in another part of the room. These days most of the 350,000 tons of olive oil consumed each year in Italy is extracted by heavy and unromantic machinery – the old mill where we went for our tasting was now a *ristorante* and the millstones had been idle for years.

'We are tasting,' said Dottore Mazzoni, 'for fragrance, aroma, flavour, sweetness, fruitiness. You don't swallow, just let it fill your mouth.' A convenient spittoon stood by, but I found the experience more medicinal than gastronomic: old prejudices die hard. For every litre of oil the Italians pour into their soups and saucepans we still only manage to force down the equivalent of an eggcup full. We prefer Mazola or dripping in the chip pan, and put more store on malt vinegar in the salad than a splash of extra virgin.

Dottore Mazzoni has been blending olive oil for Bertolli all his working life. The firm is the brand leader both in Italy and America, and it keeps out front by providing the kind of oil Italians like. 'In this country,' said the dottore, 'marketing is less important than the palate. People will try your oil once, and if they don't like it they won't buy it again.'

The firm buys its oil from some ten suppliers in Tuscany, but the best comes from Lucca. I gathered it was something to do with the microclimate, the sunny slopes of the hills that encircle the medieval walled town, and the humidity.

Olive oil varies from the rich, thick green variety, earthy in flavour and as viscous as Essolube, to lighter golden oils more suited to mayonnaise. It is classified according to its natural virtues and its acidity. Extra Virgin must be perfect in flavour, aroma and colour and have a maximum acidity of one per cent. Fine Virgin must be equally perfect, but its acidity is permitted by the International Commercial Standard to rise to 1.5 per cent. Ordinary Virgin is a lesser thing altogether; it aims to be acceptable rather than perfect and its acidity can be as high as 3.3 per cent. The fourth category is known, paradoxically, as Pure – a blend of Extra Virgin and oil which has been subjected to washing, decantation, centrifugation and filtration to make it better than it might have been.

Italians are using more olive oil than ever – last year their consumption of Extra Virgin rose by half. Firms like Bertolli are cashing in on the excellent health image of the product. 'In Crete they use more olive oil than anyone else in the world,' says the dottore, helping himself to a dash of Fine Virgin, 'and their heart disease is the lowest in the world.' On the cans of oil that Bertolli exports to America is the bold statement: No Cholesterol. Our labelling laws do not permit such statements, true though they may be. The *New York Times* claimed recently that because of the high level of monounsaturated fats in olive oil it may be even more effective in lowering cholesterol and safer to eat than large amounts of polyunsaturates.

To encourage Americans to switch to olive oil, Bertolli recently launched in the States what it describes as 'the first *new* olive oil for over 4,000 years'. Its two big selling points are its culinary versatility (it has a very high smoking point, which makes it ideal for frying, but enough character to make a good mayonnaise or to flavour a salad) and its comparative blandness when compared with the stronger oils the Italians prefer.

29. Crusading in Cornwall

Mary Martin and her sister Virginia were raised at Gooseford in St Dominic on the Cornish side of the River Tamar, a landscape of rushing streams, deep valleys, cider orchards and daffodils. Sadly, by the time Mary returned to Cornwall after graduating from the Royal Academy schools the valley had changed. Gone were most of the cherry and apple trees, grubbed up to make way for more commercial crops or brought down by strong winds and old age.

Mary and her partner, James Evans, started researching the old varieties and for the last fifteen years they have been planting almost forgotten trees with names like Ben's Red, Blue Sweet, Captain Broad, Early Bower and Limberlimb. When I went to see Mary, Virginia and James there was much talk of the past over our lunch of vegetable soup, good strong cheddar, watercress picked from the garden and bread baked fresh that morning.

James's father farmed between Callington and Launceston, Virginia's and Mary's grandfather was a miller; most of their relatives had worked the Cornish land for generations. One hundred years ago the orchards of the Tamar valley were prolific; the whole area was famous for its extraordinary variety of fruit and the springtime blossom. 'A lot of the fruit,' Virginia recalled, 'was sent by river to Devonport market but once the railway arrived at Plymouth in 1849, London and the Midlands became a big market – Tamar cherries sold all over the country at 2d and 5d a pound.'

I hadn't realized that cherries froze well. On the table was a bowl of small, black and wonderfully sweet Burcombe cherries from the 1996 crop. We talked of the long ladders needed to

reach the topmost cherry-laden branches, the predatory star-
lings which could spoil a whole orchard in half an hour and
the good seasonal food the Tamar farms produced.

'The farms and gardens here in St Dominic were almost
self-supporting. We had poultry and eggs, pigs for pork, bacon,
sausages and hog's pudding. Cows provided milk, butter and
cream; there was salmon from the river; fresh vegetables and
rhubarb used in the spring for pies and tarts until the strawberries ripened.'

A wide range of crops spread income through the year and
rotation helped maintain soil fertility without the use of artificial fertilizers.

But by the time James and Mary began their crusade to
bring back the old fruit trees of the past, local orchards had
deteriorated almost to the point of no return. Many smallholdings had been sold to incomers and folk memory of how things
were had almost disappeared. For more than a decade, like a
pair of detectives, Mary and James spent all their spare time
talking with everyone in the region who had a knowledge of
the old trees. Some even recalled the taste and flavour of old
apples and which ones were good for eating, stewing, cider-
making and turning into apple dumplings.

Then came the long years of grafting old shoots on to new
root stock. James presented friends and relatives with labelled
trees so that they became spread around the valley. Cornwall's
climate and soils produced cherries and apples completely
different from those found in Kent – it seemed an act of
vandalism to let them perish. Three years ago they bought two
nearby fields and with the help of a grant from the county
council they have laid the foundations for a new but traditional
Tamar Valley orchard.

While James planted, Mary painted. Her pictures are a
remarkable record of the yearly cycle of trees and plants. On
good days she is at her easel from eight in the morning until
dusk moving, as she says, sometimes between four or more
pictures 'following the sun's effects, feeling that special state of

excitement at the prospect of capturing something of the heartbreaking perfection and frailty of blossoming trees.'

The orchards they have created have little or no commercial value. Supermarkets will not sell their apples and cherries but the achievement is immense. The rescue of old and interesting trees was a race against time – a few twigs of an ancient Red Pear were plucked from a bonfire.

This amazing labour of love is a story told in an evocative book called *Burcombes, Queenies and Colloggetts*. Mary's pictures, Virginia's words and James's research are an inspiring celebration of what imagination and enthusiasm can achieve when wedded to a respect for nature and the accumulated wisdom of the past.

'What we are preserving', says James, 'is fruit which was on the edge of extinction. We have proved that the old varieties can be grown without chemical sprays.' It was refreshing to meet people whose concern was not for profit but for the glorious valley in which they are privileged to live. 'Now when I paint the orchard,' says Mary, 'I feel more hope and less nostalgia for, out of the corner of my eye, I can see the new trees taking their place as distinctive successors to the old ones.'

30. Pudding Lore

Cut out puddings, said my doctor scrutinizing my cholesterol readings. He told me to cut back on a lot of other comforting things – cream, butter, cheese, cakes and biscuits. So it's farewell to the pud for a bit; that's like waving goodbye to a substantial piece of our national heritage.

The pudding has changed its nature in a remarkable way over the centuries. In medieval times if you were talking about puddings, what you had in mind was a stomach of a pig or sheep stuffed with minced meat, suet, seasoning and spices and boiled for hours. The most enduring manifestation of this culinary past is the haggis, immortalized by Robert Burns as 'Great Chieftain O' the puddin' race'.

Puddings have always had understrappings of pastry and dough and although the word has broadened to include all manner of pies, tarts and light desserts a real pudding by definition is a filling experience, none more rewarding than the plum pudding prepared for Christmas which is the apotheosis of pudding.

Think of puddings and steam rises before the eyes from baked jam roly-poly, suet and syrup, toffee apple, sponge, semolina, rice, dumplings, cabinet and chocolate puddings. Recently a club was set up to celebrate the passing of the pudding. Its members meet once a month to enjoy a night of gastronomic nostalgia.

Lose a dish and you lose a little bit of your history. One of the things we've lost are all the local puddings named after the villages and towns in which they were created. *Malvern* pudding majored in apples and eggs. *Manchester* was largely jam; *Nottingham* embraced the glorious Bramley apple, *Mansfield*, sold at the annual fair in Sherwood forest, featured currants and suet, *Newcastle* was a superior version of bread and butter pudding speckled with candied peel, *Southport* of the sandy beaches had a mouthwatering pudding in which suet, apples and nutmeg came deliciously together and *Warwick* was famous for its rich confection of glacé fruits, ginger, rum and brandy. *Monmouth* was a bread and jam pudding baked in a gentle oven while *Shropshire* called for brown bread and nutmeg and a serving of brandy butter. To make an *Ipswich* pudding, you took half a pound of best blanched almonds, orange flower water, the yolks of eight eggs and the whites of four and beat it all up before baking.

Tadcaster was noted for its baked treacle suet pudding, the people of *Canterbury* enjoyed a plain sponge with hot wine sauce, retired colonels in *Cheltenham* liked baked suet with fruit and in the Roman city of *Chester* their great pudding treat was really a custard of egg yolks, chopped almonds and the juice of lemons. In *Deptford* and *Chichester* they swore by a milk and egg yolk pudding and in *Exeter* their seven-egg pudding was thickened and warmed with rum.

Some of the most popular puddings of all are based on that cheapest of ingredients: bread. Bread pudding itself, solid and shot with dried fruit, and bread and butter pudding are the two great national standbys.

Then there is a whole repertoire of batter puddings, none more celebrated than *Yorkshire* which had the dual role of being served with gravy before the main course and as a dessert with syrup or jam.

Every county seems to have had its preferred recipe for batter puddings. In *Kent* the batter was cooked over juicy summer cherries. In *Tiverton* they steamed their batter with ginger and candied lemon rind and *Tewkesbury* batters were packed with freshly picked fruits. In the little Nottinghamshire town of *Gotham* wise men and women served their batter with cowslip wine and sugar.

The heyday of the pudding must have been at the turn of the century before the motor car and central heating had softened us all up. In those days houses were cold and enormous amounts of energy were consumed in manual labour and keeping warm – you needed large helpings of pudding to fuel the body.

Lady Clark of Tillypronie, who collected recipes avidly all her life, had no fewer than 150 for puddings including countless variations on old favourites like cabinet pudding for which she offers six alternatives. Then there was a fig pudding ('get boxes, never drums of figs'), Half-Pay Pudding (raisins, sultanas, currants and treacle), George IV Pudding ('you will need 9 pancakes'), Cholmondeley Pudding ('take the sharpest possible apples') and Venus Pudding ('ornament a well-buttered mould with preserved ginger').

And the greatest of all the British puds? Surely bread and butter must be the outright winner. It has cream and eggs, crisp on the outside and soft within, it is a pudding for all seasons just as fulfilling eaten cold as piping hot from the oven.

But if I had to nominate one pudding which never fails to delight then it would be that classic lemon pudding known as *Sussex Pond*. It calls for all the things that raise cholesterol no end – flour, fresh beef suet, butter and sugar. All you do is line a basin with suet dough, fill the bottom with demerara sugar and butter, and place in the middle a whole lemon pricked all over so that the juices will be able to escape. After boiling for four hours the lemon will have almost disintegrated giving a wonderful citrus flavour to the suet crust. It may not be good for the lipids but it does wonders for the palate.

31. The Big Cheese Revival

It was a bitterly cold January day back in the late 1970s. I was standing in a stone farmhouse on mainland Orkney. Outside the rain was turning to sleet and snow but Mrs Laird's kitchen was warmed by television arc lights. We had come to film the making of a traditional cheese. Mrs Laird already had her pans of winter milk on the stove and while the cameraman was setting up she watched them with an expert eye.

'I learnt', she told me, 'when I was fourteen when I went to work at the farm. The summer cheese is the best with the new grass and everything and when the cow is new calved the milk is better I think. There's not many of the younger women interested in cheese making. They would sooner have the prepared stuff, what do you call it? Processed cheese.'

Mrs Laird's implements were simple – a few bowls, hand-presses, cheesecloth. She didn't measure the rennet that curdled the two gallons of warm milk, she added the salt by the fingerful. Cutting the curd, the draining, the moulding and maturing in the whitewashed scullery were as commonplace as making a pot of tea. And yet her cheeses were perfection, unpasteurized masterpieces.

On the following day we went to the creamery in Kirkwall to watch Orkney cheese being made on the production line. For commercial purposes the milk is heated to 160 degrees Fahrenheit, a process which kills the micro-organisms and destroys most of the enzymes which lend cheese its flavour. The high temperature shrinks the curd and produces a putty-like cheese with the two essential parameters of modern marketing: year-round consistency and a long shelf life.

So here were two cheeses both made from Orkney milk,

totally unrelated in texture and taste. The one made in the
Hozen farmhouse was crumbly and full of flavour; the other
was unmemorable and bland. There are still one or two
farmer's wives left in the Orkney islands making their cheese
by hand. I get mine from Shapinsay. It's usually made by
Williamina Russell. At this time of the year she and her
husband have seven milking cows and when the demand for
liquid milk is supplied she only has enough left over to make
about seven 2½lb cheeses a week. She is hoping that her
daughter Vera will carry on the tradition. There is one other
family on Shapinsay making cheese, a handful more elsewhere
but you get the impression that it's all very tenuous. A rural
craft that may well expire through lack of interest.

When I was a child spending my summers in Skye every
other house had crowdie on the table for tea. Who makes
crowdie in Skye today? Shop-bought crowdie from Presto,
factory Dunlop, creamery Cheddar and added value fun cheeses
have taken the place of the old local cheeses all over the
country.

If you want a date for the decline in British cheese then
1939 is a good enough benchmark. When Neville Chamberlain
went to the microphone on that Sunday morning in September
there were over 1,600 farms in Britain which were known to
be making cheese for sale and many more where farmers' wives
made it for purely family consumption. The cheese varied from
farm to farm and county to county. By the mid 1970s when I
was watching Mrs Laird at work in Orkney there were fewer
than seventy farms where cheese was being made in what these
days one must call the traditional way.

In Gloucestershire where in the eighteenth century 7,500
tons of cheese were made every summer there was no commercial cheese production whatsoever. And so the sad tale ran
all over the countryside. Farms which before the war had still
been making cheese let their moulds and presses rust. It was
easier to sell the milk than go through all the trouble of
converting it into cheese.

Patrick Rance, the good cheese guru, began his crusade against what he called 'the rising flood of plastic-smothered insipidity' twenty years ago in the days when the Milk Marketing Board held such powerful sway that many people were convinced that it was determined to wipe out Real Cheese altogether. Its marketing arm, Dairy Crest, had even had the insolence to register the two words 'farmhouse cheese' for their own exclusive use. It was a pre-emptive strike which angered the mild-mannered Food Standards Committee so much that they rapped Dairy Crest resoundingly on the knuckles. 'The word "farm" and similar expressions designed to attract the desired rural cachet', they said, 'is misleading if the foods to which they are applied have not been produced on what the general public would understand to be a farm.'

Despite the fact that the Committee – about as potent an instrument for change as a petition from the poor – deprecated this bastard use of the word 'farm' nothing of course was done. Two years later in their *Report on Cheese* they noted disparagingly that some of the larger 'farmhouses' were producing cheese in excess of 5 tonnes a day. Wouldn't the more honest word, they enquired mildly, be *industrial* not *farmhouse*?

Most of the Farmhouse cheese sold in Britain today comes from mass production creameries which bear about as much relation to a farm as a sickle does to a combine harvester. Just as bread has become wrapped sliced lint and beer has evolved into a tanker product made bearable only by massive transfusions of CO_2 so most of the cheese we're offered today is, ironically, ideally suited to accompany the wretched bread and the awful bitter in that sterile offering known as a Ploughman's Lunch.

Nowhere is this burden of mass production and automation more apparent than in the dreadful bars of soap which are sold in supermarkets as Cheddar. Once it was the greatest cheese that England produced. The Mendip Hills were as famous here as any cheese-producing region of France. Today most of the Cheddar on sale in supermarkets is an insulting extruded curd which has nothing to do with England at all.

Although Cheddar is still the most popular cheese in Britain with a 44 per cent slice of the market most of the cheese sold under that name is young, unmatured, and about as interesting as bubble gum. Cheap 'Cheddar' from Germany and Belgium has already cost us more than 500 jobs in British creameries. Nine per cent of our native Cheddar is prepared in automated factories and disgorged in custom-built blocks designed for the machinery which will chop them into cryovac-wrapped rectangles ready for the supermarket shelf.

The well-matured cloth-bound truckle is getting rarer and rarer and more and more expensive. Most of the twenty-three farms still making Cheddar in the West Country are using pasteurized milk much to the regret of enthusiasts like Patrick Rance who believe that pasteurization is death to flavour and character.

One man who does not share that romantic view is Viscount Chewton, heir to the Waldegrave Estate which makes truckles of Cheddar in the traditional manner and matures them for up to a year. 'In the early days we used unpasteurized milk and we wound up having to throw a lot of our cheese away. You have a lot of E. coli in milk and it's bound to affect the cheese. If you're just making a few cheeses a week and you're extremely careful you can get away with it but you do run into problems of hygiene. As for pasteurization killing the flavour. Well I don't know. Dear old Pat Rance makes a song and dance about it and you get other people claiming that they can tell which meadow a cheese came from. I think the reason that unpasteurized cheeses do have so many fans is that they are almost all made with loving care by people up to their elbows in milk and there's no doubt that when you're making anything by hand unless you're hopelessly inefficient it must be better than what comes out of a machine.'

The polarization between the giant automated creameries turning out cheese by the tonne and the handful of farms and smallholdings where the daily output of cheeses can often be counted on the fingers of one hand is complete. The new cheesemakers tend to be good friends of the earth and utterly opposed to additives, and they are passionate conservationists and revivalists.

A cheese folk hero is Charles Martell who almost single-handed restarted cheesemaking in the county of Gloucester which in Victorian times used to export 5,000 tonnes of cheese a year to the rest of the country. The cheese was made from the milk of mahogany-coloured cows known as old Gloucesters which after the war had along with cheesemaking almost died out. Charles Martell began making cheese at Dymock fifteen years ago as part of a campaign to save the Old Gloucester cattle. He now makes 16,000 kilos of unpasteurized Single and Double Gloucester a month and his newly revived Double Berkeley, coloured traditionally with marigold petals, triumphantly disproves Lord Chewton's theory that pasteurization is a universal panacea.

His example inspired John Crisp at Newent who also has a herd of Gloucester cattle and is now making 2,000 kilos of superb Single and Double Gloucester all year round – and, of course, unpasteurized. Former insurance salesmen, musicians and redeemed academics are numbered among the growing ranks of middle-class cheesemakers. As with the owners of English vineyards they all appear to have been remarkably successful in another career before creating their dream dairies. They produce all sorts of cheeses from the traditional to *feta* and *Brie* lookalikes. Cheeses come flavoured with whisky, coated with paprika and chives, rolled in oatmeal, flavoured with sage and onion. Some might think it's all been overdone a bit. Better though for a few eccentrics to overdo it than not have it done at all.

So successful has Patrick Rance's one-man crusade for real cheese been that last year the much maligned Milk Marketing Board as a placatory public relations exercise issued a brochure listing 180 cheesemakers using cow's milk, ewe's milk and goat's milk. The MMB had a reputation for discouraging small-scale cheese production but they are now changing their public face in these matters. Patrick Rance was so impressed by this public-spirited gesture that he agreed to write the foreword. In it he rather unkindly but quite rightly pointed out that even with the current revival only 0.45 per cent of British milk goes into cheese made by traditional methods. In some parts of the country, notably Scotland, traditional farm cheesemaking has all but perished. On the Scottish mainland, as far as I can establish, there are now only four or five farms making cheese for commercial sale. The most successful recent recruit is a Carnwarth farmer Humphrey Errington whose ewe's milk cheese is now selling all over Britain.

In the age of Walter Scott you could have bought sheep's cheese quite easily in the Edinburgh markets. Scott had himself painted with his daughters attired to go sheep milking and his Meg Dods praised the ewe's milk cheese of the Borders as an excellent substitute for Gruyère. When the Industrial Revolution covered the Clyde valley with smoke a new affluence created a demand for mutton; lambs were fattened for the table and the supply of milk for cheesemaking dried up. Humphrey Errington with the help and encouragement of the West of Scotland Agricultural College at Auchencruive began in 1985 to make small amounts of mould-ripened cheese from the unpasteurized milk of his own herds of sheep. He hired as his cheesemaker Mary Lang, the daughter of a local farmer who had been trained in the mysteries of cheese at Auchencruive. This summer production of Lanark Blue is running at 130 3½ kilo cheeses a week.

Another couple who have put the clock back successfully are the Butlers of Lower Barker Farm, who live on the western slopes of the Forest of Bowland. They weren't doing very well out of their poultry so in 1969 they decided to start making traditional Lancashire cheese. Before the war there were 200 farms in Lancashire making cheese in the old-fashioned way from two-day curd. It took time to make and was not suitable for mass production. So a new cheese was invented, harsh and high in acidity, which is called New Lancashire. Jean Butler and her husband Thomas with a milking herd of 120 Friesians are now among the four farms left in Lancashire producing what Jean would describe as real Lancashire cheese. 'This new stuff is totally different. It's white, it's dry, it's acid and sharp; ours is more buttery and creamy. I think the whole thing is misleading to say the least. We have to mature our cheese for up to six months and the way in which we make it is very time-consuming.' The Butlers produce only twenty-five cheeses a day. Small stuff compared with the brave new Lancashire creameries.

But real cheese production doesn't have to be small to be beautiful. At Chewton Mendip, nine miles from Cheddar Gorge, the 700 Friesian and Ayshire cows on Viscount Chewton's estate produce a ton of cheese a day. Cloth-bound, matured for up to a year, the cheese finds favour with connoisseurs even though it's made from pasteurized milk.

At the other end of the scale is the success story of a couple who ten years ago knew nothing about cheese at all. Leon Downey was principal viola with the Hallé when he decided to loosen the strings and buy eighteen irresistible acres in Pembrokeshire. 'We bought a cow,' he told me, 'we bought a manual and we started making cheese. We gradually found our way into hard cheese because nobody else was doing it. Then Dougal Campbell started making cheese at Ty'n Grug Farm in Llandeilo so we weren't alone.'

Today Joan and Leon Downey have eighteen milking cows which produce 70,000 litres of milk a year that is converted into 18,000 rich cheeses with a natural crust they call Llanglofan. 'We had no help from the Milk Marketing Board. We tried for grants and couldn't get any. They said, "Crikey, you can't make a living off eighteen acres," so I said, "I'll show you!"' And the Downeys have shown everyone just what can be done if you have enough enthusiasm. Last year they won every marketing award going; they've even been visited by a delegation from the Basque country keen to see how a small organic mixed farm can pay.

Paradoxically they have now been caught in the tangled web of EEC lunacies. 'To be quite honest we just can't make enough cheese to supply demand. This year our quota of milk is being reduced compulsorily so the government will be giving me a grant to produce less milk, with the result that there'll be a shortfall in our cheesemaking and the gap on the shelves will be met by imported cheese. Our plan ten years ago was to give people who don't want a slab cheese a choice. We proved there was a demand. Now the bureaucrats are clamping down on the supply.'

Many cheeses have died out through lack of people to make them. Fifteen years ago I was in Dorset looking for Blue Vinny, a hard, low-fat cheese which once was as famous as Caerphilly or Cheshire. I met old people who knew other old people who used to make it but as far as I could ascertain not an ounce could be had. When Patrick Rance came to write *The Great British Cheese Book* in 1982 he pronounced it as dead as the dodo.

Now it's been revived by Mike Davies who farms 400 acres on Blackmoor Vale. He has 160 cows and uses the less fat morning milk to make his Blue Vinny. 'We don't want it to be creamy – in fact I add skimmed milk to bring down the fat content. The milk is of course unpasteurized and that makes production more difficult, you've got to be that extra bit more careful.'

During the four years that he's been making Blue Vinny Mike has seen two other people have a try and then give up. 'You've got to be enthusiastic in this field. Quality control is a problem. A lot of people don't know how to market their cheese once they've made it – it's all uphill.'

The man who knows more than anyone in England about the new cheese revival is James Aldridge who does for good cheese what a *négociant-éleveur* does for good wine in France. He seeks it out and then matures it. As you read this 3,000 cheeses are maturing in his Kent store, cheeses he has judiciously bought from makers he respects.

He is scathing about the boutique cheesemakers who give their product a fancy name and the rest of the trade a bad name. 'In the last five years the number of people making cheese in Britain has increased more than tenfold. Seventy per cent of them are probably turning out decent cheese – the rest are making rubbish. Most people don't know the difference, especially if it's tarted up with chives or herbs.' Five years ago Aldridge was buying from about twenty different makers, now he has sixty suppliers countrywide. 'Some people make a good cheese one week and a rotten one next week. Then you get an enthusiast who makes good cheese and he sells out to someone who's only interested in money. They expand production and start turning out rubbish. People go on buying it because of the name. I'd like to see people try cheese before they buy it. I'd like to see more experimental cheeses. There's a tremendous market for cream cheeses similar to the French ones. We've got the cows, the pastures, why can't we do it?'

One of the reasons might be that there is no central advisory body to which enthusiasts can turn. When Mike Davies started making Blue Vinny he was lucky enough to turn up a recipe in some old files. No one was there to back him or advise him.

Why not create a really active British Country Cheese Authority which could help production at all stages? That could perhaps be counter-productive thinks James Aldridge. 'People who make good cheese aren't usually in it for the money. They make it on a small scale and they do it with love and great care. Once the demand grows there is always a temptation to lower standards. I've seen it happen over and over again.'

When you're buying cheese do not be taken in by fancy wrapping or high prices. Do what the French do, try a bit before you buy. There's a lot of money to be made at the moment marketing cheese – new shops are springing up in every affluent High Street. Remember anyone can make cheese – not everyone can make good cheese.

32. Cheered-up Chicken

A reader of this column who has to watch his sugar intake recently bought an attractive-looking brown-skinned roast chicken from Marks & Spencer. When he got it home he found that the ingredients included brown sugar, dextrose and sodium polyphosphates. He asked me why chicken, which his mother and his wife had always managed to roast without added sugar, needed this kind of adulteration. And what were polyphosphates doing in poultry?

I wrote to M&S on his behalf and got an immediate and helpful reply. Vivienne Jawett, their food and wine press officer, sent me a reprint of the staff newspaper for February 1989 which featured a report by a journalist who had watched the chickens being processed at a factory outside Glasgow. They are wheeled in trolleys into one of seven giant dry-air ovens and cooked to a minimum internal temperature of 85 degrees centigrade; and that's 13 degrees above the survival limit of salmonella and listeria.

The article was full of information about packing and the sophisticated systems of 'cold chain' distribution which race chilled products to the shopper in the shortest possible time. All very impressive and laudable. But not a mention of the sugars and polyphosphates. In a short accompanying letter Vivienne explained that sugar is added to aid the browning of the chicken and the polyphosphates are injected to retain the succulence of the meat.

It wasn't clear whether the brown sugar was there solely to colour the skin or to lend some kind of extra flavour. The fact that polyphosphates had to be added suggested that without them the chicken might be a dry old thing. We students of modern food technology know that polyphosphates are a widely used additive in such products as fish fingers, cheap luncheon meat, sliced ham, burgers and turkey meatloaf. Polyphosphates are manufactured by heating orthophosphates. According to an expert in these matters, Dr Tom Coultate, at normal levels of use these substances constitute no health risk 'since they appear to be hydrolysed to orthophosphates by the pyrophosphates present in most animal and plant tissues'. Dr Coultate, a senior lecturer in food biochemistry at the South Bank Polytechnic and a former research assistant in the Unilever laboratories, makes no bones about the vital role that polyphosphates play with their convenient ability to enhance the water-binding properties of muscle proteins. Products like luncheon meat, based on homogenised or macerated muscle tissues which have been tumbled and massaged in special machinery, achieve their texture largely due to these emulsifying and water-retentive salts.

What this can mean in practice was demonstrated to me many years ago in a seafood plant on the west coast of Scotland where queen scallops were being processed for the European market. The manager showed me how the tasty little molluscs are shelled and then allowed to lie in tanks, taking up as much water as their muscles can pump in. When flash-frozen in that water-inflated state they look bigger than they really are and on the scales they weigh more. When they are thawed all the water runs out, which is disappointing for the customer, but there you go. The manager told me that some processors soaked their scallops in a polyphosphate solution: 'That way they take up much more water.' No, he said looking shocked, they didn't stoop to such practices. Over a drink he told me how you could get even more water into a scallop or a prawn by dipping it into icy water a second time and giving it a second flash-freeze. They called it double-glazing and no they didn't do that sort of thing themselves.

According to Vivienne, the M&S chicken cooked in hot air is one of their most popular foods, a fact which, she claims, 'demonstrates our customers' appreciation of this high quality product'. Vivienne was very pro-active about the added sugars as well. 'Cooked chicken', she told me, 'without dextrose and brown sugar would be less appetizing and therefore we have not offered this product to our customers.' Marks & Spencer pioneered the cook-chill shopping revolution; is it beyond their resources to find a supply of naturally succulent chickens which wouldn't need to be bolstered with polyphosphates? And why not have them roasted properly so that they don't need all that added sugar?

Meanwhile I am recommending my diabetic reader to try a small local butcher if he still has one. In the last twenty years 28,000 independent butchers' shops have gone to the wall and the big six supermarkets have captured over 50 per cent of the retail meat trade; that means less choice in the high street, not more. David Lidgate, a founder of the hundred-strong Q Guild of quality butchers, assures me that none of his members colour their chickens with sugar or soaks them in polyphosphates. Any consumer with an eye on quality will wish them well in the future but small butchers' shops are still closing at the rate of forty a week and they will be increasingly vulnerable when the new Unified Business Rate comes in with the Poll Tax. Where I live the rate bill for small shops is likely to be doubled; how long will our one remaining butcher be able to survive?

33. Tea and Honey

In a supermarket the other day I was watching people choosing tea. I went there to do a little bit of research. Was it flavour that determined choice or price? Most shoppers went for the own brand packs which were a few pence cheaper than nationally advertised teas. They liked that particular tea, they told me, it made a good cup. Did they ever experiment? Now and again but by and large they stuck to the blend they always had.

It probably wasn't a very valid way to do market research and maybe I would have got different answers if I had gone into a speciality tea shop but there didn't seem to be much curiosity. Tea was tea and that was that. To really appreciate the virtues of tea and its infinite varieties you have to go and talk to the men who grow it and the experts who blend it. Over the years I've been lucky enough to visit quite a few tea estates in different parts of the world and in London I've been made privy on various occasions to the secrets of successful blending. That's made me very choosy about the teas I buy. Teas are rather like wine. You can buy something for everyday drinking very cheaply; but the outstanding vintages from the great vineyards – well, they cost a bit more.

In Calcutta not so long ago I spent a morning with Dipak Roy of the Indian Tea Board; he talks about the magic leaves with a lifetime of experience at his command.

'We in Britain', I said expansively, 'must be your best customers.'

'Well, you buy a lot of our tea and you buy a lot from Ceylon and elsewhere but sadly you don't buy our *best* teas.' More than 65 per cent of the finest India tea now goes to the

Russians. The Germans too go only for the best and the Japanese are also frantic buyers of the top teas. But when it comes to writing cheques the oil sheikhs of the Middle East sweep the board.

'This', says Dipak Roy handing me a small glass-sided silver caddy, 'is a sample of probably the highest priced lot we ever sold at auction here in Calcutta.' In 1979 seven chests of these exquisite leaves from Doolahat in Assam sold for the present day equivalent of £25 a pound.

'Mind you, it would have taken eight or nine months to collect that much tea; the very finest tips from the very finest high-grown bushes.'

Slow growth yields high quality, hence the unchallenged excellence of the tea gardens which climb a quarter of the way up to the Himalayan peaks. 'You must go and look at the best,' says Dipak Roy, 'and then you will know what real tea tastes like.' It wasn't until a couple of years later when I was back in India that I got a chance to spend a couple of nights at Namring estate whose teas had just set record prices in Calcutta.

The manager, Chaudhary Mangal Singh, met me at Bag-dogra airport which lies on the plain below Kalimpong and Darjeeling. There was a ninety-minute drive ahead. The rains had been heavy and part of the road had been washed away. The sun was falling like a blood orange in the sky as we began the ascent. Soon we were climbing in low gear and the night air was cool after the heat of the plain. Although the bulk of the tea that India produces is of average quality, exceptional teas – the first flush of the highest bushes – can fetch prices which seem unbelievable for a mere handful of dried leaves. Mangal tells me that a few months ago, a small parcel of 101 kilos of particularly delicate tea from Castleton estate at Kur-seong fetched £86 a kilo. I said we didn't pay anything like that for *our* tea. Mangal looked at me sadly. He didn't think much of the British palate and he told me that as a nation we were not interested in really good tea. Mangal is not a man to contradict. So far that year he had hit more centuries than any other manager of a tea estate in India. And I'm not talking about cricket. In the tea business if a parcel fetches more than a hundred rupees a kilo at auction, it's a century. How many centuries had Mangal scored then? 'Eighty-two! The next best? Well, there are managers who have hit about forty or fifty but nowhere near eighty-two.'

When I woke up next morning and went to the window the view was awe-inspiring. If you can imagine Ben Nevis covered with tea bushes, that wouldn't be a bad analogy. Namring, the fourth biggest estate in Darjeeling, stretches seventeen miles from east to west and the bushes range from 1,000 to 6,000 feet. Women in saris hover like butterflies among the bushes and from the long low bungalow which is the school the chant of children's voices wafts across the valley.

For breakfast there is one of the most delicious jars of honey I have ever tasted. 'Tea honey,' says Mangal. 'They say there is nothing more lovely. We have many bees and this is what they make.' With our toast and golden honey we drink not just any tea but a second flush picked in the first week in June. It is golden in the cup, not the kind of tea you would dare pollute with milk.

'This tea fetched £30 a kilo at auction – most of it went to Japan.' Mangal approves of the Japanese; they buy the best. 'Probably,' he says, pouring another cup, 'you'd have to pay 3,000 rupees a kilo for this in Tokyo.' The tea is delicate and has great depths of taste. But then at that price it must be the equivalent of a glass of Château Lafite? 'Much better than wine,' says Mangal loyally, 'the best tea in the world.'

I don't know whether it was the best tea in the world but on that fine morning with the sun falling on the peaks of the Himalayas it was quite an experience. Perhaps we ought to be a bit more adventurous when we have tea for breakfast. Not just throwing a teabag in the pot, but selecting the right leaves to make the perfect infusion.

In India you drink Indian tea. In this country we have traditionally been very lucky. We have teas from almost every country in the world to choose from – China, Sri Lanka, Indonesia, East Africa, Kenya, Malawi, Tanzania and Zimbabawe. We're currently drinking a tea grown in the Cameron Highlands of Malaysia. It's a tea we got very fond of when we lived there. I've never seen it on sale in Britain but if you know anybody coming from Malaysia ask them to bring you a quarter. It stands up splendidly to London water and is equally good at breakfast or in the afternoon.

Are some teas better than others? It depends what you mean by better. Take Earl Grey. Now Earl Grey is really looked upon as the Rolls-Royce of teas; it has overtones of butlers bearing breakfast trays down the long corridors of country houses. Nobody quite knows what role Earl Grey played in creating this very idiosyncratic blend but one story is that an emissary of the noble Lord, while travelling in China, saved the life of a Mandarin who in gratitude sent back to England a delicately scented blend which forever after bore the name of the second Earl. The Earl Grey on sale today is usually made from fine Darjeeling blended with teas from China and oil of bergamot. Bergamot is citrus in origin so Earl Grey is not improved by the addition of milk – a slice of lemon would not come amiss.

Whether you like Earl Grey or not it is a unique experience, better perhaps in the afternoon than with a heavy breakfast. Perhaps the most famous of all China teas is Lapsang Souchong. Large-leafed and reminiscent of autumn bonfires, it is a light greyish-green in colour and its immediately recognizable smokiness might well remind you of the aroma of grilling bacon. Again this is a tea which would be mortally offended and terminally wounded by milk. Drunk best on its own perhaps. I once tried it with a plate of smoked salmon but that wasn't the answer either.

One of the finest black teas from China is Keemun which in the days of the Imperial court rivalled Oolong from Formosa. Whatever the fragrance of an orchid is, then Keemun is deemed to rival it. The tea comes from Anhui province and is nutty on the palate. Two green teas from China are Gunpowder and

Jasmine. The liquor of Gunpowder is straw-coloured, the flavour delicate and the aggressive name was bestowed on it by
early British merchants who thought it resembled lead shot – in
appearance that is, not taste. Jasmine tea is a blend of green and
black teas aromatized with dried jasmine leaves; a feminine
and almost voluptuous liquor which deserves to be drunk in a
contemplative manner. China Pouchong, an Oolong tea with
a lower than average caffeine count, is blended with various
blossoms including jasmine and gardenia; mild and almost pink
in colour it would be ideal on a long hot summer afternoon.

These are fairly expensive teas for special occasions but
worth seeking out. Michael Smith recommends Yunnan tea,
deep-toned and golden-hued, as being ideal for the making of
tea punches or served well chilled. Do not be misled by the
term 'Orange Pekoe'. Not an orange-flavoured tea this but a
descriptive term. Pekoe comes from the Chinese *Pak-ho* meaning white hair; a characteristic of the tender top two leaves and
bud of the tea bush is the fine white fibre on the back of the
leaf. Orange Pekoe is a rolled leaf wiry in appearance. These
are top grade teas from Assam and Darjeeling.

The teas of Assam are strongly coloured, big in flavour and
ideal for the early morning cuppa. Darjeeling teas are the clarets
of tea, so perfect that they can be drunk on their own and are
ideal for drinking after dinner. Most teas are improved by
blending and many of the 1,500 blends on sale contain between
twenty and forty different teas, some there to give strength,
others flavour and others to lend colour. You can make your
own blends to suit your own palate. Ceylon, bright and golden,
is most often blended with Indian teas to produce the perfect
breakfast cup but Darjeeling and Assam blends are equally
bracing. A small pinch of an expensive and egregious tea like
Oolong can work wonders with an inexpensive brand and if
you find Earl Grey too scented on its own try it added in
moderation to your own favourite blended tea. Just as the teas
of China are unbeatable with Chinese food so over the decades
we have grown accustomed to the taste of tea with a whole

range of good food. I wouldn't dream, for instance, of taking a Loch Fyne kipper at breakfast with anything other than a cup of tea. Bacon and eggs were designed for tea and in the afternoon would you really want thin cucumber sandwiches and scones with anything other than tea? And that great invention of the British – High Tea – is exactly what it says it is: afternoon tea elevated to the status of dinner with savoury dishes, but always with a hot pot of tea at the ready.

It is perhaps the refreshing but not overwhelming properties of tea which make it so universally appropriate. A creature of habit, I am loath to begin the day without a cup of tea. Being a rapid riser I'm in the kitchen before anyone else doing it all just as the book says. Run the tap until the last vestige of stale water has gone; warm the pot, let it infuse. And then the delicious first taste – hot and strong, energizing. A transfusion on which to build the day. Others may go on to other beverages at breakfast but I stay with tea. Croissants with coffee I'm sure are just the job but I'm a marmalade man and marmalade calls for tea. In the middle of the morning while others spoon powder into cups I'm at the tea again. What is so perfect on its own and so right with so many things? Last thing at night it's tea again; something fragrant and light from a special tin. It may be fashionable to drink other things but there is a rightness about tea, a fitness of taste and substance which makes it more ubiquitous than any other beverage.

And memorable too. I've taken tea with muffins in Boston, tea with Peking duck in Singapore, tea with curry on the hill railway to Nuwara Eliya in what in those days was called Ceylon. I've drunk tea on the banks of the Tay and in lonely crofthouses in the Outer Hebrides. Tea with fried haddock in the Isle of Skye, tea with poached salmon in Skibbereen, tea at the Ritz and tea with baked beans on toast in that very good Pull Up on the old A1.

But enough of that. Time, I feel, to put the kettle on.

34. A Peruvian Delicacy

The humble raisin has been around for at least 2,000 years but it hasn't always been very popular – particularly in the US where novelty is all when it comes to food. Behind the rise of the wrinkly no-hoper to its current status as a hip, healthy snack lies an absorbing tale of modern marketing.

This autumn I visited the San Joaquin Valley in California where almost half of the world's raisin crop is grown. In this fertile, irrigated region which is roughly the same size as the Netherlands, there is an abundance of fruit. Peaches, apricots, plums and nectarines nestle amid thousands of acres of vine, originally planted for table grapes and wine.

In the summer of 1873 there was an unseasonal heatwave in the valley – so intense that it shrivelled the grapes in every vineyard. The growers appeared to be facing ruin until one bright spark hit on an idea. He took a wagonload of the spoiled crop to San Francisco and passed it off as a Peruvian delicacy. It was a sell-out, and the Californian raisin industry was born.

This year the UK will import 28,000 tonnes of raisins – that's five times the figure of a decade ago. Yet, in recent years, raisins have suffered from an image problem, which seems odd in the health-conscious US. After all, what could be more natural and nutritious than a deliciously sweet grape dried by the sun? Low in fat and sodium, rich in minerals and fibre, the raisin contains virtually no fear-inducing cholesterol.

The simple fact is that American consumers regarded them as boring, which is why 60 per cent of the crop had always gone into products like bread and biscuits.

Research revealed that people were prepared to buy raisins, but only as an ingredient for the store cupboard. Even then, they would only put in a brief appearance in puddings and cakes at Thanksgiving and Christmas. Little old ladies who had relished home baking were a dying breed and the younger generation simply couldn't relate to raisins.

Small wonder that the US marketing industry was finding it hard to sell the idea of the raisin as an all-day snack.

In 1985, the advertising agency Foote, Cone & Belding conducted a series of surveys to discover how the younger sector viewed these 'little nuggets of sunshine'. Compared with other nutritious foods, they fared badly. Perceived as 'weak' and 'lonely', one respondent went so far as to condemn raisins as 'embarrassing to be seen with in public'!

Lorna Wood, a promotion activist working for the industry, gave me the full shock-horror story: 'People knew raisins were good for them. They liked them, but they were regarded as wimpy and very uncool. Eating raisins just wasn't the neat thing to do. They needed a total personality make-over.'

What happened next has passed into advertising legend. Through the wonders of animation, the dancing raisins campaign was born. As they strutted along to Marvin Gaye's Motown smash hit *I Heard it Through the Grapevine*, these wrinkled little fellows captured the hearts of American youngsters. 'Kids kept insisting on actually meeting "The Raisins", so they were brought to life for celebrity appearances in New York's Thanksgiving Day Parade – and even for the presidential inauguration,' said Ms Wood. 'We persuaded people to think of raisins as warm, funky and cool – and it worked.' Needless to say, sales rocketed.

The manufacturers have a high regard for their product. Take food technologist Garry Obenauft: 'Raisins plump up during cooking whereas sultanas fall apart. And they are a great enhancer of shelf-life. Put them into a product and you can take out most of the preservatives.'

Raisins were first included in American cookies only six years ago, but the idea has caught on dramatically. 'People from the UK are astounded when they walk down a cookie aisle in the US, as it may be 60 feet long. Not all contain raisins, but a great deal do,' said a marketing mogul. He explained that every biscuit has to have a different flavour and must be new or improved, as Americans have a short attention span: 'The food here is a bit like the film industry; you always have to come up with something else.' So, with such a fast turnover, there's plenty of scope for raisins.

However, there is another problem – drought. Before the wells were sunk in the nineteenth century, the San Joaquin Valley was as dry as the Sahara. Even now the irrigated patches are surrounded by arid desert. 'We're in our sixth year of drought,' said farmer Joe van Gundy. 'No new water supplies have been developed in twenty years.'

If rain doesn't come soon, there will be no vines or raisins and the desert will swallow up the fertile land. At the moment that is not a future anyone is prepared to consider in the happy valley of San Joaquin.

35. In Praise of Venison

My acquaintance with venison began late in life – I don't recall eating it as a child in London or in the Hebrides. In shooting lodges and Highland castles they ate it by right; ordinary folk were not encouraged to enjoy it.

Deer were stalked not for meat but for their magnificent head and antlers. For landowners, a deer forest was a status symbol; and the more land values rose, the harsher the game laws. Gone were the days when, in the words of the old Gaelic proverb: 'A fish from the pool, a tree from the wood and a deer from the mountains are a theft no man was ever ashamed of.'

You needed a licence to handle game. Small wonder that there is no culinary tradition in ordinary homes for venison or any other sporting game.

It is not without social significance that we export 80 per cent of our venison to Europe, and in particular Germany, where game is not regarded as the preserve of a particular social class.

This lack of interest in venison is a great pity. The wild herds of the British Isles are multiplying at a rate that places enormous pressure on the land. It is estimated that the population of red deer in Scotland alone will have to be reduced by at least 100,000 to prevent long-term damage to natural woodland. So there's no shortage of deer, a food which fulfils all the criteria for healthy eating. The animal feeds naturally and hasn't a gram of surplus fat. It is also one of the most flavourful meats, and a young hind or stag properly hung is as delicate as lamb or beef, and much cheaper.

A venison steak is a gastronomic treat, but there are other bits that make even tastier eating. I remember some twenty years ago eating deer liver for the first time. I was roaming Deeside researching a television documentary when I met a couple of stalkers busy disembowelling – or gralloching – deer on an estate.

The hearts, lungs and livers were to be thrown out for the dogs. We had our sheepdog with us and this looked too good to miss – could we have some? They were only too happy to give us the 'umbles' for which, presumably, there was no commercial demand. We boiled the heart for the dog and sliced the liver almost paper thin, which we lightly floured and seasoned. Just shown the heat of the pan, it was tender, full of flavour and unlike any liver we had ever tasted.

A couple of years ago, Safeway made a valiant attempt to persuade customers to eat more wild Scottish venison, but it doesn't have to be wild to be enjoyed at its best. John and Nichola Fletcher started the first twentieth-century deer farm in the late 1960s. John is a vet who was awarded a doctorate for research into deer on the island of Rum. And in her book *Game for All* Nichola tells us that rearing deer for sport and the table has a long history; in mediaeval times there were 1,900 deer parks in England.

At their farm in the Howe of Fife, the Fletchers keep 300 red deer. In the summer they graze on grass; in winter their feed is supplemented with hay and potatoes. They are reared compassionately and killed by a single rifle shot to the brain, with far less stress than in a slaughterhouse.

Most of the Fletchers' venison is sold at around eighteen months and hung in a chill room for two to three weeks. The carcass may have as little as five per cent fat; and whether from red, roe or fallow deer or my favourite, the sheep-sized sika, venison is as versatile as any domestically reared meat.

When I visited the Fletchers, I had the pleasure of eating deer liver once again. Nichola put a little oil in the pan, floured the slices and, as she put it, gave them a fright in the heat. With a salad, fresh bread and a glass of red wine, it was as fine a feast as you could imagine.

Whether roasted, prepared as steaks or collops, made into stalker's haggis, potted or hashed, turned into spicy sausages, rich soup, a terrine or pie, venison is not to be missed. The famous French chef Alexis Soyer rated venison second only to turtle soup in the hierarchy of great British dishes. It is high time to reinstate it.

36. 'When the Herring are in the Loch . . .'

I was brought up eating herring – you couldn't live in the Hebrides and not be aware of this enormous bounty from the sea. The 'silver darling', as it was known, kept whole communities in good health and prosperity, which is reflected in the old Gaelic saying: 'When the herring are in the loch, the doctor is out of the house.'

In the 1920s, cargo vessels came from Hamburg, Stettin, Danzig and other Baltic ports to fill their holds with herring, and boats packed with barrels of cured fish sailed from the tiny island of Barra to New York. The herring was so remarkable a source of prosperity that the boats coming from all over Europe to collect their share at the time of the Gold Rush in the Klondyke became known as 'klondykers'. Today's klondykers are vast factory ships that process fresh herring on the spot, but what they take is a tithe of the immense trade in herring which reached its peak in the Edwardian era. In those days, around 2,500,000 barrels of cured herring, weighing over 250,000 tonnes, were exported to Europe every year.

Eight thousand boats crewed by 44,000 men and boys went to fish. On shore an army of 21,000 women and girls followed the boats and, with bleeding hands, gutted and packed the barrels.

Between the 50s and 60s the herring catch fell by half. By the early 70s, changes in the sea bed, availability of food, the salinity of the water and the ruthless efficiency of the purse-seine nets – some the size of a football pitch – had contributed to a further decline in stocks. It wasn't until 1977 that the

North Sea herring fisheries were closed, and in 1983 the ban was extended to the west of Scotland.

Although there is now a relatively stable supply, we have lost our taste for it – which is a shame because a plump herring contains more vitamins and minerals than any other fish, flesh or fowl.

The herring is a fascinating and beautiful fish that moves about in 'families', each with its own distinct patterns of migration and spawning. Streamlined and camouflaged as the colour of the sea, the herring is far too fly to take a baited hook. The only way it can be caught is, unsportingly, in a net.

In the Baltic countries it was said that every girl who went to the altar knew a hundred ways of preparing a herring! In Germany a scholarly tome was devoted to the herring. To this day, the Scandinavians pay far more attention to it than we do: in towns and cities like Copenhagen, it comes in many guises and the recipes are closely guarded.

The fat flesh of this versatile fish lends itself to marinating. Whether you bake, grill, fry or pickle it, the herring remains a fish for all seasons. And I haven't even mentioned its glories when kippered.

'How extraordinary that a fish of such character is so difficult to sell in the restaurant,' writes Rick Stein, owner of the Seafood Restaurant in Padstow. 'If I were to serve fresh herring fried in oatmeal with bacon, I doubt I could sell two on a busy night.'

We now export 85 per cent of the catch, preferring it seems to eat a frozen fillet of haddock. Research reveals that people don't like the smell of herring, have never learnt how to fillet it and find it far too bony.

The inhabitants of Lewis, who once supported themselves on the annual herring shoals, now manufacture capsules of fish oil. Nineteenth-century travellers in the Hebrides were amazed that the natives – who appeared to exist on only herring, potatoes and oatmeal – were so healthy. Scientists now know why: herring and mackerel are rich in Omega-3 fatty acids which protect against heart disease. But instead of visiting the fishmonger for our ration of fatty acids, people today buy their protection from the chemist.

The herring gulls still wheel over Mallaig – once the premier herring port of Europe – but they may be all that remains of the romance that surrounded the heyday of the drifters.

37. The Right Size of Apple

I was down in Herefordshire in October looking at the formidable 1989 apple crop. In a packing station I watched as the Cox's were graded. The right-sized good-looking apple fetches significantly more than a wrong-sized good-looking apple. Taste doesn't at this stage enter the calculation.

'Shoppers don't want apples that don't look nice,' the foreman told me. 'These are too small, they'll go for juicing I expect.' The small apples looked delicious – they were just the right size to give a child to take to school.

'If the apples are too big people won't buy them either. So what you're really looking for is a consistent apple of the right size.'

That seemed to me to go against all the principles of farming. Surely what the apple-grower wanted to do was produce apples with a good taste and flavour? I went a couple of miles down the road to a small farm where Ian Pardoe was moving towards organic growing. 'I gave up artificial fertilizers seven years ago and all we use now is a small amount of fungicides, as little as possible.'

What it's meant to the Pardoes is a substantial saving in their bill for chemicals but Ian Pardoe is finding that the supermarkets don't have much interest in his product. His fruit doesn't look as good as apples cosseted with growth regulators and all the other sprays that make an apple look good.

I'm not sure that the supermarkets have got it right. If Ian Pardoe's Cox's are a bit misshapen and vary dramatically in size, does that really matter? What is the virtue of having carrots, potatoes, pears and apples all the same size?

The virtue is solely commercial. If you are trucking fruit and veg all over the country in pre-packed see-through bags the filling of the bags is almost impossible if the product isn't of uniform dimension. You might end up with one bag containing eight carrots of medium size alongside a bag with two big carrots.

In the old days when carrots and apples came in wooden boxes the greengrocer could provide exactly what you wanted. If it was three large potatoes for cooking in their jackets you could have those; if you wanted big apples for baking all you had to do was pick them out.

When supermarkets trumpet the tremendous choice they have brought the consumer what they really mean is a choice of what is commercially convenient. If you want expensive exotica like mangoes, rambutans, lychees, star fruit and papaya you can have them all the year round. You can have strawberries from January to December as well and all sorts of luxuries air-freighted in from the Third World.

But produce which is not available in quantities suitable for national distribution is being edged out. I discussed this with a supermarket executive who vigorously denied that bulk buying meant the elimination of real choice.

'We encourage all our managers to buy small quanities of local fruit and veg if it's top quality; we don't want to see regional specialities disappear.'

In practice not much of that happens. In Kent I was taken round an apple orchard where twelve different varieties were growing. 'There's not a supermarket in the country which could cope with all this. They want a whole container load of Golden Delicious or a thousand cases of Elstar. I could give them twenty boxes of Lambourn's, thirty boxes of James Grieve, I've got six Allington Pippin trees – they don't want to know.' This particular grower is happily selling to local greengrocers and does a big trade in his own farm shop but he is not of much use to the supermarket industry.

Perhaps it isn't the fault of organizations like Sainsbury's,

Tesco, Waitrose and Marks & Spencer. They aim to give the public what the public wants.

'If it won't sell then we can't stock it,' said a produce buyer patiently explaining his dilemma. 'Housewives buy with their eye and you can go on as long as you like about carrots grown in manure but if the carrot looks all gnarled and twisted there's no way we can shift it.'

But who is dictating what finds its way on to the shelves? Many farmers will tell you that they can only sell fruit and vegetables which are grown to the supermarket specification. 'That specification goes mainly for looks – they want cauliflowers all the same colour and size, they want each tomato to weigh the same as the others in the bag and above all they want it to look pretty.'

Perhaps it's our fault. When did you last take a plum back and complain about its lack of flavour? When did you last return a pear because it had no taste? The choice the supermarkets offer is immense when it comes to breakfast cereals, packets of dessert mix or snacks. But real choice has been systematically narrowed in the last twenty years as far as fresh produce is concerned.

If you want two potatoes on a polythene tray all scrubbed and covered in clingfilm then the supermarket is where to find them. If you want four tomatoes beautifully presented and lovely to look at you know where to go. But is that really what we used to know as choice?

I would like to see a move by shoppers to exercise their power more decisively. But maybe we've left it too late. Traditional fishmongers, bakers, game dealers, butchers and greengrocers are closing down every day because they are unable to compete with the convenience, the banking facilities, the cheque cards and the cheap petrol pumps of the out-of-town hypermarkets. Before long there won't be many small food shops left. And not long after that our last chance to exercise real choice will have disappeared.

If you think I'm exaggerating just look around your own

High Street. Is there a fishmonger left? An independent butcher? How many greengrocers are there? In the part of London where I live eight small food shops have closed in the last few years – three of them shut their doors within months of the opening of a brand new supermarket. The prospect of a Britain where we'll all be eating the same standardized food does not appeal to me. Time perhaps for a redefinition of what we really mean by choice.

38. The Acceptable Face
of Smoking

In rainswept Scotland from early times curing food over peat or wood fires was an essential method of preservation. Most families who lived near the sea were skilled in a light smoke which not only kept fish for a week or more but imparted taste and flavour to what was an often monotonous diet.

The joy of smoking in the days before computer-controlled purpose-built kilns was its infinite diversity and it is individuality which the new breed of Scottish craft smokers are going for today. They would understand Kate Archy, widow of the gardener at Inverewe who in the nineteenth century smoked her fish in an almost bespoke fashion. 'Who nowadays', wrote Osgood Mackenzie of Inverewe with reverence, 'could settle like her the exact quantities of salt, sugar and smoke each dried salmon and grilse required to suit the date of their consumption, whether immediate or deferred, confidentially imparted to her by the dear calculating mother? Until salmon close time ended the family was never disgraced through being out of salmon or wonderful kippers, not to mention venison and venison hams.'

Meat, whether it was venison, beef or mutton, lent itself to long, slow curing in the chimney, usually in the smoke rising from a peat fire. Shetland is still noted for its 'reestit' mutton from which pieces could be cut to flavour a soup or make a stew.

In Sir Walter Scott's day the Borders were renowned for their mutton hams carefully pickled with salt and a little coarse sugar and hung for months in a shepherd's chimney. 'No sort of meat', said the talented Isobel Johnstone writing under the pen name of Meg Dods in 1826, 'is more improved by smoking with aromatic woods than mutton.'

History books give the honour of inventing the kipper to an Englishman, John Woodger of Seahouses in Northumberland, but writers as early as Martin Martin in 1703 described how the people of the Western Isles 'kippered' their herrings by hanging them in the rafters of their stone and thatch houses to cure in the smoke of the peat fire. Wherever the herring were landed what wasn't consumed immediately was either pickled or smoked, and of all the herring the ones that fed in Loch Fyne were considered to be the plumpest and the tastiest.

Marian McNeill, author of *The Scots Kitchen*, recalled staying one summer on the shores of Loch Fyne. She used to watch the boats sail in at dawn and unload their crans of herring which were run straight up to the kippering-sheds. 'Here the fish were plunged into a brine bath and hung up to smoke over smouldering oak chips while their colour changed slowly from silver to burnished copper. We ate them fragrant and succulent for breakfast next morning with buttered baps, crisp oatcakes and hot tea.' Once she sent a box of these white (lightly smoked kippers) to a friend in London who wrote back by return saying: 'Gold would not buy these here!'

While the west coast became famous for its Loch Fyne, Mallaig and Stornoway kippers the east coast perfected three different kinds of cure for the ubiquitous haddock – the Buckie, the Arbroath and the Findon which were originally smoked over smouldering seaweed after being split and immersed in brine. According to Sir Walter Scott the seaweed imparted 'a relish of a very peculiar and delicate flavour'.

It was the fishermen of Auchmithie who were the first to behead, gut and wash small haddock, tie them two by two, brine them and hang them on rods over oak chips until they were coppery-brown on the outside and creamy within. By the beginning of the nineteenth century the haddock smokers of Arbroath had eclipsed their rivals in Auchmithie and ever since haddock cured in this way have been known as Arbroath smokies.

The doyen of the smokers is Bob Spink whose family firm was established as fish curers and merchants in 1915. They hold two Royal warrants (one for the Queen and the other for the Queen Mother) and, fiercely proud of their fifth generation inheritance, continue to smoke in the traditional way despite a skirmish with Brussels back in 1992.

The European Commissioners wanted Arbroath's twenty-seven smokers to swap their traditional wooden poles hung in brick pits for more hygienic stainless steel. Arbroath councillor Alex King claimed the Brussels bureaucrats had hygiene on the brain. 'Send them over here,' he roared, 'and let them try to pick up poles from an oven!' At the eleventh hour the newfangled regulations were altered and the wooden poles reprieved. Each firm was given £5,000 to satisfy the EC on smaller matters but the old traditions were preserved.

Elsewhere in Scotland a great deal of money has been invested in pleasing the Eurocrats but I'm happy to say that a lot of swashbuckling individuality survives. I was talking to a fishmonger in the Borders recently who showed me the small cupboard under the stairs in which he smokes wonderful salmon and white fish. 'It's the build-up of the tars', he said proudly, 'that make our fish so tasty.'

All smokers have their own favourite cures and rituals. In Biggar the Simpsons, mother and son, cold-smoke prime locally caught soles over oak chips after marinading them in lemon juice, salt, rosemary and libations of silver birch wine from Moniack Castle. The Fletchers of Auchtermuchty in the Howe of Fife who farm their own deer cure venison haunches for about three days in a salt, pepper, red wine and root ginger brine before smoking. At the Colfin Smokehouse near Portpatrick they cure trout, herrings and salmon in a brine flavoured with brown sugar, dark rum, juniper berries, black peppercorns and bay leaves before smoking over oak chips and sherry cask sawdust.

Fergus and Shona Cumming of Dinnet in Aberdeenshire dry salt their fish which they prefer to brining, while in gloriously remote and beautiful Achiltibuie the innovative Keith Dunbar prefers brining because he claims it offers him greater subtlety of flavour. The international reputation of the smokehouse at Achiltibuie was founded on the traditional Scottish sweet-cure achieved by marinading sides of salmon in a brine with rum, molasses and juniper. Then there's the Glen Moray malt whisky cure and salmon cured in the Edinburgh fashion by dry salting them overnight and lightly smoking them over smouldering oak sawdust.

Near the pier in Mallaig Andy Race smokes almost everything the boats bring in from lemon soles, turbot, halibut, cod, monkfish, haddock and even whelks, and on the shores of Loch Fyne Andy Lane and Johnny Noble smoke cod's roe, mussels, trout and herring. Andy is currently Chairman of the Scottish Salmon Smokers' Association some of whose members export up to 80 per cent of their production. What is angering them at the moment is the nefarious trade in imported Norwegian farmed salmon which is often smoked north of the Border, dressed up in tartan wrappings and passed off as Scottish. They are taking court injunctions but with Norwegian salmon at its cheapest ever the temptations to dissemble are pressing.

All the more important to know your smoker. One who exports to Europe, Japan, the United States and Hong Kong is Debbie Hammond whose attitude to her fish informs the whole process. At the Shetland Smokehouse in Skeld they dry-cure their salmon and give it a moderate smoke. 'The most important thing is that the fish must be absolutely fresh. We choose the fish we're going to work with; what we do afterwards is minimal. We use premium sea salt and because we find oak too overpowering on its own we use quite a lot of beech which leaves a delicate, distinct aftertaste.'

Denis Wilson who smokes local produce at Eckford near Kelso agrees with Debbie. 'We specialize in smoking eels and the first secret is to start with a good specimen.' Mr Wilson's son Hamish is the official eel-catcher for the river Tweed and they select only prime eels for smoking. 'It may sound inhumane but we starve them for two to three weeks to get rid of any unwelcome residues from their diet. Brining rather than salting – that's the real secret. Salting is much quicker but we like to do things slowly.'

Over in Galloway Allan Watson goes in for a full strength smoke, heavily pronounced, powerfully strong. 'We use good quality salmon and we cure it with rum and dark syrup. Then we smoke it for a lot of time, maybe thirty-six hours over oak sawdust from Grant's distillery.' Allan told me that he was not interested in supplying supermarkets. 'All they want for their mass market is an acceptably bland taste.' At the Galloway Smokehouse they have opted for a deep flavour of wood and an attractive sweetness. 'If you like it, fair enough, if not, go somewhere else – and there's plenty of places to go.'

Another smoker who shares Allan's enthusiasm for a good strong smoke is George Jackson of Mermaid Fish Supplies at Locheport on North Uist. He dry-cures local farmed salmon and smokes it over local peat. It bears an uncanny resemblance to heavily peated island malts like Talisker, Laphroaig and Lagavulin. Salmon smoked over peat is quite an experience.

In the last two decades the number of small independent smokers has grown astonishingly. There is an uncounted band of hoteliers who have installed kilns to smoke local catches and every enterprising fish merchant has a smokehouse at the back of the shop. The range of food smoked has also been endlessly extended. If you want smoked grouse or pheasant, wild boar, scallops, lobsters and crab, it's being done somewhere. Whether it were best perhaps not done at all is a question I'll leave hanging in the air. Although salmon, haddock, herring, mutton and ham lend themselves to the smoke cure I'm not so sure that the new spirit of enterprise – 'if it moves smoke it' – is always defensible. Adding value with smoke may make commercial sense but I've had some products where the smoke-screen hasn't worked at all.

But pick carefully and you'll not be disappointed.

Part Two

☙

THE FOOD WARS

1. On Being Cast Down

'It is', an American travel writer said to me recently, 'your expectations that are so low. You have sacrificed the real to the pretentious.' He had been touring Britain looking for good simple food and everywhere he had been offered what is known in the trade as 'ovenable' and 'microwavable' frozen dishes, most of them presented as if they had been prepared on the spot. Why, he wanted to know, when our home-grown fruit is so good, should we have taken the passion fruit and kiwi trail? 'In the height of your pea season I was given imported mange-tout, and when I wanted home cooking I got a fake pizza or a fake lasagne or a fake moussaka. What's the *matter* with you people?'

I think it's got something to do with our priorities; we prefer durables to perishables. And it's nothing, for once, to do with class. The well-off frequently feed themselves and their friends abominably. A peer I know, impoverished by death duties, told me how he and his wife were once invited to a shooting party by a Scottish duke. Not having any money of their own, they looked forward to the luxury of staying in a rich man's castle and getting stuck into top people's food. 'You're not going to believe this,' he said, 'but when we came back in the evening absolutely famished after a day's stalking, the starter for dinner was cold chopped-up bacon and eggs left over from breakfast!'

At a stately home a couple of weekends ago there was a rally of Rolls-Royces – cars, some of them, worth a sheikh's ransom. I saw a party of four bring out their hamper from an elegant Silver Cloud. What equally splendid meal would they produce? It turned out to be a tin of pork luncheon meat, tomatoes, processed cheese and a bottle of Liebfraumilch. Not drinkable Liebfraumilch like Blue Nun or Crown of Crowns, but the kind of sugary rubbish you buy in a back street. Perhaps keeping the Rolls in the manner to which it was accustomed had bankrupted them and rubbish was all they could afford.

Or maybe like everyone else they're not that interested in what they eat as long as it doesn't take up too much time or interfere with the worthwhile things in life. Even on holiday most of us aren't bothered – as in 'What would you like for lunch?' . . . 'Anything, really, I'm not bothered.'

Recently Butlins invited various travel writers to sample their new-style package, and I was interested to read what Peter Black, who went on behalf of the *Daily Telegraph*, would make of the experience. We have fed him ourselves and we know what he likes – fresh, real food in reasonable quantities at a reasonable time with a reasonable glass or two of wine. Unleashing a perceptive and witty man like him on the 53 acres of Butlins Bognor was rather like sending Anthony Burgess a review copy of the latest Mills and Boon or asking Elisabeth Frink to comment on a display of garden centre statuary.

Mr Black was a model guest; he observed the rules punctiliously. 'Because of the early dinner time, it was only five o'clock when I ordered a vodka and tomato juice ('Did you want Worcester sauce? We haven't gorrany.'). To make way for important things like bingo and the glamorous grannie contest, dinner occurred at 5.45 sharp: 'Destiny brought us pea soup, triangles of soft white bread, a chop with bacon, peas and chips, and, for pudding, a triangle of cake with custard poured over. I was downcast by this meal. It recalled a similar meal I had eaten in Bunnerong Migrant Hostel outside Sydney in 1964.'

Being cast down is more often than not the traveller's lot these days when most of the meals on offer are foilpak and boil-in-the-bag dishes which can be thawed in minutes and presented as 'gourmet specialities of the house', a claim that raises expectations seldom fulfilled.

Recently the marketing director of a chain of middle-range restaurants asked me if I would try a meal and tell him what I thought of it. The set lunch was £9.95; not cheap. We chose as starters a crab patty (soggy pastry and a gungey filling which certainly didn't taste of crab) and an avocado mousse cleverly moulded in the shape of an avocado – it had unfortunately been dyed the colour of a bottled mint sauce, and again had no identifiable flavour. As on-the-spot cooking is phased out of all but the most expensive restaurants we shall be faced with more and more frozen 'designer' dishes like these, all froth and no substance. Already far too many cookery books are appearing with unnecessarily elaborate recipes which give the impression that the presentation and garnish is more important than the ingredients. For decades now our food has been over-processed; now it's becoming overdressed and tarted up to a farcical degree. At a recent dinner given by a provincial branch of the International Wine and Food Society (people you might expect to know better), the starter was the mandatory and overrated avocado taken to its ultimate absurdity: 'Ripe avocados are sieved, mixed with whipped cream, gelatine and lemon juice, then set in a long pâté dish. Down the centre of the mousse is set a courgette stuffed with a finger carrot. The whole is served on a bed of radicchio with lemon wedges and tomato butterflies' – gnome cookery for gastrognomes.

We must start fighting back. Meanwhile I'm making a collection (rather on the lines of 'small earthquake in Chile') of catering claims least likely to arouse interest. Here are two which qualify: 'Bar Meals Served All Day' and 'Top chefs swear by Uncle Ben's'.

2. Saving for the Future

They call themselves Seed Savers and they are found all over the world. One of the most enthusiastic is a Frenchman who lives in northern Australia. It was love that started it all; a young woman called Jude who is now Michel Fanton's wife.

Michel was lecturing in England recently and he told me how he got the seed saving bug. 'I wanted to make Jude an authentic *Ratatouille Niçoise* to impress, and show my love for her but I couldn't.' He searched for a meaty tomato that cooks well but all he could find was the tasteless supermarket kind. 'I wanted special capsicums and chillies, the flavoursome *Courgettes de Nice* and a powerful garlic.'

Many of these seeds were not for sale in Australia, so he had to advertise for them in gardening magazines. 'The response was overwhelming – an embarrassment of seeds came our way, and we just had to share them with other food lovers.' And so the Seed Savers' Network was born.

It was in Iowa that Kent and Diane Whealy became involved in the seed saving movement. 'We were planting our first garden together,' Kent recalls, 'and in the autumn Diane's grandfather gave us the seed of three garden plants that his family had brought four generations before from Bavaria.' When the old man failed to make it through the winter, Kent realized that if the seeds were to survive it was up to him to save them for future generations. From that realization came Seed Savers' Exchange, now one of the strongest seed saving organizations in the world. They are doing great work safeguarding the vegetable heritage of Eastern Europe and the former Soviet Union.

In Austria Nancy Arrowsmith runs Noah's Ark and in the Netherlands in a small house behind Utrecht railway station there are more than 30,000 seed samples. It is an immense collection of what are known as minor crops: endangered *wild* plants used by people from Tibet to Timbuktu. In England there is the remarkable seed library of the Henry Doubleday Research Association. Its footsoldiers are the Seed Guardians practising conservation through utilization; they plant the seeds and harvest them for future use. The Heritage Seed Library is a thriving enterprise with more than 5,000 members dedicated to preserving biodiversity.

The arguments for preserving as many plants as possible are compelling. If all the plants in a field are identical and a pest or disease evolves which threatens them you could have a total crop failure. This happened in the 1840s in Ireland. At that time all the potatoes growing in Europe were descended from two strains and the blight went through the potato fields like lightning.

The trend today is to minimize variety. In the European Union all plants have to be registered on a National List. As this costs about £2,000, with an annual renewal fee of £250 to keep them on the list, the temptation for the seed companies is to register only the varieties that will sell in bulk. So it is the commercially profitable carrots and peas that get on the list, not the little-known seeds that provide wonderfully tasting produce for the garden or allotment.

As Jeremy Cherfas, founder of the UK Heritage Seed Programme, says: choice is important for all of us. 'I do not mind if the supermarkets wish to stock their produce counters with uniform, tasteless products. One of the reasons I garden and grow my own food is precisely so that I can have something other than that.'

What sticks in the throats of all modest gardeners is that everything not on the National List is forbidden. You cannot market or trade in any seed which has not been registered. 'That alone', says Jeremy Cherfas, 'is enough of a motivation to save your own seeds. When I grow food from seeds that I have saved I feel a powerful connection with the entire history of agriculture. A chain links one season to another, one generation to its parents, right back to the first people who deliberately decided to look after the plants they ate. When I sow my saved seeds, I am part of that chain.'

The story of seed saving is told in an exciting book originally written by Michel and Jude Fanton in 1993 and adapted for British readers by Jeremy Cherfas, and in addition to its gazetteer of vegetables worth seeking out, it offers some salutary parables for our irresponsible times. One story in particular illustrates the price the poor often have to pay when they embrace the brave new technologies of the western world. In 1970 Norman Borlaug was awarded a Nobel Prize for developing short-stemmed, high-yielding varieties of wheat and rice, miracle seeds which, when planted with agrichemicals and watered with massive irrigation projects, would turn the Third World into a wondrous rice and bread basket.

What actually happened was indeed a Green Revolution but it required crippling investment and it left behind a legacy of poisoned soils, foreign debts, the destruction of village traditions and an admirable eco-system sacrificed for short-term gain. The growing of large fields of cereals and the creation of monocultures undermined the structure of entire communities. Herbicides killed weeds but they also destroyed taro, water spinach and water chestnuts which villagers fed on – food for free. The small fish which swam in the paddy fields and were an essential protein supplement in the diet of rice growers disappeared, victims of chemical sprays.

All the more important to preserve seeds which deliver the nourishment and pleasure small gardeners need; plants that can be reared without recourse to chemicals; plants grown for taste and flavour, not profit.

3. It All Adds Up

I have detected an interesting new counterblast to those who raise anxieties about chemical residues in food and it's one which lifts the debate into the realms of mathematical fantasy. It began with the eminent and respected Dr Colin Berry, professor of morbid anatomy at the London Hospital and chair of the Advisory Committee on Pesticides. Dr Berry proclaimed at the height of the controversy about the growth-regulating spray Alar that you would need to eat 6,000 Alar-sprayed apples a day before you suffered any noticeable harm.

Six thousand apples a day? My enfeebled mind could not take this thought in. How would you get 6,000 *peeled* in a day, let alone down your throat? I sped to my lightning pocket computer and did a few swift calculations. A skilled apple-freak could peel a Pippin in 30 seconds, thus being able to prepare and core 6,000 apples in 50 hours. By the end of day one, provided that the peeler could work for four hours non-stop, only 2,880 apples would be ready for mastication, leaving 3,120 unpeeled and, more to the point, uneaten.

In the interests of scientific research I ate a peeled apple, chewing it thoroughly before swallowing, as recommended by experts in the workings of the digestion. It took a good three minutes to demolish an average-sized grade one Laxton. At twenty an hour, even the most compulsive eater could only dispose of 480 apples a day, certainly nowhere near the 6,000 proposed by Dr Berry. I assumed that his dismissive and jokey figure was plucked from the air purely for its shock effect. What he was actually saying was that it is physically impossible to be harmed by the residues in an apple.

For those worried about pesticide residues in chocolate, the

Biscuit, Cake, Chocolate & Confectionery Alliance has worked out an equally unattainable EDDD, or estimated daily danger dose. They say that a child weighing 20 kilograms would have to force down over a tonne of chocolate a week to reach even the periphery of pesticide poisoning. Of course the yuk or throw-up factor would operate much earlier on; domestic trials suggest that even a healthy child could only stomach seventeen chocbars in a good day without being violently ill. A similarly lunatic statistic has been posited for the long-term build-up of additives in the body – you are more likely to die from being struck by a meteorite, it says, than by all the additives eaten in a lifetime.

The cumulative if unintentional effect of all these statements – the 6,000 apples, the tonne of chocolate – is to make all opposition to the continuing high usage of pesticides seem neurotic and hysterical. Good news for the agrichemical industry, but where does it leave the consumer? Looking rather foolish; laughed out of court. And yet doubts remain. There has never been any research in Britain into the effects of a lifetime of accumulated additives and residues on the body and, so far as I know, no research is contemplated.

In the United States they are more inquiring. The Natural Resources Defense Council, which includes in its environmental protection programme the safeguarding of food and drinking water from toxic contamination, started in 1986 the first-ever study in the Western world to determine whether levels of pesticide residues pose a hazard to young children. Their findings, published a year ago, make disturbing reading. They claimed that a wide range of fruits and vegetables contained pesticide residues which put toddlers and pre-school children at more than average risk. They described this health risk as intolerable. At least 17 per cent of the pre-school population, or three million children, received exposure to neurotoxic organophosphate insecticides from raw fruits and vegetables that are above the level the federal government considers safe. Pre-schoolers, according to the NRDC, have greater exposure to pesticide residues than adults because they eat more food relative to their weight and have a far greater physiological vulnerability to toxic chemicals than adults because of the immaturity of their body systems.

True or false? Who can say? Such alarming conclusions are not reflected by our own working party on pesticide residues. Their latest word is that the average intake of such residues in Britain is low and considerably less than the ADIs (acceptable daily intake) laid down by the Codex Alimentarius Commission. The ADI is defined as the amount of a chemical which can be consumed every day for an individual's lifetime in the practical certainty, on the basis of all the known facts, that no harm will result. In this country, ADIs are based on the body weight of a ten-stone person, not on a toddler. If we did research on the exposure of small children to pesticide residues, would we find the same 'intolerable' risks that the NRDC has in the United States?

In our society such issues would be difficult to raise. Americans are not only allowed to register their concern about the indiscriminate use of chemicals on crops but are listened to seriously. Here protests are brushed off with the tonne of chocolate and 6,000 apples a day response. Residues? Don't worry! Everything is safe and stop rocking the boat.

4. Seeds of Profit

There's nothing more British than cabbage; except perhaps a cup of tea. Both, like almost everything we eat, came originally, or are still imported, from overseas. Parsnips, broccoli, celery, asparagus, artichokes, dill, fennel and mint are Mediterranean in origin. Carrots, cucumbers, onions, garlic, spinach and rhubarb came from Central Asia. Central and South America gave us the potato, tomatoes, avocados and pumpkins. Without China we would never have had radishes, chives, pears and peaches. The Welshman's leek came from the Near East, the Scotsman's neeps from China, the English apple from Asia. And it's the same story with meat: goats, pigs and sheep came from the Near East, chickens from India, turkeys from North America, and cattle from Eurasia and North Africa.

Our indebtedness continues. At this moment Cambridge biologists are investigating the possibility of developing three Andean tubers – the ulloco, oca and mashua – for use in the UK. One man at least reckons that the rich, developed countries of the North should be repaying the Southern countries, from where two-thirds of our plants came, in more than kind. He is Pat Roy Mooney, author of *Seeds of the Earth* and a recent series of articles which charts the way in which, since colonial times, we have relied heavily for our political and economic domination on the exploitation of the plant resources of the Third World.

We have always drawn on the botanical treasures of more climatically favoured countries to lend variety to our farms and gardens. By the time Queen Victoria ascended the throne, the British Isles were growing 13,000 species of exotic flora. Our lucrative rubber industry in South-East Asia arose from twenty-two rubber seedlings smuggled out of Brazil in 1876. Cinchona seedlings taken illegally from Ecuador started rival plantations in Asia; Mexican sisal transported from the West Indies to German East Africa eventually dwarfed the original production.

The new plants which were switched from country to country founded the fortunes of the industrialized West, changed the textile and chemical industries and, according to Mooney, 'utterly transformed the agricultural economy of the world'. Mooney's thesis is that the manipulation of the countries of the Southern Hemisphere is continuing today. The new green revolution offered by genetic engineering continues to dominate the lives of peasant farmers in the Third World, which are increasingly influenced by the West's desire for cheap food.

Even the seeds which the Southern countries plant are often controlled by the transnationals of the North. Large petrochemical and pharmaceutical firms, many of them directly engaged in the manufacture of fertilizers and pesticides, have been busily acquiring seed firms in the last decade. 'For those interested in pesticides,' writes Mooney, 'there was an obvious advantage to adding seeds to their repertoire, since the same advertising and distribution channels were employed . . . the government that subsidized seeds might also subsidize agrichemicals for those seeds.'

Research is now producing seeds and biocides that 'need' each other: spin-off carried to its logical commercial conclusion. It's a world of high technology which has even produced fluorescent maize which can enable a farmer to see what he is sowing at night! CIBA-GEIGY's 'Herbishield' is a textbook example of the multi-sell. They have enrobed their sorghum seed in three chemicals: 'Two are to protect the seed from the encroachment of grasses, while the third is to protect CIBA-GEIGY's seed from CIBA-GEIGY's leading herbicide – Dual. Dual is normally toxic to grain sorghum. The entire package allows CIBA-GEIGY to sell more Dual.'

Mooney sees such dovetailing as alarming for the developed

countries of the North, but 'in the South it can be disastrous to peasant economies'. According to Silvi Bertalomi of Zurich television, CIBA-GEIGY has already attempted to market this package in the Sudan. Sudanese officials tell us that they have now refused the deal.

Western control of plant gene banks, its training of overseas students to use expensive technology in their own peasant economies, and the appropriation of fertile land and cheap labour in Third World countries to provide luxury foods for the West, is making an eventual confrontation between North and South more and more likely. Meanwhile, in an effort to redress the balance, Ethiopia has banned the export of germ plasm and Indonesia has suggested a seed tax in the West which could be distributed among the poorer countries. The FAO at their twenty-second session tabled a commitment which would use all our plant genetic resources for the benefit of all mankind. Behind the potato and the cabbage on your plate is a world of concern.

5. Unnatural History

The Epcot Center is a permanent international showplace covering 260 acres in the grounds of Walt Disney world, which itself sprawls over 46 square miles of Florida. The jewel in its ambitious crown is a theme area called Future World, a series of visions of the decades to come which have been made possible by the generosity of multinational companies. It is through their corporate filter that various manifestations of the human spirit are expressed.

Thus the World of Motion ('a rib-tickling ride through the evolution of transportation') is masterminded by General Motors. This paean of praise for the internal combustion engine peddles the myth that 'mankind's progress has been directly related to worldwide innovations in mobility'. It is the kind of questionable assertion that could only be offered within the context of the Mickey Mouse view of life which pervades the entire place with the odour of rotting illusions.

A portentous gallery entitled The Land has been assembled by the giant Kraft corporation whose malign contribution to Third World hunger goes discreetly unrecorded. The mysteries of the seas are seen through the eyes of United Technologies Corporation and an upbeat exhibit called Universe of Energy comes from Exxon, the transnational which brought the world the Alaskan disaster.

Wandering round Epcot a couple of years ago I thought how lucky we are in Britain that the public perception of reality is not orchestrated by big business. I spoke too soon. This Christmas thousands of schoolchildren have been trooping round the new £1.2 million Food for Thought gallery in Kensington's Science Museum which has been largely funded by our most successful family of grocers – Sainsbury, with additional donations from British Sugar, the National Dairy Council and Tate & Lyle.

The very first exhibit visitors see when they enter the new gallery is a Sainsbury's check-out. Round the corner is a mock-up of a McDonald's burger outlet and just beyond that, to reinforce the retail image, is a 1920s Sainsbury's shop. Sainsbury's certainly got a remarkably full return for their investment. When I pointed out on *The Food Programme* this interesting invasion of a government-funded museum by private enterprise the museum itself was a bit miffed. They didn't seem to comprehend that the anodyne and unquestioning view of the world of food they had laid out was slightly dishonest. Nowhere in the new gallery is there any hint of the disquiet felt by a growing number of shoppers about the manner in which their food is produced.

You will see a machine for making sausages but there is no mention of the dubious process for mechanically stripping a carcass to produce the sub-standard slurry that goes into so many bangers and pies. I accused the new gallery of ducking the important issues of the current food debate and, by adroitly brushing under the carpet tiles the concern many adults felt about the food they are eating, offering no food for thought at all.

In the December issue of *Museums Journal* Maurice Davies has written a thoughtful article about the issues raised by the growing need for commercial sponsorship and in particular the effect it has had on this new food gallery. He was told by Jan Metcalfe, the project co-ordinator, that my comments had been 'rather ungenerous' and that 'you can't mention everything'. Mr Davies quoted staff of the Science Museum who told him that the Meat and Livestock Commission, who also coughed up sponsorship money, 'was unhappy about there being any mention of slaughter in the display, preferring to perpetuate an image which suggests that meat travels untouched straight from the field to the dining table'.

Another company which provided cash was Mars and they were rewarded with a Mars Bar display 'as a familiar example of snack food' – a gratifying piece of product placement which acted as an endorsement rather than a serious attempt to discuss the rise of the snack food industry.

Maurice Davies points out that the Natural History Museum has accepted £1 million for its Global Ecology display from BP and that British Nuclear Fuels is giving £73,000 towards an Energy for the Future gallery at the Greater Manchester Museum of Science and Industry. Researching his article Davies found that exhibition organizers recognized that accepting money from interested parties could lead to a real risk of self-censorship. 'It could be said', writes Davies, 'that museums prefer to duck the issues of real concern to their audience and concentrate on safer subjects . . . in the final analysis it is worrying that Britain's museums risk jeopardizing their role as providers and interpreters of authoritative and balanced information because they are being forced by government to rely too heavily on sponsorship.'

I certainly wouldn't rely on Sainsbury's or the Sugar Bureau or Mars or the meat industry to tell me what was happening to our food. Neither would I go to Disneyland. Turning our museums into public relations exhibitions for commerce and industry may be good for commerce and industry but it doesn't inspire the kind of confidence and intellectual independence we have traditionally associated with those museums.

6. Contented Palm Trees

'I do believe,' said a spokesman for the margarine manufacturers Van den Berghs, 'that one shouldn't throw terms at the public which they don't understand.' He was talking on *The Food Programme* about a recommendation made by the Committee on Medical Aspects of Food Policy that products containing trans fatty acids should state that fact. Van den Berghs markets a comprehensive range of edible fats and oils including Krona, Outline, Blue Band, Summer County, Stork, Echo, White Cap, Cookeen and Spray. Some are no doubt high in unsaturated fats, some are inevitably high in saturated fats, but with food labelling legislation the way it is and an industry reluctant to bombard consumers with information they might not understand, how are we to know?

The right to know what one is eating has become a major issue in recent years. It has now been established beyond reasonable doubt that we are eating too many saturated fats.

There are various theories about the precise events which shunted us on to the wrong track. Professor Michael Crawford, head of the nutritional biochemistry unit at the Institute of Zoology, believes the foundations for a disastrous diet were laid by the Enclosure Acts of the seventeenth and eighteenth centuries. Before that time animals ate not only young green grass but fully grown plants containing seeds and natural supplies of oil. By selective breeding fat cattle were developed. A lot of the fat went to make candles, and hard manual work kept meat eaters fit and lean. But a diet high in fat is no longer appropriate for people who drive to work by car and sit in overheated rooms.

There have been other significant developments which have

changed our eating habits drastically. Dr Geoffrey Walsh, a retired GP, wrote to me recently pinpointing the invention of the steam drifter as another crucial milestone on the road to coronary heart disease. When the people of Northern Europe ate large quantities of herring, he says, they were getting all the essential fatty acids they needed. With the arrival of trawlers and seine nets there was a massive surplus of herring. Much of it went for fishmeal; from the rest fish oil was extracted to make margarine. Unfortunately, fish oil oxidizes and goes rancid very quickly; the only cheap way to give it long shelf life is to hydrogenate it. But hydrogenation converts the healthy unsaturated fish oils into hard saturated oils and they are not good news. Cakes, crisps, biscuits, pies and sweets all contain large quantities of saturated fat. When you heat a liquid oil with hydrogen some of the polyunsaturated fats are also changed into trans fatty acids which inhibit the body's capacity to metabolize essential fats.

Hence the growing popularity of supplements containing gamma-linoleic acids, such as evening primrose oil, which are being marketed as essential to health. It is ironic that on the island of Lewis, where the natives once lived on fresh herrings, a factory has just been set up to manufacture capsules of herring oil – an expensive way to counteract a diet high in hard saturated fats.

The best way would be to move towards a balanced diet which would not require any supplements at all, but in a consumer society geared to highly processed food it's a difficult goal to achieve. Professor Crawford thinks that one of the saddest aspects of present-day life in Britain is that we have almost turned our backs on the natural harvest of the sea. 'It's not so long ago that cockles, mussels, shrimps and seafood of all kinds were the traditional fare of Londoners and people in cities all over Britain – food full of essential fatty acids.'

Having moved away from fresh food to convenience food, it's vital that such foods should not be described in misleading terms. The food and health lobby in the United States is currently battling to have what it calls the tropical oils properly identified. Palm oil is 51 per cent saturated fat, coconut oil is 92 per cent saturated fat. On labels containing these oils you will see the specious claim 'made with 100 per cent vegetable shortening'. The word 'vegetable', say the campaigners, encourages people to believe that the oil is healthier than an animal fat, when in reality it is far more saturated.

Palm oil and coconut oil are widely used in this country too. I once addressed a convention of ice-cream makers and suggested that they would do their customers a favour by putting the slogan 'our ice cream comes from contented palm trees' on the wrapper. A suggestion greeted with dignified silence. But why not? Would it be all that misleading to insist on the industry adopting a code of health warnings for potentially harmful products? Meanwhile, remain distrustful of labels which do not specify exactly what the food contains. You can be sure that if the packet just says 'vegetable oils' or 'edible oils' someone has got something to hide.

7. Processing for Profit

I have just surfaced from a long weekend immersed in food trade journals and am so confused that I'm finding it difficult to dissociate fantasy from reality. It's a world in which educated men offer the fairy gold of gastronomic junk and ingredients are commended not for their nutritional value but principally for their packet-filling potential. How do you fancy a tonne of low-calorie bulking polysaccharide pea concentrate, 'a particularly good base to use as it has a neutral flavour'? The most persuasive argument for another low-cost ingredient is that the bag it comes in can be easily disposed of.

I was sorry to have been a week late to send a cheque for £155.25 which would have gained me admission to a one-day conference at a hotel in Ealing where a posse of food engineers from various chemical companies delivered papers on acidulants, thickeners, flavours and colours in an attempt to allay fears 'from the consumer lobby with its call for more natural foods and fewer artificial additions'. The advertisement for this educational day out appeared on a page devoted to such mouth-watering substances as '10lb of cooked lamb suitable for high-speed slicing', speciality phosphates, non-dairy creamers with excellent whitening power, flavoured emulsions and clouding agents.

Much of the literature concerned chemicals which seemed to have been developed solely for the benefit of the manufacturer. Could we consumers, I wondered, do without the Dow Chemical Company's current contribution to food happiness, Methocel Premium Food Gums? These are not something you suck when bored but a substance ingested willy-nilly in just about anything from strawberry shortcake to fried onion rings.

Methocel is a boon in the factory. It lowers pumping-energy costs, reduces heat-exchanger fouling and boosts productivity so that soups and sauces 'become nice and thick after they're packaged, but not while you're processing them'. Their astonishing thermal gelation allows food batters 'to set up more solidly on the product, reducing batter "blowoff" and extending cooking-oil life'.

Methocel is almost as versatile as Brasso. In baked goods it results in a stronger cell structure 'so cakes are less likely to fall apart when handled by fast, automated equipment'. All very well, you may cry, but what does it taste like? Is it good for you? Few of the trade journals concentrate on such marginal matters; their remit is to examine innovations which enhance productivity and profits and help the machines run more efficiently.

I was in one of Europe's largest packet-soup complexes the other day, going through the ingredients with the Production Director. 'And this one?' I asked.

'Ah, that's to make the contents flow into the sachet.'

'Is that what the consumer insisted on?'

'Oh no, it's to facilitate production.'

The growth market in food at the moment lies in what people can be persuaded to eat between meals. At the European Chip and Snack Association Conference in Frankfurt last year, keen interest centred on the pellet-based snack with its gratifyingly long shelf-life and an inherent ability to be expanded using very little oil or indeed none at all. Using the technology of HTST (High Temperature Short Time) all manner of new-looking enticements can be extruded by cutting and crimping. The value of the snack-pellet market alone is estimated to be $25 million and one cannot help thinking that more money is currently being spent on pushing back the frontiers of snackdom than on cancer research.

Equally astronomic sums are to be made in the quest for low-calorie sweeteners. In the pipeline and hoping to compete with the world leader aspartame are a handful of new products including a chlorine derivative of sucrose known as Sucralose and a stereosimer of sucrose tentatively called 'L Sugar'. Watch out, too, for polydextrose, a bulking agent for ice cream, instant puddings and candies which can reduce calories by up to 90 per cent without sacrificing texture, palatability or 'mouthfeel'.

In the past, television has shown itself to be highly skilled at creating programmes which exploit the skills of cooks like Raymond Blanc, Anton Mosimann, Claudia Roden, Delia Smith and Madhur Jaffrey. The excellent *Take Six Cooks* is a case in point. There's nothing more fascinating than to see an expert at work. Surely it's about time television mounted an investigative series looking at how the packets and tins on which most of us live are manufactured? I'm sure the food industry, which has nothing to be ashamed of, would welcome cameras into their laboratories and processing halls. It could be compulsive viewing. No hassle with the title either – how about *Take Six Chemists*?

8. Fat Lot of Good

There is a flourishing tradition among the industrialized nations of exporting their surpluses to what are optimistically known as the developing countries. In recent years, they've also become a lucrative dumping ground for products which have come under suspicion among Western consumers.

As smoking declines in America and Europe, the tobacco giants are focusing their marketing skills on the Third World, where the illiterate have not yet heard that cigarettes are lethal. Excess baby milk floods the clinics of shanty towns with the dubious message that expensive nourishment from a tin is better than milk from the breast.

Pesticides which are no longer acceptable in the northern countries are shipped to Asia and Africa and in no time boomerang back as residues in cocoa and vegetables. Despite the evidence that, with pesticides, less is best, the British Nutrition Foundation – a body funded by the food and chemical industry – has just framed a powerful plea for agrochemicals.

In its latest newsletter, Dr David Conning, director-general of the BNF, claims that it is 'truly amazing how, with full bellies, some have started to worry about the nature of the food we consume to excess'. Under the headline 'Enter the Luddites', Dr Conning lashes out (I think that might be the phrase) at those who question the presence of pesticide residues in their food. This, suggests Dr Conning, 'creates anxiety, undermines any confidence the public may have in food safety and leaves the food producers in something of a dilemma'. Not to mention the pesticide producers.

Dr Conning's commercial argument is that without a strong

market in developed countries there is no incentive for chemical manufacturers to stay in business: 'Alar and DDT are good examples of what happens when the market for a chemical is reduced for whatever reasons.' What happened when the potent carcinogen DDT was finally banned in the US after an intense legal battle with the major producers was that it continued to be sold in the rest of the world. Incidentally, with our customary faith in the integrity of our advisory committees, DDT was allowed to be used in Britain until 1984 and there are few of us whose bodies do not contain DDT residues.

When there is an outcry against a particular pesticide, says Dr Conning, 'the tragedy is that the serious consequences occur, not in our backyards, but in Africa or the Far East.' The spectre of a Third World famine fuelled by lack of sophisticated chemical agents is a PR scenario devised and enthusiastically documented by the agrichemical companies. It is strange to see it being promoted by the BNF, whose patron is that untiring Third World traveller, the Princess Royal. She might be the first person, if asked, to tell the Foundation from her own personal observation that few of the dilemmas of the poorer countries will be solved by digging a deeper grave of debt with the help of international agribusiness.

An event which may have passed unnoticed by the BNF – and one of interest to any student of big business on the make – was the conference held in March in that famine-haunted corner of Asia, Bangladesh. It was organized by the Washington-based National Renderers' Association, which works closely with the US Department of Agriculture.

The thrust of the conference was to persuade the Bangladeshis to buy the edible tallow which sensible American consumers are avoiding like the plague. 'We believe', said Eugene Matern, a leading Chicago renderer, 'we can make an important contribution to your economy and your country's food supply.' And, he added disarmingly, 'Bangladesh need not be confused by the claims of self-appointed consumer advocates.'

A major function of the conference was to rubbish evidence that it might be unwise to eat a substance normally used to make candles, soap and laundry items. Just as the American tobacco industry has had to seek new markets, so the domestic meat industry has found that it needs new consumers for the saturated and suspect carcass fat cholesterol-conscious Americans will no longer eat.

According to the American renderers who produce what they are careful to call not tallow but Beefoil, the relationship between blood cholesterol levels and coronary heart disease is 'so weak it has no practical importance to at least 95 per cent of the population.' They cite a Californian scientist, Dr Russell Smith, whom they describe in their latest bulletin as having 'no specific credentials in either medicine or human nutrition', who talks wildly of a 'lacework of conspiracy in the current national war on cholesterol'.

Meanwhile, McDonald's, who have traditionally cooked their French fries in edible tallow which is 25–30 per cent cheaper than vegetable oil, are now being forced by consumer demand to change to oils less high in saturated fat. A commercially wise move which will make even larger supplies of American edible tallow available for the hungry peasants of Bangladesh.

9. A Liking for the Lowfalutin'

I was interviewing Nicholas Coleridge for the *Meridian* book programme the other day. His book, *The Fashion Conspiracy*, is a gruelling read. Can people really be that self-centred and be taken seriously? It suddenly occurred to me that there are remarkable analogies between the world of *haute couture* and the world of *haute cuisine*. If you're wealthy and want frocks, you go to fashion houses in Milan, Paris and New York; if you're wealthy and want food you go to Eugénie-les-Bains, Roanne and Talloires. The Troisgros brothers, Chapel and Bocuse, do for sauces what Balmain, Chanel and Givenchy do for frocks.

Coleridge describes how the top fashion designers license their names for use on luggage, sunglasses and aftershave. Megastar chefs lend their names to bottles of wine, jars of quails' eggs and boxes of chocolates. With dresses, the colours and the style change from season to season; with food, too, there's the same compulsion to innovate – one year *minceur*, the next *nouvelle* and, waiting in the wings, *cuisine naturelle*.

I went once to a very highfalutin' restaurant in France noted for its elegant restraint – elegant restraint was that year's fashion. Nothing much happened for about forty minutes apart from the appearance of an *amuse gueule*, a smidgin of *foie gras* about the size of a bee's knee. Then a platoon of waiters appeared with gold and sable plates as big as dustbin lids. On each was a perfectly poised *moule* which had undergone a lot of elaborate culinary engineering. It was the apotheosis of mussel, but not really much to get your teeth into. This singular first course was greeted with the same gasps of delight that might be bestowed on a breathtaking Ungaro garment gliding down the catwalk in the Avenue Montaigne. One felt restrained applause was called for. Other small morsels on large plates made their appearance, separated by long dramatic intervals. At one stage the great chef himself moved graciously among the diners, bowing slightly. The bill, when it came, was astronomic.

Both fashion and food depend on a small circle of *prominenti* who have the time and the money to indulge their whims. Without women able to spend $30,000 on a dress there would be no designer billionaires. Food comes cheaper, but in the five or six great restaurants of Europe where designer menus reach the status of art nobody is bothering about the bill. The fashion set flying from collection to collection is mirrored by the Foodies rushing to book in at the latest chic eating place.

Chic has afflicted hotels, too. In the last twenty years Britain has produced a small number of country-house hotels in which comfort borders on luxury and the cooking is faultless. Most of them are a treat to spend a night in, but do try to avoid the drawing-room after dinner; here, inevitably, the travelling pests who seem to spend their life driving from one Country House Hotel to the next gather to establish some kind of wretched pecking order.

Last summer we stayed at a very grand CHH and were soon made aware that we had stumbled on a travelling circus of CHH habitués. A retired couple who had arrived in a beige Rolls were going on about Cliveden, where they had been fed and watered the night before. 'Fabulous,' they said, 'the ultimate experience.' Everybody else was a bit put down by this; none of them had yet made it to Cliveden. They had been trumped. Someone on the sofa threw in Inverlochy Castle. A palpable ace. The quality of the bathrobes at Gravetye Manor, the trouser presses at Hambleton Hall, the bibelots at Sharrow Bay and the bath fragrances at Chewton Glen were all subjected to minute analysis and future plans were revealed. Some were speeding north to Miller Howe (fabulous breakfasts) and others to Le Manoir and its memorable hot dinners. It sounded like hard work, calling for lots of plastic money.

In her book about the pleasures of working and cooking in the Mediterranean, *Honey From a Weed*, Patience Gray reminds us that good food is not about conspicuous consumption or the display of wealth but 'the result of a balance struck between frugality and liberality . . . homemade bread rubbed with garlic and sprinkled with olive oil, shared – with a flask of wine – between working people can be more convivial than a feast.'

The best meal I ever had was as simple as that. We had been visiting a vineyard owner in Sicily and he and his daughter pressed us to stay for lunch. There was bread baked that morning, home-cured charcuterie, cheese from his own sheep, olives, olive oil, salad and tomatoes from the farm. With the meal we drank the owner's red, white and rosé Cerdese wine and, sitting in the cool of that medieval kitchen, we ended the meal with figs and peaches and grappa from his own still. It was lowfalutin' food at its best. 'In my experience,' writes Patience Gray (and who could disagree with her after feasting like that?), 'it is the countryman who is the real gourmet.'

10. Defying Nature

If any television producer is looking for a riveting fifty minutes he might do worse than take a film crew up to Aberfeldy, Tayside, where Walter Yellowlees and his wife Sonia spend a lot of their retirement growing vegetables organically. They wouldn't come away with a gardening programme; Dr Yellowlees is good at compost, but, more importantly, he has been a lifelong campaigner for good, fresh food. He speaks with the authority of thirty-three years as a family doctor in a practice which covers a big area of the upper Tay Valley.

During his years as a GP visiting patients he was repeatedly appalled, in his own words, 'at what I saw on the family table: tinned meat, tinned vegetables, very seldom any salads; masses of white bread, scones, biscuits, cakes, sweet drinks, packeted milk puddings, margarine instead of butter, and, in place of porridge, the ubiquitous packeted sweetened breakfast foods.'

He had ample opportunity to observe in his rural practice how the growing and eating of fresh food had almost entirely ceased. He used to go and see an old lady of ninety who described how they had plenty of everything on their farm in her childhood. 'We had cows and sheep and hens. We made lovely cheese and lots of fresh butter.' Now the pastures have gone out of cultivation – 'some of them have been blotted out by the Forestry Commission's dark green conifers. The farmhouse is the weekend cottage of a professor of economics.'

The picture he paints could apply to almost any rural part of Britain where industrial farming and monoculture has killed the rural roots of the country. Round Aberfeldy 70 per cent of the arable land is growing barley for brewing and distilling or for animal feed. 'The arable farmers are heavily dependent on soluble chemicals and machines. Hardly any of our food now comes from local farms. All our milk has to be brought from a central creamery thirty miles away.'

Dr Yellowlees's simple message is that health cannot be created without good food based on sound agriculture. But after three decades spent trying to persuade anyone who will listen that faulty food plays an enormous part in causing disease, he often finds that his audience, which frequently includes medical graduates and undergraduates, hasn't grasped his message. He thinks that the dazzling success of drugs, which began in the mid-1930s with the discovery of sulphonamides and moved on to penicillin and all manner of magic pills, has blinded the medical profession to the fact that many of the diseases which this antibiotic arsenal is used to treat might never occur if only we ate more sensibly.

Dr Yellowlees is profoundly depressed by the way in which our concentration on industrial expansion at the expense of agriculture has brought us none of the lasting benefits which the Victorians anticipated. He would place the blame on our unnatural food chain – an overuse of pesticides and synthetic hormones by farmers, an over-refining of carbohydrates, over-cooking of processed food and the excessive use of additives by manufacturers.

We have the headline-grabbing virtuosity of transplants and a medical technology which was unforeseeable when Walter Yellowlees graduated from Edinburgh in 1941, but also a growing incidence of degenerative diseases, from diabetes to diverticulitis, all associated with an unhealthy diet. Dr Yellowlees is scathing about the way in which Western society connives at disease and then spends millions treating it. He also thinks that we are tackling the problem of disease far too late in the day. He is opposed to the mass fluoridation of water to inhibit dental caries, preferring to see a diet which would have the same effect without all the bother. He is an opponent of the current campaign to persuade people to eat 'unnatural' polyunsaturated margarine instead of natural butter. Surely, he argues, there must be a simpler solution and he cites the words of James Lind, the naval surgeon who in 1753 suggested that scurvy at sea could be prevented by an issue of lemon juice. 'Some persons,' Lind wrote later, 'cannot be brought to believe that a disease so fatal can be prevented by such easy means. They would have more faith in an elaborate composition dignified with the title of an anti-scorbutic golden elixir or the like.'

And so today many medical persons cannot understand that the way to good health lies in a fundamental change in our eating habits – not the nibbling of raw carrots or spoonfuls of bran but a national policy to produce and market healthier food. As a first step Dr Yellowlees would like to see a law passed which would compel any lay or medical contributor to the current debate on diet, nutrition and health to reveal whether they were being funded by or receiving a salary from any partisan sector of the food industry. He would like to see financial incentives given to farmers so that they could produce food free of toxic residues or other additives.

As a start, he suggests that medical schools should be more aware of the importance of the ecology in the origin of disease: 'Seldom in the writings of our highly skilled specialists is there a glimmer of the truth that there is a unity in the health of the soil, the health of plants and animals and of man. The worship of technology finds little time for a comprehension of nature's laws, or for the humility to understand that we cannot defy nature without being punished.'

11. The Black Museum of Cantonment Road

Cantonment Road, palm-lined, cooled by sea breezes, was once an exclusive address in Penang. Here, in more prosperous times, merchants built large, verandaed mansions from which they commuted to their counting houses in Georgetown. Number 87 is shabby now, full of office furniture and old typewriters. The staff, however, are young and burning with zeal. This is the headquarters of the Third World's most successful consumer pressure group. CAP, the Consumers' Association of Penang, was founded in 1969 and it has campaigned on a wide range of issues, from pollution of water supplies to the exploitation of estate workers.

One of its main concerns is the safety and quality of food, and not an edition of its monthly newspaper, *Utusan Konsumer*, is without some new cause for concern in the food chain. CAP lashes out at filthy abattoirs, horrific food-processing practices, carcinogenic dyes in soft drinks, industrial chemicals used to flavour ice cream, and lead in milk powders.

CAP is handicapped both by the Malaysian government's permissive attitude to food manufacturers and a deep-seated belief among Malaysians that imported products have magical properties not possessed by local food. In Cantonment Road there is a black museum of bottles and packets claiming to promote health, which do the reverse, and products presented in a manner which would invite criminal prosecution elsewhere. One of CAP's research team, Mary Assunta, pointed to a tin of condensed milk which advertised in large letters that it was 'ideal for babies'. 'In rural areas,' she told me, 'you find mothers giving new-born babies condensed milk, in the mistaken belief that it's better for them than breast milk, and of course they end up with terrible malnutrition problems.'

Nutritionist Norinda Khor showed me a herbal tea made by Milupa in West Germany which had a picture of an impossibly healthy-looking white baby on the packet. When CAP analysed the contents it was found to be 90 per cent sugar. 'It was basically glucose and yet they were recommending it as a food for babies from the first week of life!' CAP wrote to the manufacturers and also raised the issue with the Malaysian health ministry, but nothing seems to have happened. 'Our problem is that our code, unlike the WHO code, only applies to infant formula foods – so all these manufacturers of cereals, baby foods and herbal teas can say what they like about their products.'

Norinda Khor relates the decline in breastfeeding in Malaysia to the way in which Western food companies are dumping surplus milk products on the Third World. Countries like Malaysia, with their tolerant import regulations, present an ideal market for all sorts of dubious foods, ranging from health foods with misleading and insupportable claims to foods which contain additives now banned in Europe and the United States.

It's not only potentially harmful foods which are being imported into Malaysia. CAP alleges that some thirty dangerous chemicals banned in the West are still on sale in the Third World; as a result, there are five times more pesticides in the body of an average Malaysian than in the body of an average American. DDT, Dieldrin, Chlordane, Heptachlor and Aldrin are all freely available. Ungku Abdul Aziz, South-East Asia's leading authority on rural development, is horrified at the way in which these toxic pesticides and weedkillers are being abused: 'Farmers here have no idea of the implications. When they're in a hurry they just dump a sack of pesticide on the field; they load it up with really toxic quanitites and then, as you know, in Malaysia it rains a lot and it all finds its way into the streams and we have this problem of pollution.'

Before I left Penang I talked to the founding president of CAP, Inche Mohamed Idris, a prominent community leader and a former muncipal councillor. There had just been a parliamentary election in Malaysia. Had their eighteen-year struggle on behalf of the consumer borne fruit? Was consumerism an issue in that parliamentary election? Mohamed Idris shook his head sadly. 'Unfortunately, no. We are very sad, because the real issues of the people have never been properly discussed and pursued.' So what drives him and his team on? 'Faith in the long term, faith that change will come.' The president of CAP pointed out that these days every political or commercial action caused a reaction somewhere else. 'Take the pesticides we use. We export the food to you and that has an effect on your health. Overall, the world is one. So we must all join together to bring about the right climate for all of us to live as healthily as possible.' A simple and logical approach to international cooperation and harmony; a message the West would do well to take to its heart.

12. Eating Words

By next Sunday, it's estimated we will have got a good way through some 17,000 tonnes of Easter eggs. According to the Biscuit, Cake, Chocolate & Confectionery Alliance, we spent £142,434,000 on chocolate eggs last year, well over £9 million more than we spent in 1988.

These figures dropped through my letterbox just after I'd finished reading *Ill Fares the Land*, a new and revised collection of essays on food, hunger and power by Susan George. They perfectly illustrate the divide between the kind of society which we inhabit, where the pressures to overconsume are continuous, and large tracts of the Third World which hover on the edge of famine.

In her first book, *How the Other Half Dies*, which appeared in 1974, Susan George analysed the reasons for world hunger with great clarity. She followed this in 1979 with a study of the corporate control of food, *Feeding The Few*, and two years ago she tackled the burden of debt which shackled the Third World – a staggering trillion dollars which was fuelling oppression and despair. *A Fate Worse Than Debt* put forward the highly acceptable thought that the financial crisis of the developing countries was far too important to be left to economists or indeed politicians . . . least of all to politicians.

In between her books Dr George has made many combative sallies from her base as associate director of the Transnational Institute in Amsterdam; slim and elegant, highly articulate, she has fired audiences all over the world with her logically ordered message that it's high time ordinary people became involved in an international scandal of catastrophic proportions.

She has the gift, not being an economist, of making the

issues overwhelmingly clear. When she came to London two years ago to give a lecture to the Guild of Food Writers, she asked her audience to think for a moment. 'In all the pictures of all the famines you're ever seen,' she said, 'have you seen a single one of a Third World army officer or cabinet minister starving to death?' Inequality is not, she points out, just a manifestation of the gulf between the rich north and the poor south. The way in which national wealth is shared internally, even in the most deprived countries, compounds the miseries. Unlike others who write about poverty and hunger she realizes that the international economic system encourages malnourishment in the most unlikely places. In 1985 the US Physicians' Task Force of health professionals carried out a nationwide study which concluded that at least 20 million Americans were going hungry and lacking adequate calories, proteins and vitamins.

The results of economic imperialism are, of course, more overt in the developing countries. Stories from Brazil concentrate on the effect the destruction of the rainforests will have on the global climate by the end of the century. But this arboreal holocaust which has enabled Brazil to become the world's second-largest exporter of agricultural produce has created a society in which two-thirds of the population – some 80 million people – are malnourished.

Dr George's thesis is simple; she believes that the fundamental disparities between rich and poor are caused almost entirely by the pursuit of power and profit. She describes the realities of Third World poverty created by an alliance of the banks, the IMF, the debtor elites and the OECD government protecting their own banking networks.

Susan George has relentlessly exposed the fruits of injustice, but what would she do about it if given the chance? She got the chance at a conference in Canada in August 1983. Invited to give an after-dinner speech she outlined an imaginary co-operation programme for a Utopia in which human rights, human dignity and human needs would be the touchstones of theory and the goals of action. She refined this theme at Ottawa University in March 1985. First, she suggested, every developed country needs to review food-aid policies which undermine people's right to feed themselves. Human rights demand a reordering of power. All too often the non-producers have seized power from the producers and are depriving them of their means of subsistence. The villains in this scenario are corporations and banks, development-aid agencies, absentee landlords and local usurers – a combination of corporate interests and state policies which helps to depopulate the countryside and perpetuate hunger.

There are the ultimately serious questions still to be asked. If we believe that everyone has a right to food, would we also accept that the first right of those deprived of food is to resist the forces which violate their rights? Do we believe that the right to food overrides the right of property? And more directly, do we recognize that the right to food for all cannot be ensured without political conflict? The final question in this disturbing book concerns us all. 'Are we ready,' asks Susan George, 'to stand up to the forces in our own societies that deprive people of food, even indirectly? The right to food and the freedom to resist injustice are inseparable. There is no freedom without bread, and no bread without freedom.'

13. Getting Fresh

I spent an invigorating day last week with the inner caucus of the Women's Farming Union. Six of them had gathered in London before an audience of produce marketing executives to solicit support for their latest campaign to highlight the virtues of British food. They're going to call it 'Get Fresh', and they propose to cash in on the growing interest in the countryside by drawing attention to the high quality and freshness of home-grown produce.

Their national chairman is Elizabeth Browning, married to a Kentish fruit-grower and one of the small ginger group who founded the WFU seven years ago, when the French began invading Britain with their heavily promoted and subsidized Golden Delicious. 'It was Anne Humphreys who started it all. She rang round the country until she was hoarse and said: "We're going to do something, our husbands don't know what to do – the apple industry is going to be wiped out." '

The wives organized themselves into a lobby and began to battle for the English apple. 'What the French were doing in subsidizing their growers was illegal and we had to go and prove that to MPs, Euro-MPs, and the Ministry. We went to the public, too, and told them about English apples.'

The Ministry must have been impressed: after a year they gave the apple-growers £300,000 to set up an organization to improve the grading and packing of fruit. 'They also gave us money to restructure the industry, take out old, useless orchards and replant with young trees.'

I asked Elizabeth Browning why it had been left to the womenfolk to take action. She rallied bravely: 'Well, it was in the picking season and the men were working from daylight until dusk, weren't they?' As a result of their defence of English apples, phone-calls began flooding in from other farmers' wives. 'They said, "My goodness, at last someone's speaking up," and we got enquiries from a lot of dairy farmers' wives who were going through a bad patch. So we set about trying to help them, too.'

The next move was to devise a surveillance scheme to see that British farm produce was given a good showing in the shops. 'We got people all over the country to send us reports. If anything was wrong, we got in touch with the heads of retail chains and said; "Can we help you? We hear that a lot of the Bramleys you're selling are bruised." They didn't like it for the first year but now we have a very good working relationship with the shops and supermarkets and they ask us to ring them the minute we see a problem.'

There are now 2,000 members of the WFU, all keen to improve consumer relations. They talk to Women's Institutes and Townswomen's Guilds, they go on radio and television trying to build the image of British food and present it in the best possible light. They are also anxious to protect the image of farming itself. They are naturally worried about issues which present the farmer as a greedy ravager of the land and a polluter of the environment. 'I think it's important', says Elizabeth Browning, 'that the public should know us as friends and individuals who don't come from a different world. We too have children with measles, fussy husbands, and we live under pressure.'

Despite *The Archers* and *Emmerdale Farm*, the image of the farmer remains unflattering: 'Most people see farmers as well off, driving big cars, having a shoot or a party every week, living in fabulous houses. I should think nine per cent of the farmers in this country can afford to do that, and jolly good luck to them! We think it's up to the women to go and talk to the public and say: "Come and visit us, come and see the small dairy farmer who works round the clock every day of the year and is really struggling."'

Elizabeth Browning is convinced that attitudes in the countryside have to change. 'Farming is very traditional. But look at what's happened in other traditional industries: coal, steel, textiles. We mustn't bury our heads in the sand – we must be ready for change and, above all, we mustn't whine.' In view of the tremendous impact wives were making, I asked Elizabeth whether they were brighter than their menfolk, more willing to have a go? 'Women', she said, 'are very determined and persistent. A woman just doesn't give up. We're terriers!'

The terriers of the WFU are launching their 'Get Fresh' campaign on 28 April, when they'll be inviting a hundred opinion-makers to a slap-up lunch of real, fresh British food at Butchers' Hall. There will be a vast range of farm produce on display from Britain's second-largest industry and a lot of very determined women ready to convince you of its excellence, quality and flavour. And they're not likely to accept lack of interest for an answer.

14. A Breakfast Egg

Two Sundays ago I boarded a British Airways Boeing bound from Barbados to London. Ninety minutes out of Heathrow, the cabin staff began laying the tables in the first-class forward cabin. Crisp linen, elegant cutlery and Wedgwood china. There was seasonal fresh fruit, yoghurt, grilled lambs' kidneys and sausages, grilled tomatoes or kipper fillets. And eggs of course – freshly scrambled or boiled to your liking. Where would a traditional British breakfast be without eggs?

But, along with every other British Airways plane in the air that morning, our flight was eggless. The menus had been printed before John Taylorson, the airline's Head of Catering, and the British Airways medical advisers decided to stop serving eggs because of the health risk. Taylorson happened to be on board the plane and he told me that, like all other airlines, they were in constant touch with the WHO and, weighing up the evidence, they had decided to ban eggs two days earlier.

When I arrived back in London it was to find that hospitals and schools were taking similar decisions. Egg sales had fallen in the supermarkets by 10 per cent or 15 per cent depending on which paper you read. It had taken a long time for the facts about *salmonella enteritidis* to enter the public consciousness. It was last August that an article in the *Lancet* revealed the difficulties the egg and broiler chicken industry had got themselves into. Salmonella had been endemic in the flocks for two years, the article said, but it was only belatedly that the Department of Health issued its warning: raw eggs were to be avoided; all eggs should be thoroughly cooked.

What surprised me about the egg story was the way in which the industry refused to admit the gravity of the situation.

I was reminded of the old Radio Armenia joke about the listener who rang up the studio helpline. 'Comrade,' he asked, 'what are we to do in the event of a nuclear attack?' The reply was reassuring. 'Do not panic, comrade. There is no possible reason to be alarmed. In the event of a nuclear attack, put on your shroud and walk quietly to the nearest cemetery.'

In the forefront of the 'nothing to worry about' lobby was the British Egg information Service, known in the circles in which I move as the Egg *Dis*information service. Opening my mail on the morning I got back I found a press release headlined, for ease of comprehension, 'Eggs are safe, say BEIC'. The BEIC, paid spokespeople for the egg producers and packers, bravely put its head on the block. We reaffirm, they said, 'that eggs are a safe and wholesome food'.

One of the few establishment figures who dared to flout what you might call the Armenian Shroud convention and actually alert the public to the truth was Edwina Currie. Predictably, the farming MPs turned savagely on the lady who, for once, made a perfectly accurate and scientifically defensible statement. 'Most of the egg production in this country is now infected with salmonella,' she said. Too true; but what a gaffe. The public is considered too feckless by Whitehall to be allowed to weigh up the evidence and decide for themselves whether or not to run the risk of being made ill by an egg.

The evidence, unfortunately, see-sawed between minimal risk and high risk, depending on whom you listened to. What was irrefutable was that from now on reaching for an egg was going to be like playing Russian roulette. The fact that only 12,000 eggs eaten every day in Britain are infected with salmonella still makes it a risky proposition.

The egg crisis and the parliamentary embarrassment it has created highlights not only the long-term perils of intensive farming, but the confusion that occurs almost daily from having two quite separate government departments dealing with food and health. *The Food Programme* recently uncovered an Alice in Wonderland situation in which comfrey, known to cause liver damage, is banned from use in herbal medicines by the Department of Health while being sanctioned for sale in the form of a herbal tea by the Ministry of Agriculture.

It would be comforting to think that somewhere in Whitehall plans are being made to merge the Ministry of Agriculture (which far too often appears to labour under the delusion that its prime role is to defend the livelihood of the farming and food industry) with the Ministry of Health – it could perhaps be called the Ministry of Food and Health. Had such a Ministry been in existence twenty or so years ago, it might well have banned totally any move by the egg farmers to cut costs by feeding hens on contaminated broiler-waste, processed feathers and faeces.

Ironically, the campaigning organization Compassion in World Farming is now being seen by more and more people not as neurotic loonies but as a level-headed group who saw very clearly that forcibly turning chickens into cannibals and rearing them in conditions which make daily doses of antibiotics essential was both morally and medically wrong. The coming year will undoubtedly reveal further instances of practices in the food and agriculture industry which are clearly not in the public interest. One can only hope that there will be more openness, less shredding of the facts, and a greater commitment to act in the interests of the general public and consumer than we've seen in the present egg farce.

15. Fudging the Food Figures?

'Eating habits are getting healthier', ran a headline in the *Daily Telegraph* last month. Other papers, also quoting the latest figures issued by the Ministry of Agriculture, told the same comforting story. We were eating less full cream milk, beef, pork, lamb, eggs, butter and sugar, and more skimmed milk, chicken, fish, wholemeal bread, fruit juice and fresh fruit.

How does the government know all this? The story begins before the last war, when surveys like those of John Boyd-Orr in 1936 and B. S. Rowntree in 1937 underlined the poor diet of what was called in those days 'the working class'. In 1940, when the health and fitness of workers became vital to the war effort, a survey was set up to monitor the effectiveness of rationing and to provide information which would enable the government to formulate its food and farming policies to the best advantage.

In those days interest centred almost exclusively on lower-paid urban workers but in 1950 the National Food Survey, as it was now called, was broadened to include a cross-section of the whole country. It's a survey which has become the envy of the world; every year some 7,500 people, mostly housewives, fill in a questionnaire recording in great detail the food they buy for use in the home, how much they pay for it and when and by whom it is eaten. Four times a year the NFS publishes a summary of trends and a 250-page book comes out annually, packed with tables and statistics. These are used by Whitehall departments to make many of the vital decisions affecting the social and welfare services and to provide long-term forecasts about the future nutritional and food needs of the nation.

But how accurate is the National Food Survey? It relies for

its data on the goodwill of volunteers and to find out just
how it works *The Food Programme* in June appealed to any of
its listeners who had taken part to get in touch with us. One of
those who did was Christine Hill, who lives in Cheshire. One
Monday morning her doorbell rang and there was a woman
from the NFS. After she'd asked about the size of the family,
whether Christine had a deep-freeze, where she shopped and
so on, she produced a booklet and said that she'd like Christine
to fill it in for the next seven days.

At this stage, half the people approached decline. Christine,
being public-spirited, accepted but, as she told *The Food Programme*, she had no idea just how much work was involved:
'Imagine coming home from the supermarket laden with boxes
and bags, and you can't put any of it away until it's been noted
down for its price, weight and its brand name. Then you have
to write down everything that every member of the family
eats. I've got three children, and by the end of the week I was
wishing they weren't so fastidious in their likes and dislikes – it
would have been a lot simpler if we'd all eaten exactly the
same thing at exactly the same time.'

About five per cent of householders who agree to fill out
the 15-page booklet give up after a few days; it is a demanding
exercise which not everyone would be capable of undertaking
successfully. In a recent article in *Nutrition & Food Science*, Dr
Judith Frank of the School of Science and Society at Bradford
University suggests that unless the people contacted are representative of the population as a whole and the information
gathered is accurate, the results of the NFS must be approached
with caution.

Certain minority groups like caravan-dwellers are not eligi-
ble for inclusion in the survey, which used to draw on the
electoral register but which, since last year, has been based on
the postal-address file. As Dr Frank told *The Food Programme*,
the way in which the 7,500 respondents are selected can place
a bias on the results. 'For instance, there is a large proportion
of people in the United Kingdom who have difficulty in

reading official material and they would decline to take part in the survey. In one analysis of the results, it was possible to see that single-parent households or households where there was unemployment were more likely to be non-respondents.'

When the National Food Survey started in 1940 people still took most of their meals at home. There were works canteens and fish-and-chip shops, but the multimillion-pound fastfood industry and the replacement of domestic meals by snacks taken on the move was not envisaged. The NFS still takes no account of meals taken outside the home and although the form-filler is asked to note the number of meals eaten out, no breakdown of the cost or content is required. Neither is there any record of soft drinks, confectionery or alcohol consumed. Is it possible that, as social habits change and the formal meal is replaced by snacking, the NFS is getting out of touch with reality?

Dr Frank's interest in the survey was aroused in the mid-1970s, when inflation was at its peak. She was concerned about the way in which families on a fixed income were managing. 'I started looking at the National Food Survey then to see if it was possible to tell from the results whether there were families suffering from malnourishment. As a matter of fact, you can't pick them out, although at that time it was well documented that there were certain families whose intake was less than desirable.'

The NFS is recognized by the government as being primarily a source of economic information – detailed nutritional evaluation would involve a much more complex series of questions and analysis. Collecting information for the NFS and processing it currently costs £500,000; in terms of the money spent by the food industry on market research into the latest packet of crisps or bar of chocolate it is a relatively small amount of money. But there is a snag – even asking someone to help provide information may well influence their shopping patterns.

As Christine Hill admitted: 'By the end of the week I was avoiding the shops and thinking twice about going in to buy anything at all. I imagine that the NFS want a large degree of accuracy from the survey if they're asking for so much detail, but I wonder, as it's so time-consuming, whether this doesn't militate against people being accurate in what they put down – they must surely get rather careless as the week goes on.'

And pride too, particularly among those on a low income, must play its part in fudging the figures. Nobody wants to admit that they don't know how to feed themselves and their family properly. Dr Frank claimed that elderly people asked to fill out the form go out of their way to make special purchases for that week: 'One example that I heard of was not of a special purchase, but there was an elderly gentleman completing his survey sheet when his daughter called round, just to check that everything was all right. He'd put down that he'd had sardines on toast for his tea and she said, "But you didn't have sardines, Dad," and he said, "No, but I *should* have done."'

Perhaps Dr Franks's most disturbing conclusion is that although the NFS compares the aggregate nutritional value of household food with aggregated estimates of nutritional need, it does not really reveal the plight of those most in need. 'The method of summing up and dividing to produce an average, although sufficient to meet the requirements of administrators, obscures nutritional reality. Averages assume a credible acceptability . . . but, really, averaging distorts actuality.'

16. Fat Chance

It's not often that BBC1's consistently rewarding and watchable
Q.E.D. manages to combine low farce, tragedy, pathos and
social comment in one half-hour, but it did do so rivetingly in
its report on a New England summer camp for the young and
overweight.

Camp Shane (or Camp Shame as many of the youngsters
who are despatched there must see it) tries to slim down child
victims of the junk food war by controlling their diet and
subjecting them to almost endless exercise. The head counsel-
lor, an extrovert called Barry Hye, has based his public persona
on an amalgam of the frock-wearing corporal in *M*A*S*H*
and Robin Williams's manic *Good Morning Vietnam* disc jockey.
At the camp's microphone he wears furs and is seen presiding
over a meeting of the staff with a three-foot sawn-off safety pin
clamped on his head.

The manic Barry apart, the documentary was far from
humorous. American families spend $65 billion a year on junk
food and its young victims were obscenely maimed. The girls
had thighs like sequoia trunks, the boys had faces of melting
lard and unmanageably wobbling breasts. In one painful
sequence fourteen-year-old Josiah Traeger, an aspiring actor,
described through choking sobs just what it was like to be a
constant target for derision. Another lad, Scott Butler, who saw
himself as a beached whale, had been attending the Rochester
Nutrition Unit since the age of three. He lost eighteen pounds
in his three weeks at Camp Shane. 'I worked out', he said with
the honesty of the child, 'that it cost my folks $80 for each lost
pound.'

Three weeks at the camp cost £1,140; nine weeks is

£2,300. For Josiah and his parents it was money well spent. He shed thirty-four pounds and a few weeks later signed a contract to appear in a TV series. Not all the children who leave the camp enjoy a long-term benefit. Within weeks Marissa Maimoun, an attractive youngster, had put on another six pounds. 'What was really extraordinary about the camp,' Barbara May told me, 'was the camaraderie. Here were youngsters who had never been picked for their school team doing well. Many of them felt relaxed for the first time in their lives.'

By coincidence, in the same week that *Q.E.D.* was looking at Camp Shane, *The Food Programme* examined the problems of the overweight in Britain and the way the food industry has reacted. Diet drinks, butter and spreads laced with water, calorie-counted convenience meals, artificial sweeteners, and (a treat to come) the wonder polyester sucrose fat that will enable everyone to eat and eat and not add a calorie.

The cynic may well ask whether creating expensive artificial foods to enable people to stay slim isn't going about things in the wrong way. It is, of course, the right way to make money. Findus has proved that with its palatable Lean Cuisine. Launched in 1985 it has been growing in sales by 30 per cent a year and is now worth £50 million a year. Birds Eye was a bit miffed at missing out on this lucrative and untapped sector of the 'anxiety' market. The Findus meals keep to a maximum of 300 calories and are a bit meagre – the Birds Eye boffins refer to it as Mean Cuisine and believe that their formula is more likely to hit the jackpot. 'Healthy Options' sell for £1.50 – you get more food and of course more calories; the portions vary from 400 to 500 calories.

According to Dr Ann Robinson, a family doctor who featured in *The Food Programme*, only about three per cent of the UK population are what you could call medically overweight – weighing in at 13 stone and more when they should perhaps be ten. But a significantly larger number of people suffer from some kind of eating disorder. Julia Buckroyd, who has written a book on the subject, believes that problems with food, with eating and with what that implies for size, weight and shape, are now endemic in the female population. She deals with the manifestations of anorexia and bulimia, the bingeing followed by self-induced vomiting, which she describes as 'the most secret, the most shameful, the most isolating and desolate of all food misuse'.

Meanwhile, the pressures to overeat the non-nutritional junk foods that lead to the grotesqueries of a Camp Shane are growing in this country. Snacking on convenience products high in fats and sugars blunts the appetite for the fresh foods that in the past provided us with a healthy and balanced diet. Worried by our bulging waistlines we turn not to fresh fruit and vegetables and the lean meat and fish recommended by the Health Education Authority, but to the slimline meals and low-calorie nibbles with their specious promises of a sylph-like rejuvenation.

Perhaps the most depressing image of the Q.E.D. programme came when the fat children of Camp Shane were unleashed for the day and given a dollar to spend. Counsellors cautioned them that it was only to be spent on 'diet' Cokes. Curing the ill-effects of the Coke civilization with allegedly less harmful junk drinks doesn't make sound nutritional sense. It's good, though, for the food and beverage industry and what's good for them must be good for us. Junk still rules.

17. Raising Questions

The Ministry of Agriculture sends me all its press releases. I am the grateful recipient of masses of useful information about meat gel agents, ruminant feed orders, salmonella, lead in milk and the daily doings of ministers. Baroness Trumpington has only to visit the world's premier sweets and biscuits fair and I am rushed a summary of her pep talk to the assembled chocbar executives and boiled sweet boffins. When Food Minister David Maclean cuts through Brussels red tape ('Government Fights For British Mince'), I get the news instanter. Every time Mr Gummer lashes out at distortions about food safety in the media, a release outlining his surreal views comes winging through the post.

What didn't come winging through the post at all at the begining of March 1990 was a very important piece of news indeed. For the first time the Government had approved the commercial exploitation of a genetically modified organism. You might have thought that this historic decision would have merited a major press conference so that we could meet the members of the three advisory committees who had given MAFF the green light. Not a bit of it. The information was released quietly at 17:18 on 1 March on a Whitehall wire service. There was no customary press release put in the post – officially I have still not heard the news.

When *The Food Programme*'s Jane Rea investigated the implications for the consumer, she found that there were all sorts of groups who were disturbed at what had happened and the manner in which it had happened. The organism itself has been developed by a Netherlands company based in Delft. Using DNA technology, their research scientists have created a

mutant yeast which will make dough ferment faster. Debarred
from manufacturing the yeast in their own country, the firm
has built a factory here in Britain. At Felixstowe, with the
approval of MAFF, they have erected a factory as wide as a
football pitch and as tall as a house, which will be able to
produce up to 900 tons a week of the wonder yeast and in due
course supplies will be shipped to other European countries
and to Japan and the USA.

According to Dr Julian Kinderlerer, a biochemist at the
University of Sheffield and a member of the Advisory Committee on Genetic Modification, all the Dutch have done is to
help nature achieve what might well have eventually happened
naturally: 'It's like taking a word in a sentence on the screen of
a word processor, moving it along and putting it back in.
There is nothing added, nothing taken away.'

Environmentalists are concerned that if these yeasts enter
the atmosphere they could present a peril. Dr Kinderlerer
admits that science does not yet know what makes a yeast like
candida, which does present a health hazard, different from a
yeast used in raising dough. 'If we did, we would have no
concern whatever. The concern that it could produce a path-
enogenic yeast is there but it's small.' So small he reckons that
you are probably talking about a .000001 per cent risk.

But there is more than risk at stake. No information about
the new yeast was made available before it was approved; the
decision was taken behind closed doors. Ironically, on the same
day that the announcement was made about the mutant yeast,
the Department of the Environment issued a three-page statement reaffirming the right of the public to have access to just
this kind of information before government decisions are made.

Dr Roger Straughan, a moral philosopher at the Unversity
of Reading who has written a paper on genetic manipulation,
believes that the public should be given a chance to debate
whether or not this yeast should be commercially manufactured. Consumers, he says, need basic factual information about
what scientists are doing. 'They also need to be made aware of

the broader issues involving social, moral, political and religious concerns and they need to be involved in the debate.'

The UK Genetics Forum, angered by the Government's stance, point out that the Environment Protection Bill which is now going through Parliament does not make it obligatory for the Government to release information about genetically engineered organisms. There is no provision in the Bill for the public to offer comments on work in progress involving genetic modification. Nor are the three advisory committees required to consider the social or ethical implications of new research. The UKGF believes that public interest bodies should have the same right as the biotechnology industry to nominate representatives to committees looking at genetic modification experiments.

The Felixstowe factory has permission to make bread and sell the mutant yeast anywhere in the United Kingdom. There is no obligation for bakers to reveal that they have used the yeast in their bread. Equally questionable is the inadequacy of the supervision which is available to monitor organisms like the new yeast. There are only three specialist health and safety inspectors to keep an eye on what's going on and they have to cover the whole of the UK. Bearing in mind the number of genetically modified substances which may be released in the next few years, the lack of supervision seems irresponsible. It is above all the secrecy in Whitehall that is alarming consumer groups. Once again the Government has revealed its contempt for open debate.

18. For the Good of
the Community

I spent a stimulating evening last week with some of the members of the Canterbury Farmers' Club which, in 1993, will be celebrating its bicentenary. It is one of the few survivors of the wave of agricultural societies which came into being during the Agricultural Revolution.

When it was founded in 1793 the Society undertook to encourage improved husbandry, livestock breeding and the better care of animals. It also promised to support 'those things likely to conduce to the prosperity of Kent in particular and to the good of the community at large'.

Once a month, as many of the 500 members who are free gather together to eat a modest supper – it was bangers and chips last Monday – and listen to an expert holding forth on some improving subject. They had invited me to try to tell them why farmers were getting such a bad press at the moment.

In the audience were hopgrowers, fruit farmers, dairymen, fertilizer and pesticide salesmen, seedsmen and academics. The biggest farmer in Thanet was there – a man whose family works 2,000 acres – and there were small tenant farmers wondering how long they were going to survive.

If I have ever used the phrase 'farming lobby' I shan't do so again in a hurry. Farmers must be the most discrete group in the country. There were men in the room whose farms were as computerized and mechanized as they could make them. There were others who practised agriculture in a manner which would warm the heart of any conservationist. What did, perhaps, unite them was a feeling that whatever they did would be wrong. After the egg crisis the fear of hormones and anti-biotics, the issues with ominous initials like BST and BSE, the charges of contaminating the land with nitrates and slurry – how could they win back the confidence of the public?

There were those in the audience who felt that organizations like Friends of the Earth were creating unnecessary alarm about chemical farming. 'We use very low levels anyway and everything is thoroughly tested,' said one member. That sparked off a bit of a barney. It was all very good-humoured and my fears and doubts about factory-farming were treated with great courtesy. I was conscious that there were quite a few people in the room who, were a move to organic farming possible, would take that route with alacrity.

We discussed the influence of the supermarkets on crop production and I felt a consensus in the hall that, although it was comforting to have a big contract and know that cheques were coming in regularly, the demands made on a farmer for consistency and cosmetic perfection were not really what farming was all about.

One farmer told me that, these days, you only applied fertilizers and pesticides as a last resort: 'In the boom time you sprayed everything in sight as an insurance against something that might never happen. Now when I walk the fields with my consultant, both of us are really looking for options which don't involve any unnecessary application of a fungicide or an aphicide. Too damned expensive.'

There are fears that asset-stripping and set-aside may turn the countryside into little more than a theme park for towns-folk. One man whose family have kept their land in good heart since the sixteenth century lamented the policy of cheap food which had led consumers to put price before quality, taste and flavour. 'In Britain,' he said, 'people just won't pay the proper price for an egg or an apple. You talk about battery egg production. Nobody in their right mind would practise such methods. Nobody in this room does. But it happens because people demand rock-bottom bargains.'

The dilemma which many farmers find themselves facing may be of their own making. As you drive down from London to the coast the vast acreage of rape now in full flower is tangible proof that most farmers will grow anything as long as it yields a profit. People who live in towns prefer to ignore the fact that farming is a business like any other. We have a romantic notion that time should have been artificially arrested in an unchanging rural panorama of picturesque barnyards, free-ranging chickens and golden cornfields. Strangely, I found just such a scene in deepest Kent the following day. There were calves happy not to be in boxes, cows untouched by bovine somatotropin, an air of contentment in the stock. I'm told that more and more farmers are keen to return to the traditional logic of mixed farming and rid themselves of a dependence on monoculture. I was surprised to learn that as yet no official encouragement is being handed out to farmers who want to go organic. I have seen estimates which suggest that, in the past, subsidies for farmers cost up to £20,000 per farm per year. If we were once able to pay that kind of money to increase production, why can't we find similar sums to enable farmers to make a decent living without being forced into practices which are not, in those words of 1793, 'to the good of the community at large'?

19. *Unfood for the Unfit*

Procter & Gamble, the Cincinnatti multinational, is into almost everything from diapers to detergents, and deodorant to dentifrice. It has 120 plants scattered worldwide and corporate sales of over $12 billion. Apart from its toiletries, P&G is big in food. Walk down any high street past the ventilators of fast-food outlets, and that smell of burning fat will probably be P&G's market-leading, heavy-duty frying oil, Prep. P&G majors in cake and pastry margarines, speciality shortenings and bulk refined oils; the brands have enigmatic names like Fair, Blaze, Fay, Deepio, Vortex and Freedom.

It also pioneered the soft chocolate-chip cookie, but, according to a consultant, it was so unrewarding that the package tasted better than the product. In 1983 it had been hoping to sell $400 million worth of cookies, but last September it began to cut its losses and was forced to sell off $100 million worth of unused plant. All may not be lost, however; forecasters predict that P&G could well rebound into the market with a new 'diet' cookie incorporating a chemical additive which has been in the research-and-development pipeline for twenty years.

This new substance, a man-made sucrose polyester, is the ultimate 'unfood' for a society which has an insatiable appetite but deep neurosis about obesity and heart disease. According to P&G, olestra, as it proposes to call the substance, provides the rich taste of full-calorie fats and oils but is so non-intrusive in its passage from palate to anus that it leaves no calories behind. Olestra can be liquid or solid; it could be used to replaced saturated fats in margarines and salad oils, in ice creams, cakes, snacks and, of course, cookies.

Olestra, made from sugar and edible oils, contains no cholesterol, and P&G has been bombarding the media with its virtues for some time now. Visions are being held out of a future where you can eat as much as you like without putting an inch on your waistline, and the medical benefits are carefully stressed. The claim is that olestra will reduce dietary fat and calories and lower the risk of heart disease. It is, P&G insists, an important aid to nutrition and health because 'it enables people to enjoy the great-tasting foods they want while helping to reduce their intake of fat and calories'.

So confident is P&G that it is on to a winner that it has devised an all-embracing patent which will prevent any other manufacturers from cashing in on olestra's future success. Stock market experts are convinced that fat-free fats could be an even bigger seller than artificial sweeteners. Burnham Lambert, a leading analyst, thinks that olestra could have sales of $1.5 billion a year in the US alone, and international royalties could make P&G's future profits astronomic.

On 7 May 1987 P&G filed a petition with the US Food and Drug Administration requesting approval of olestra as a replacement in everyday foods. To assist the FDA, it handed over its extensive scientific research which, it claims, proves olestra is beneficial and safe to use. But last summer, using the Freedom of Information Act, the Washington-based Center for Science in the Public Interest acquired the data which P&G had submitted to the FDA and passed it on to an independent toxicologist for assessment. The CSPI admits that olestra could lower cholesterol levels by replacing a portion of the saturated fats in the nation's diet, but it points out that cholesterol isn't the only substance washed out of the body by olestra; Vitamin E literally goes down the pan, too. P&G counters that criticism by planning to fortify olestra with additional Vitamin E.

The CSPI also recommends that until P&G produces more persuasive safety studies, olestra should not come into the marketplace. Dr Michael Jacobson, director of the CSPI, has passed a summary of its misgivings to Whitehall, where the

Food Advisory Committee has been considering whether there is a 'case of need' for olestra to be cleared as a safe food. If it agrees that there is a 'need' then it will be up to the Committee on Toxicity to pronounce on its safety. All this will take many months.

There is certainly a commercial need for olestra; after twenty years' expensive research on it, P&G needs to have it cleared. But do we really need this no-calorie, fatless fat food? Aren't we eating enough as it is? Olestra will almost be a licence for the fat and greedy to eat more and more. The nice foods (like doughnuts, cream buns, ice-cream sundaes and, of course, cookies) will no longer be naughty: Guzzling might become respectable. The commercials almost write themselves: 'Lower your cholesterol with just one more non-fattening olestra pecan pie.'

On a planet which has not yet learnt to share its limited food resources fairly and with dignity, olestra seems to me like something we could well do without. It would be nice to think of the FDA and our own Food Advisory Committee giving it the thumbs down, not on grounds of health or safety but for purely moral reasons. We don't *need* more heavily processed food in the West; we need less.

20. The Roots of Hunger

No human right is more clearly enshrined in international agreements than the fundamental freedom not to go hungry. In 1974 the superpowers assembled for a World Food Conference and, flown with rhetoric, proclaimed that 'within a decade no child will go to bed hungry, no family will fear for its next day's bread'.

Today estimates of the number of chronically and severely malnourished people in the world range from the Food and Agriculture Organisation's conservative 500 million to the World Bank's one billion. Not only has the problem not gone away; it has been compounded by the inability of official agencies to address the political issues which nourish the roots of hunger.

Despite the fact that for the last decade the FAO has promoted an annual World Food Day to draw attention to its failure to feed the hungry the world remains preoccupied with other matters. Many of the questions raised at that 1974 conference are still unanswered.

The FAO has admitted that there is no shortage of food in the world. The prodigious surpluses produced by western countries demonstrate, if demonstration were needed, that agritechnology can achieve miracles of overproduction if there's enough financial incentive. In the short term intensive farming with all the attendant depletion of the earth's mineral and fossil fuel resources and the frequently irreversible damage to the environment could fill empty bellies from Bangladesh to Ethiopia. But that is surely not the way ahead.

When the distinguished Indian economist Amartya Sen researched the causes which contribute to famines he came to the conclusion that 'starvation is the characteristic of some people not having enough to eat. It is not the characteristic of there not *being* enough food to eat.' Although famines make the headlines and the television food aid marathons raise millions of pounds, the attention bestowed on them by the media conceals far more dramatic realities.

We have created a world in which the responsibility for implementing the thoroughly worthy aims of the United Nations no longer appears to have any political or moral urgency. Although we pay lip service to the brotherhood of man and the right of all to eat, nothing much is being done about it.

Perhaps the rich countries of the north are too indoctrinated with the idea that crop failures are acts of some malign deity and the inability of farming communities to grow enough to feed themselves is a direct result of fecklessness, laziness or worse.

The pressures on the poor countries of the world to conform to the west's idea of what constitutes the best solution to their problems frequently produces compromises which only make matters worse. High inputs of chemical fertilizers, hi-tech intensive farming systems, the growing of cash crops to pay for foreign imports are well attested recipes for disaster. And yet this treadmill of misery revolves without any hope of release.

Today the State more often than not protects the rights of property against the right to eat. Food aid inevitably sabotages the infrastructure which would enable people to feed themselves. It is a prescription for starvation applied from without; not a cure which would remove the causes of hunger and poverty.

A world system which encourages overweight and obesity in the rich countries and malnutrition in the 'developing' countries is demonstrably inadequate. It has been estimated that the Third World imports some 25 billion dollars of armaments from the well-fed industrialized countries every year. The interest which the poor countries are paying the rich for their 'development projects' and their military hardware is a burden which in many cases has strangled the will to create a society which could be self-supporting.

Western science and western economic theories have failed to feed the hungry. 'Off-the-shelf' technology has been seen to fail in so many instances that you might think intelligent people would have lost faith in it. But that is not the case. If transplanted western solutions do not work in African or Asian contexts the blame is all too often put down to the inadequacy of the receiving society – lack of literacy, bad climate, poor soil – but never the folly of exporting inappropriate farming systems to environments in which they could not have the slightest hope of success.

It is difficult to resist coming to the conclusion that answers to world hunger are not being sought with the energy that the crisis demands because those solutions would challenge the prerogative of the rich nations of the world to order the destiny of the poor nations.

But there is hope ahead. More and more people in the west are coming to see that they cannot go on consuming massive amounts of foods while others starve. All it needs is a concerted political shove and we may well achieve that grand dream of 1974 . . . 'no child will go to bed hungry, no family will fear for its next day's bread'.

21. A Conspiracy of Silence

In the last few months we have become all too aware of the risks we face from eating contaminated food but we still remain remarkably ignorant about how most of the food we buy is actually produced.

What is the level of pesticide residues in that good-looking lettuce? Does the milk in that carton contain the genetically engineered growth hormone, bovine somatotropin? Those raspberries which look so inviting in the punnet – did they ripen amid a constant fallout of lead from a nearby motorway? The flesh of that salmon is coloured pink with canthaxanthin but what else was it fed on during the course of its unnatural life? How many additives are in that bottle of *appellation controlée* burgundy? Was the chicken you are about to eat reared on a diet of poultry offal and antibiotics? How much aluminium is there in the tap water and how much nitrate in the cabbage? Has that pound of potatoes been treated with a chemical to inhibit sprouting? What has been applied to the skin of that orange to make it shiny? Has the meat on your plate been contaminated with the disease they call bovine spongiform encephalopathy? How many preservatives and improvers have been added to that kilo of flour? What are polyphosphates doing in those frozen prawns and how do you know they haven't been exposed to irradiation?

The questions are endless but the answers are hard to come by. Why is it that of the 3,500 additives used by the food industry in Britain fewer than 300 are regulated? And why is it that the Norwegian government has banned all the seventeen artificial colours permitted in the UK? Do they know something we don't? For decades mineral hydrocarbons distilled from petroleum have been sprayed on sultanas and prunes to prevent them from sticking together. Suddenly in February the government decided to ban these hydrocarbons. So what new evidence has been unearthed to make them a health risk now and how many more weapons in the food industry's arsenal of additives would be banned if we knew more about their toxicology? How soon before the rest of the questionable colourings, flavouring, foaming agents and aids to food processing will also be banned? Do we really need shellac in our sparkling orange drinks, refined microcrystalline wax in chewing gum, carnauba wax on our chocs and L-glutamic acid in our Farmhouse Country-Style meat-flavoured pie?

Most of the additives still used by food manufacturers are presumed to be safe because they have not been the subject of the kind of scentific evaluation that we might reasonably expect. Whenever I see the verdict 'presumed to be safe' against one of the chemicals used in food processing I'm reminded of Ralph Nader's assessment of a universally popular German car – 'unsafe at any speed'. I refuse to give additives the benefit of the doubt. 'Unsafe in any quantity' should be the criterion.

If that sounds irrational and alarmist I am remembering the long list of chemicals (like the now banned mineral oils) which have been used by the food industry and are now thankfully illegal. One of the central dilemmas of the present food debate is the shroud of secrecy which veils the industry and its activities. We just do not know what our pigs are being fed on or to what extent our salads are being drenched in chemical sprays or why we need all those humectants, anti-caking agents, antioxidants, stabilizers, thickeners, bleaching agents and assorted cohorts of additives which should have been outlawed years ago.

For reasons which do not stand up to responsible scrutiny the Official Secrets Act is used to conceal the special relationship which the food and agricultural industry seems to enjoy in Whitehall. As the Tory Euro-MP Richard Cottrell has unkindly pointed out the food industry is the only one in the country which actually has a seat in the Cabinet. At the industry's insistence large areas of information on the safety and toxicity of food additives remain secret. Information revealed at meetings of COMA, the Committee on Medical Aspects of Food Policy, is subject to all the rigours of the Official Secrets Act and the same applies to the deliberations of the Food Advisory Committee.

It is a cosy keep-it-dark arrangement calculated to deter all but the most tenacious investigator. Geoffrey Cannon spent months storming the impenetrable ramparts of Whitehall while writing *The Politics of Food*. His researches became a masterly indictment of a system of government which allows its food policy to be manipulated by a closed circle of commercially motivated businessmen and a group of consenting civil servants.

Whitehall's farcical handling of the *salmonella enteritidis* epidemic in the laying flocks is a classic illustration of the inability of civil servants to admit what's going on. At that time we had the respective Ministers of Health and Food running around like chickens with their heads cut off. The confusion created was due not to a shortage of information – there was plenty of that being kept desperately under wraps – but a reluctance to admit what a timebomb the chicken and egg industry had created in their efforts to cut the cost of production to the bone.

The policy of trying to keep prices as low as possible has created two kinds of food. There is the cheap and nasty stuff – wretched sausages made with mechanically recovered gristle and slurry, non-nutritious packets and tins of highly coloured rubbish and snacks rich only in empty calories – and the expensive foods which attract the words *real, natural, organic, traditional, pure, handmade*. But shouldn't all food be as safe and as pure and as fresh as possible? Why have cheap bad food at all?

I find it outrageous that we don't have access to better food and the sort of information which could lead to better health for all. The most flagrant recent instance of the government's fear of offending the food industry was their handling of the NACNE report which revealed the extent of diet-related disease in Britain and called for a radical change in dietary habits. This important document prepared by the National Advisory Committee on Nutrition Education was hastily shelved by Whitehall and would never have been seen at all if its contents hadn't been leaked to Fleet Street.

That was in 1983. Six years later we are still victims of the same climate of concealment and secrecy. There have been suggestions that the name of the Ministry of Agriculture should be changed, that Food and Health should be made a joint responsibility. I see no virtue in that. They will still continue to be run by the same prevaricating *Yes, Minister* civil servants – a group of Whitehall warriors entrenched behind barricades of stony silence.

In a democracy is it defensible that so much of the truth should be wilfully withheld from public scrutiny or doctored to make it less politically explosive? At the time of writing the government is still sitting on a report prepared by Professor Richard Southwood of Oxford University's zoology department revealing the true extent of the danger to humans from eating meat infected by bovine spongiform encephalopathy. How long will we have to wait to be told what to do about this new and terrifying threat to our health?

We have a right to know what is being done to the land and what is going on in the factory farming sheds. To have this kind of information subject to the Official Secrets Act makes a mockery of the democratic process. What we urgently need is a revolt against this conspiracy of silence by our elected MPs. Until very recently food was not regarded as a political issue or a subject which won votes at elections. Now food is on the political agenda we must keep it there. If we want to ensure that our food and drink is as safe and as healthy as possible then we as consumers must take more interest in the way it is produced. We need more vigilance and more commitment to a responsible system of food production. We need to spend huge sums of money putting our food and farming house in order if we want to enjoy the pleasures of the table in the years to come. We have never bothered much about food in the past and I have grave doubts that we have the will to change the fate that awaits us. I hope I shall be proved wrong.

22. Fresh from the Pod

'I will be with you before curfew,' wrote Pitt one summer day despatching a messenger from Westminster to his friend William Wilberforce in Wimbledon, 'and expect an early meal of peas and strawberries.' It is the taste of those early, green, succulent peas, their freshness from the pod, that we, with all our resources and our high technology, have almost lost.

There is nothing to compare with them. Certainly not the dried pea nor the canned pea surfeited with sugar, nor the green-blue dyed marrowfat bullet tasting of sulphur and the chemistry lab. Nor, alas, the frozen pea; least of all perhaps the frozen pea which raises visual expectations it never satisfies.

It looks good, it retains its shape and texture, it is tender in the mouth. Unfortunately the pea the frozen food industry chose for mass planting and harvesting in the flatlands of Lincolnshire and Humberside has great commercial advantages but no taste at all. None. And even when in desperation the marketing men added an artificial hint of mint (NEW, NEW, NEW!) it couldn't redeem that bland forkful of inoffensive nothingness.

Had they only taken the delicious garden pea and frozen that, then all would have been well. But they needed a freezer pea – a species which would grow well, crop well and be disease resistant. In the producing of the Wonder Pea the plant geneticists bred the flavour out of it. A whole generation has now been reared on this neutral cultivar, a generation which has never shelled a fresh pea in its life and has come to believe that the specious frozen pea is what peadom is all about. The acreage under fresh garden peas has fallen dramatically. In the part of the world where I live you can no longer buy peas in the pod. Soon I predict they will be a universal rarity like quinces, persimmons, samphire, mulberries and Jerusalem artichokes.

The bland freezer pea which sends no stimulating messages to the tastebuds is a classic example of the way in which commercial imperatives manipulate raw materials so that eating becomes an exercise in marketing not in joy and pleasure. Soon there will be, I'm told, a designer freezing strawberry that won't disintegrate into a mushy watery mess when it thaws. It will look like a picture book strawberry and photograph superbly for the TV commercials. But what about its flavour? Will the New Strawberry like the New Pea be just another mouthful of nothing? And how long will it be before the only strawberries available will be the frozen variety?

Already technology has mutated even the simplest foods so that the taste is smothered or replaced by the far from natural. It is becoming increasingly difficult to find fresh milk in public places; its place has been usurped by little plastic tubs of metallic-tasting UHT 'milk' or sachets of chemical powders which 'whiten' tea or coffee. Potatoes are mixed into a tasteless and frothy mash from powder; ice cream has the soapy taste of palm oil; fish is battered and crumbed, beef is burgerized, steaks become additive-rich steaklettes, chickens are nuggetized, veal is chopped into choplettes. Raw materials are massaged and minced and steamed and pasteurized and extended with ersatz bulkers. And because the end result is characterless, flavours are sprayed on and artificial colours are added to create a spurious authenticity.

These new value-added foods, debased with salt and sucrose, are nasty but never cheap. Frequently the advertising budget costs more than the raw materials so you end up buying an edible equivalent of the Emperor's clothes – rubbish masquerading as a desirable and scrumptious treat. The vinegar-flavoured crisp is not a contradiction in terms: it is the logical and inevitable end result of the sterile philosophy of over-processing.

And what isn't over-processed and over-refined and bombarded with synthetic fragrances is by a process of unnatural selection gradually robbed of all taste. A perfect partner to the frozen pea is the cosmetic carrot, a designer product if ever there was one – lovely to look at but flavourless on the palate. And for all I know the plant breeding research stations are even now developing all manner of handsome turnips, raspberries, plums and apples which will pack well, travel well and have a profitably long shelf life. And once again taste will be of little importance.

Time perhaps that we formed a Society for the Preservation of Taste. There are plenty of bodies preserving trees, disused mineshafts, trams and ospreys. Help the poor pea, that's what I say. Help milk, potatoes, kale and carrots. Before it's too late.

I'm convinced that if there is a strong and insistent demand for food that actually has real taste then there will be market gardeners and farmers who would get great pleasure out of satisfying that demand. But we must play our part. Badger the greengrocer, bend the ear of the superstore manager, get them enthused too. If we just take what is handed out then the handouts will become progressively more bland. It's up to us.

23. Irradiation Overdose?

In September 1986 representatives from nine nations met in the Holiday Inn in Ottawa to work out a strategy to persuade the world that irradiation technology was not only acceptable but highly necessary. The delegates were told that to foster a common international acceptance of irradiation they should use public relations skills and the persuasion of marketing men to stress the benefits of the process.

Since that meeting great progress has been made in furthering the cause of the nuclear industry which stands to make a great deal of money if its waste products can be used for the irradiation of food.

This summer the UK government announced that it was to push ahead with plans to legalize food irradiation in Britain. It was all to do with freedom of choice: 'The potential benefits are important and consumers should be free to enjoy them if they choose . . . No one will have to eat irradiated food if they do not want to.'

The British Nutrition Foundation published a short statement applauding the government's decision. It's a perfectly safe technology, it said, echoing Whitehall, and it dismissed as 'crackpot' the notion that there was anything wrong with giving food a nuclear fix.

Even the suggestion that irradiation counterfeits freshness and causes nutritional changes was rubbished. Scientific concern about the vitamin losses caused by irradiation was reduced to the level of farce: 'Whoever eats strawberries because they need vitamin C?'

Readers of this magazine who know that the prestigious-sounding British Nutrition Foundation is funded by the food industry will wonder why the industry is so anxious to have irradiation legalized.

Irradiation extends the shelf life of perishable foods by destroying any micro-organisms which might contaminate it. It prevents the sprouting of potatoes, onions and garlic; kills salmonella and campylobacter; inhibits the development of mould on soft fruit; and delays the deterioration of seafood. It can also be used to reduce the hazard of food-borne parasites in processed food. There is no doubt that it would have many commercial advantages.

But is this technology absolutely safe? Many scientists believe it is an unnecessary tool for the food industry and one that is potentially hazardous to health.

At an international meeting of consumer groups in Canberra last November, serious doubts were expressed about the wisdom of allowing irradiation to be used at all. It was suggested that some governments had signed secret deals to accept expensive food irradiation plants as gifts or had been offered such plants by international agencies.

There are now two irradiation plants in Indonesia, and rice, wheat, onions and potatoes have been irradiated intermittently in Japan since the mid-1970s. Early consumer protests centred on irradiated potatoes which had been treated under the guise of animal feed and then used in baby food by a prominent Japanese food manufacturer. Research in Japan has revealed growth retardation in rats fed on irradiated food and a high mortality among rats fed continuously on irradiated products.

Although Japan is often cited as a prospective customer for irradiated foods the meeting was told that consumers there will not buy food if they know it has been irradiated. The New Zealand government has adopted a firm stance against the new technology which it believes unncessary, expensive, damaging to the condition and flavour of foods and likely to ruin New Zealand's market image if it were ever accepted.

In Australia there is the National Coalition to Stop Food Irradiation which has pointed out that food irradiation plants are extremely expensive to build and have substantial maintenance costs. That outlay has to be recouped from the consumer.

Dr David Murray, who has written a book about the problems of irradiation, told the meeting that there was a significant protein loss when food was irradiated. 'On cooking, irradiated meats lose higher proportions of soluble minerals and vitamins as "drip loss" than ordinary chilled or frozen meats,' he said. Dr Murray also pointed out that attempts to encourage people to eat more fresh fruit would be undermined by the vitamin C loss endemic in the irradiation process.

He believes that far from being wholesome, 'irradiated foods suffer immediate deterioration in every conceivable parameter of quality: unattractive flavour, discoloration, ruined texture and cooking behaviour and an added burden of potentially carcinogenic radiolytic products'.

But wait a minute, you must be saying, the government's Advisory Committee on Irradiated & Novel Foods, which based its views on detailed international studies and experience, claimed that irradiation would not significantly change food nor would it prejudice its safety and wholesomeness.

Yet Dr Richard Pugh, Tesco's head of science, told me he had grave reservations about the process. He gained his doctorate from a thesis on irradiation.

We do not know, Dr Pugh said, enough about the way in which irradiation may affect bacteria on the surface of food. That's why Tesco and most of the other supermarkets will not be selling irradiated food.

The problem is that they may well buy unknowingly food that has been irradiated in other countries. The Netherlands is one of the thirty countries which endorses irradiation and it virtually controls the spice trade in Europe. For some time now it has been using irradiation as an alternative to the suspect fumigant ethylene bromide. On balance you might well be better off eating irradiated pepper than pepper cleaned up with a fumigant which is about to be banned for safety reasons.

But that bonus does not apply to the wide range of food

which will be irradiated from now on. The Minister of Agriculture says you will have the choice *not* to eat irradiated food, but I do not believe that this choice will always be available.

I would like much firmer guarantees about safety and wholesomeness. Supposing an operator overdoses food? Could that happen and if it did how would one be aware of it? There is no universal test to determine if food has been irradiated.

No mention has been made by the government about the price the consumer will have to pay for the long shelf-life and the 'convenience' of food that stays ever-fresh. It has been estimated that you might have to pay up to 15p per pound more for radiation-sterilized meat.

The key question about irradiation, apart from its long-term safety, is whether it can be used to give a semblance of freshness and safety which actually conceals inner dangers. Though irradiation can kill bacteria in food it will not remove toxins already created by bacteria.

Never has it been more important for shoppers to know the facts about their food; there are too many doubts concerning irradiation to make it an acceptable risk. We're back, I'm afraid, to *caveat emptor* – let the buyer beware.

24. A Better Biscuit?

Don't put your faith in statistics and what they say until you have carefully considered what they don't say, said William W. Watt. He also observed that facts are stubborn things, while statistics are rather more pliable.

So many statistics arrive with the morning post that you almost begin to feel bludgeoned by disinformation. Practitioners of public relations sprinkle statistics into their press releases with an abandon reminiscent of chocolate chips in cookies, no doubt working on the principle that a golden nugget of astonishing magnitude can lighten a load of pure verbal dross to great effect.

I'm talking about those impossible-to-disprove bits of information that provoke the response, 'Well, I'll be darned!' And they frequently centre around that abstract entity – the Average British Household. We might be told that the ABH buys 3.2 bananas a week, consumes 3.85lb potatoes and cooks 2.8oz pasta.

The figures are always presented in baffling fractions or decimals. Thus the Tea Council – a body convened to promote the consumption of tea – will tell you that every man, woman and child over the age of ten drinks 3.77 cups of tea a day. You will also be told that this mythical man/woman/child only drinks 1.82 cups of coffee in a similar 24-hour period.

So the British drink 196 million cups of tea a day – but how many un-drunk cups do we pour down the sink, and if the old lady next door actually drinks fifteen cups a day, whose share is she swallowing? And further, how do you actually pour 3.77 cups of tea and not exceed your norm by accidentally consuming 3.78 cups? No wonder such statistics are hard to swallow, yet the food industry finds them irresistible. What set me thinking about all of this was the handout that landed on my door-mat last week. It was from a public relations company called Adwise – a good name that, with its overtones of wisdom.

It turned out that Adwise was writing on behalf of Burtons Biscuits of Bracknell in Berkshire. I always thought that Burtons specialized in those low cost three-piece suits, but this Burtons had just launched a range of healthy eating low-fat biscuits.

'As a nation,' Adwise revealed, 'we love biscuits.' This was followed by – you've guessed it – a statistic: 'Every day we munch through no fewer than 100 million.' Imagine all those biscuits sliding down the national throat – and even if you ignore those slipped to the dog, that's still 657 a year.

What Adwise is gung-ho about is the health benefits embedded in these new biscuits, which are designed to 'help you keep in trim'. How successful they will be is anyone's guess – but a dark, uncommercial thought crosses my mind. Maybe we could keep in trim more effectively by halving our consumption of biscuits – that is, struggling by on 50 million a year instead of 100 million. Or perhaps we could go the whole hog and replace the lot with a few glasses of mineral water – surely that would revolutionize our health?

I'm only asking because it would seem that if 70 per cent of us prefer less fat in our diet, we could achieve that overnight by eating fewer biscuits and replacing the aching void with fruit, vegetables and cereals. We'd be reducing our sugar intake too.

Here's another statistic, for what it's worth. More than half of all men and four out of ten women in this country over the age of forty are overweight, and that potentially damaging burden stems largely from the hidden fats and sugars in processed foods – like biscuits.

While it's true that some firms have been reformulating their recipes by cutting back on the ingredients and additives which are perceived to be undesirable, it's not enough to make a significant difference. It would actually need a major revolution in the food industry. But at least the problem is being approached as Burtons has recognized that there is a demand for healthier products – so half fat has to be a step in the right direction.

25. Eels at Risk

I was invited to give a talk on World Food Day to a group of extra-mural students at one of our newer universities. There was a sprinkling of lecturers and researchers in the audience. I chose my words carefully and gave what I thought was an unemotional and balanced account of the way in which our food is produced. At one stage, I suggested that in view of our past experience it would be advisable for the future well-being of the world population that we should restrict the use of pesticides and potentially dangerous chemicals to a minimum. I gave examples of the way in which the heavy input of chemicals into the soil and the atmosphere was polluting not only the areas in which they were being applied but parts as distant as the poles. None of what I said was unsupported by scientific research nor was it very revolutionary. Friends of the Earth, the Pesticides Trust and other bodies alarmed at our abuse of the environment have provided plenty of well-documented evidence that what is called 'conventional' farming, and what in the interests of objectivity many of us prefer to call chemical farming, has dealt a body blow to the environment from which it may never recover.

As soon as I sat down I was vehemently corrected by an imposing dark-suited figure in the front row. Without artificial fertilizers and pesticides, he said, the Third World would be faced with famine. Our own food would cost infinitely more and we too would face massive shortages. My analysis, he claimed, was not only alarmist but irresponsible. All pesticides were exhaustively tested before being put on sale and were to all intents perfectly safe.

Chatting afterwards to the vice-chancellor of the university,

I found out that the gent in question was the professor of chemistry and much of his research money came from the chemical industry. His arguments were not new to me – I had heard them expressed on many occasions by spokespersons for the international chemical companies.

In 1977, the government belatedly established a working party on pesticide residues whose function it is to co-ordinate all information relating to pesticide residues in the food we eat, our body tissues, in wildlife and in the environment. This body is responsible to the advisory committee on pesticides which reports directly to ministers of agriculture. Due to a shortage of funds monitoring is patchy and the news emanating from Whitehall is calculated not to alarm the public. It is frequently hedged about with conditional phrases involving words like 'might' and 'may'.

After a survey carried out between 1986 and 1987 into chemical residues in wild eels it was suggested that some consumers who frequently eat eels *might* consider restricting the number of wild eels they eat. Eels live for a long time and they are a fatty fish prone to the accumulation of residues of fat-soluble compounds such as organochlorine pesticides, many of which have now been phased out of agricultural and industrial uses.

Now a new government survey has found sufficient dieldrin in eels from various parts of the country to issue a stronger warning. Eels from the Humber, Yorkshire Ouse and inshore Thames fisheries are so high in residues that consumers are being advised to restrict their consumption of eel meat to no more than four ounces a week.

Nothing to worry about there, especially if you don't eat eels anyway and don't intend to, but such announcements reinforce the high price we are still paying for chemicals which were once thought to be perfectly safe and no doubt rigorously tested. There is a growing movement to demand a higher level of responsibility in the production and processing of food. At the moment, much of what is done is done despite public unease. Pesticides are being phased out as biogenetic engineering is being phased in. We are assured that the new technologies will be perfectly safe and rigorously tested before being unleashed on the world. But we've heard that before.

As power is consolidated into fewer and bigger units, so anxieties grow. One solution will be explored this coming October when the Soil Association meets in public to discuss a new model for food and farming. What it is hoping to explore is a method of producing food in a sustainable way which pays high priority to care of the environment, health and local communities. In other words, involving ordinary people more decisively in the way in which their food is produced.

Nobody any longer believes that the Common Agricultural Policy will reduce surpluses let alone improve the quality of food; sensible husbandry has been displaced by the need for high output which in turn calls for a high energy input. This is not a philosophy which is likely to be reversed overnight. Unless consumers and producers can forge new links to promote saner farming, says the Soil Association, the agricultural crisis will deepen. It believes that organic farming creates a new trust and confidence in healthy wholesome food and is good for people and the land. Already in Japan consumer cooperatives are dictating a more rational approach to that country's limited resources and in the United States the success of farmers' markets in capturing public enthusiasm suggests that food production and distribution in the next century could be saner and more sustainable than it has been for half a century. It could be good for eels too.

26. Room for Complaint

I was chatting the other evening with a hotelier, who told me the most depressing stories about the endless capacity of his guests to make his life a misery. He's certainly no paranoiac, but an hour spent with him would put you off all thoughts of buying that little gem of a country inn for your retirement.

To cheer him up, and remind him that the British have always had an insatiable appetite for not enjoying their food and drink, I sent him a spare copy of Fothergill's *My Three Inns* in which that long-suffering and frequently insufferable eccentric chronicled the extraordinary behaviour of his patrons. John Fothergill kept, with varying degrees of impecuniosity, the Spreadeagle at Thame, the Royal Hotel at Ascot and the Three Swans at Market Harborough, and was crucified almost daily by the insensitivities of those who descended upon him.

There were majors with numbed palates who swore that the lamb was beef, swells who patronized him, commercial travellers who quibbled about pennies and country folk who used his premises as a public lavatory. John Fothergill, a martyr to complaint, recalled with relish the story of the Edwardian gentleman involved in a train crash in Germany. 'With the place littered with fallen coaches and human beings and amidst the cries of the wounded was heard that of an Englishman calling for the complaint book.'

Fothergill built a considerable local reputation for not suffering complaints gladly; neither did he knowingly lose an opportunity to put the verbal boot in. He once observed a businessman pouring Worcester sauce into his plate of soup. Before the wretched man could lift his spoon, Fothergill was there, the crystal buckles on his shoes radiating ill will, the monocle glinting cruelly. 'Next time you come I wish you would telephone to me when I would make some special soup for you out of blotting paper so that you could flavour it yourself.'

I thought of Fothergill the weekend before last, when I was staying in a small country hotel in Somerset. The food was excellent, the wine list outstanding. The kind of place where room for complaint was minute. But not a bit of it. One guest, after eating a particularly excellent dinner there, had pronounced it with a hearty laugh to be 'almost up to Berni Inn standard'. Another, on being presented with the bill, said the entire operation was a rip-off. Even more cavalier were the party who arrived with their own champagne which they insisted on drinking at dinner, and then retreated upstairs with their coffee to kill a bottle of Grand Marnier in their room.

The English don't change. Fifty years ago Fothergill recorded the antics of a couple who walked into his hotel, ordered two 10d tots of rum, and then settled themselves in the lounge with a Revelation suitcase, from which they produced a flask of coffee, a chicken and various other items on which they proceeded to lunch. Fothergill put them out, but first, of course, he put them down.

He was indeed a master at the put-down, but I have never observed it more elegantly done than by the proprietor of a Kensington restaurant with an impeccable reputation for good food. Welcoming two people, he showed them to a table and handed them menus. While they were trying to make up their minds what to order, the owner suggested that they might like some fresh Dover sole which had just arrived in the kitchen. 'I wouldn't have that, darling,' said the man in a voice that carried round the room, 'they're bound to be frozen.' The owner summoned a waiter. 'Bring this lady and gentleman their coats,' he said, and that was all.

There used to be an excellent restaurant in Eastbourne, in a street which raised few gastronomic expectations. But it was to Seaside Road that the last working pupil of the great Escoffier had come in the twilight of his life to astonish the natives with his skills. M. Maurice Ithurbure quickly won his way into the guides, and in due course, when he retired, his place was taken by a fellow Swiss, Alphonse Bertschy. Talking to M. Bertschy one day after a lunch of succulent early-summer plaice, he told me how suspicious the English were and how distrustful. The previous week he had recommended some salmon-trout to a party of four. 'It had come on the train fresh from Billingsgate that morning. Perfect. So I cooked it for them with new potatoes and a little mayonnaise. Perfection. When I gave them the bill they said they weren't paying. The salmon was frozen; they had been cheated.' Alphonse visibly quivered as he told me the story. It had ruined his week. Ever since then I have been more careful than ever not to cause offence to those who cook and cater.

Last Sunday, in a country inn, I had with my carbonated pint of bitter and ploughman's a hunk of Vienna loaf which was frozen solid in the middle. 'Did you enjoy that?' asked the barmaid, clearing the plate. And because she smiled and looked as if she really cared I told her what a treat it had been and went on my way uplifted by the lie.

27. Cheesed Off

It was cold in mid-April in the medieval town of Brignoles. There is nothing more chilling than the bare terrazzo floor of a Côte d'Azur hotel when there's no heating and the rain is beating against the shutters. 'It always rains for the fair,' Adrian Fontana told me. They've been having a fair in Brignoles every April for as long as anyone can remember – thirty-seven years, if you want precision. It's not as important as the fairs of Avignon or Marseilles, but in a landscape almost entirely dominated by vines and olive trees, an exposition devoted to wine and olives is an event of absorbing interest – even when it rains.

The principal happening on Tuesday was to be a presentation of British cheeses partnered with the wines of the Var. Adrian, in his role of High Commissioner for Industrialisation in the Var, was instrumental in suggesting it: 'At the Royal Show last year, we found your English cheeses went very well with our wines, so we asked Food From Britain to help us put on this special tasting.'

According to M. Charles André, director of the EEC press bureau, it was the first time in the short history of the Common Market that two member countries had got together to present their products in harmony. 'If it is successful,' said Charles, 'there will be many more events of a similar kind.'

The occasion augured well. Provence, although awash with wine, is not really noted for its cheeses. They are mostly made from goat's and ewe's milk: Brousse de la Vesubie is the best known; soft, creamy and mild, it goes well with the white and rosé wines of Provence. But in those parts they have nothing which would really do justice to a big, tannic Bandol or the other powerful red wines made from the grenache, cinsault and Mourvèdre grapes. Adrian told me he thought Caerphilly was the perfect cheese for Bandol. I looked forward to agreeing with him.

Other combinations leapt to mind. I visualized a challenging array of real cheese which would astonish the French, used only to their mild white cream cheeses. In the vanguard would be a noble truckle Cheddar, perhaps a year old, setting off a rich ripe Stilton. Then Britain's oldest cheese, a perfect piece of Cheshire. There would, of course, be cheese from the dales: Wensleydale, white and blue; Cotherstone, too; single and double Gloucester; Derby Sage; Lancashire; cheese from Orkney and Galloway.

The impending communion of British cheeses and the best wines of the Var was announced on posters all over the town. Fifty French journalists were speeding to this unique gastronomic event. But disappointment was in store. The wines were there and the wine-growers, but where was the cheese? In a corner of the conference room, two harassed girls were cutting up a couple of Dairy Crest cheddars, young, immature stuff, mass-produced for the supermarket trade. It had the all-too-familiar cloying texture and the bland taste that makes it so perfect a partner for a saloon bar 'ploughman's' or a seaside café salad.

Later in the morning a vacuum-packed kilo of Dairy Crest Stilton was produced and that wasn't much consolation either. What had gone wrong? There were two conflicting stories. On the spot I was told that the cheeses hadn't turned up and in panic the organizers had rushed to the local supermarket, which fortuitously was having a British week, and picked up the kind of cheese which such events feature.

There was no representative of Food From Britain present; no literature describing the glories of British cheese. Her Britannic Majesty's Consul-General from Marseilles, David Gladstone, put a brave face on what the assembled journalists from Britain saw as a humiliating fiasco. He thought the cheese was very tasty, he told me, and until I had drawn his attention to the poor quality and lack of variety, he hadn't realized anything was wrong.

There was, of course, a post-mortem. Andrew Colvin, who runs Food From Britain's operation in France, claimed that the event was not sponsored by them. 'They asked us to send them some cheeses and we did.'

It was unfortunate that what was sent was largely of inferior quality and didn't materialize at the tasting. What happened at Brignoles was predictable. Food From Britain, compared with its opposite numbers in Europe, has a minute budget. The French have nearly twenty staff in this country, seeing that we eat and drink more and more food and wine from France. Our sole ambassador over there is Andrew Colvin, and he is grievously overstretched. Things are not likely to get better. The Government expects Food From Britain to be largely self-financing and the only people who seem willing to put their hands in their pockets in the future are the giant food-processing firms, producing food in bulk at the lowest possible price. It is a sad comment on Food From Britain's commercial dilemma that their recipe book published last week featured a 'Best of British' shopping basket on the front cover prominently displaying a bag of granulated sugar and a can of peas.

If that's the best Britain can do, it might be better not to bother at all.

28. Health and Wealth

Among the fitted-kitchen outlets, the greeting-card shops, the film-developing franchises and the offices of building societies, a new amenity has opened in our main street. It's a large shop selling nothing but cheap confectionery. You move mesmerized from tubs of toffees to boxes of jelly babies, filling your basket on the way to the cash-desk. In the window a large notice announces what must be the Dental Disaster of the Year: 'Win your weight in sweets'. Is this the last desperate stand of the sugar industry, or is it the start of a new form of promotion – win your weight in fish fingers, win your weight in cornflakes?

Nothing surprises me any more – not even the Malton Bacon Factory's witty way of turning the 1986 food-labelling regulations to commercial advantage. At Malton they kill over 7,000 pigs a week, processing them into ham and bacon. Some of the hams they make contain up to 15 per cent added water, a fact which up to now has not been revealed to consumers. The water means you get 15 per cent less meat, but according to the manufacturer it produces a more succulent product, which a lot of people like. If you want watery ham, Malton's ham with 'added water' is available in most supermarkets.

I say nothing surprises me any more, but I did do a double-take when I heard that the Minister of Agriculture, Fisheries and Food had decided to go down to Brighton to open the ninth Fast Food Fair. Much of the stuff on display at the fair is what you could legitimately call 'fun food' or what the cynical might describe as 'junk food'. Sugary doughnuts and cookies, slush drinks, potato products extruded in novel shapes and sprayed with artificial flavours, budget burgers, carbonated cokes and colas – a whole range of colourful snacks engineered for easy eating.

Mr Jopling descended among the hamburger franchisees, the pizza retailers, the fried-chicken tycoons and the bun-makers, and appeared to be most impressed. 'Looking about me here today,' he said, 'I am conscious of a distinct wave of optimism for the future of the fast food sector.' He did not exaggerate: the heavily processed world of fast food has become a multimillion-pound market in the last decade. It is now one of the most profitable sectors of the entire food market. The joy of the operation is that a franchise can be run cheaply on unskilled labour, and the franchisee needs no professional skill, beyond the ability to raise the right amount of cash.

Fast food has come in for a great deal of criticism from the health lobby, which is increasingly worried that a growing section of the community is using convenience and fast food as the staple of their diet. It is not a prospect that worries Mr Jopling. 'At a time of growing consumer interest in healthy eating,' he told his delighted audience, 'the mistaken idea that fast food like hamburgers and pizzas has no place in a balanced and nutritious diet must be challenged.' He wanted, he explained, 'to draw attention to a misconception in some quarters that fast food does not provide the consumer with a nutritious meal'. The record, he said, needs putting straight. Mr Jopling straightened it by pointing out that the basic ingredients of a fast-food meal – beef, chicken, fish, cheese or potato – are all to be found in a normal balanced diet. Fast foods, therefore, 'as well as fitting conveniently into the modern lifestyle, can contribute to promoting good nutrition'.

It was a speech which was greeted with enthusiastic applause by the fast food industry, but it raised many questions. The raw materials Mr Jopling mentioned are undoubtedly good for you when taken as part of a balanced diet. Poached fish, boiled potatoes, roast chicken, a slice of lean beef – what could be healthier? But in fast food terms, potatoes usually come as chips, and chicken, fish and beef are fried. The average fast-food meal is rich in empty calories, and accompanied not by fruit and vegetables but by further providers of non-nutritional energy – the very kind of diet that the DHSS and the Health Education Council are advising us to avoid.

I wonder if Mr Jopling had time during his brief visit to Brighton to look closely at the heavily processed foods which he was commending. Had he noted the high incidence of additives, colourings, flavourings and preservatives in many of the best-selling lines, he may well have had food for further thought.

29. Words in the 'Best' Order

Like coinage, words have different values at different times; some become debased, others, like the farthing, disappear altogether. In his *Dictionary of Changes in Meaning* Adrian Room charts the history of some of the more interesting verbal ups and downs.

Nowadays, we put bulbs in sockets or expect them to produce flowers in the spring; in the sixteenth century a bulb was an onion. Custard in the fifteenth century was not made out of cornflour and put on a pudding, but an open meat pie, and a pudding itself was almost invariably savoury. In Chaucerian times 'diet' was not something you made your life a misery with but food in general; although even in those fat times the nun in the *Canterbury Tales* was clearly a medieval weight-watcher: 'No deyntee morsel passed throgh hir throte ... Attempree (moderate) diet was al hir phisik.' The first use of the word 'vegetable' to describe an edible root or herb commonly eaten with meat didn't appear until the late eighteenth century. Gray could write in 1737 of vales and hills covered with 'very reverend vegetables' without evoking an image of a landscape covered with cabbages and carrots.

Originally gingerbread meant preserved ginger from the French *gingembras*; porridge was once a meat and vegetable soup; pineapple was a pine cone; a pearmain was not an apple but a pear; junket was not a dish of curds but a fish basket; and gourmand had no pejorative overtones. Adrian Room quotes an ambivalent line from Charlotte Brontë's *Villette*, written in 1835: 'Fifine was a frank gourmande; anybody could have her heart through her palate' – or, as we would say today, she was anyone's for a bag of crisps.

Gravy, crumpet, lollipop, pastry and blancmange meant very different things hundreds of years ago, and these changed usages reflect all manner of social and technical innovations. There is perhaps an appendix to be added to Adrian Room's book on the way in which adjectives are now made to play a marketing role totally unconnected with any accepted meaning.

I was in a country pub last Sunday, one of the 5,100 owned by the brewing giant Courage, and they had two real ale beers on sale. One was described as best bitter and the other as Director's. I asked for ordinary bitter but there was no ordinary bitter on sale.

Did Courage make only *best* bitter? I asked the hired help. He didn't know. If what was on offer was 'best', it implied that it was better than some lesser bitter the brewery produced; but if so it was not possible to do a comparative tasting.

I was reminded of the evidence given at the inquiry after the collapse of the Tay Bridge on a stormy night in December 1879. Ninety lives were lost and interest during cross-examination centred on the workmanship and the quality of the iron used by the contractors. The investigators were categorically assured that only the *best* iron had been used. It subsequently emerged that there were other grades available. Better than 'best' was 'best best' and even better was 'best best best'.

I rang Courage and they told me that it was only best bitter they sold in their southern pubs. It had an original gravity of 1039 and Director's (best best best?) was 1046. Why did they call it best bitter, then; why not simply bitter? They always had called it best bitter.

'Best' has become one of those words from which, in food-and-drink circles, all meaning has leached. In Germany there are very strict regulations about the adjectives you can use to describe beer; we are less particular. Best bitter, best butter, best end of neck, best eaten before 5 June; such degrees of meaning are best left to the imagination.

Perhaps before it's all too late an Adrian Room should begin collecting all the sterile words which appear on labels;

words which are there solely to fill space and raise expectations. Next time you're in an off-licence, cast your eye over the serried ranks of Scotch whiskies which excel in the employment of adjectives whose beauty is solely in the eye of the bottler. Is 'fine' better than 'rare'?; is 'select' a better buy than 'choice'? 'Supreme', 'superior', 'de luxe', 'special', 'private stock', 'antique', 'three star'! Some no doubt are better than others, but which is best best best?

30. Anglo-Saxon Attitudes

It's interesting what images the prospect of a Channel tunnel has conjured up in the press. Not a mention of the pleasurable benefits which will accrue from being in more immediate touch with all that Gallic gastronomy. Contamination is the uppermost fear – packs of rabid dogs fanning out into Kent to lay waste the countryside, as the Normans did nine centuries ago, hotly pursued, no doubt, by infectious French persons smelling of garlic, their Renaults full of snails.

If past performance is anything to go on, we shall remain icily isolated, unmoved by all attempts to make life cheerier. The cross-fertilization of attitudes to eating and taste in England and France is the main theme explored by Stephen Mennell in a vigorous new book called *All Manners of Food*. He investigates our very different development from the Middle Ages onwards and comes to the conclusion that although our social histories are not all that dissimilar, when it comes to eating we remain miles apart.

Although the teaching of domestic science was introduced into schools in both countries at about the same time, it entrenched attitudes not changed them. A recipe book used in Manchester schools in 1889 advised students to boil carrots for an hour and cabbage for up to an hour and a quarter. What wasn't imprinted early at mother's knee or later in school tended to be derived from magazines. In France *Le Pot-au-feu*, founded in 1893, survived until 1940. It concerned itself with practical cookery and its appeal was intended to be classless. Stephen Mennell compares it with our *Woman's Life*, founded in 1895, which amalgamated with *Woman's Own* in 1934. The French magazine was enthusiastic about cooking, devoting most of its space to the kind of provincial or country dishes popularized in this country at a later date by Elizabeth David.

English cookery writers were at the same time 'ringing the changes on a huge repertoire of heavy puddings'. The rest of the food was plain but wholesome: fishcakes, mutton stewed with vegetables and cornflour mould with jam. Ploughing through magazines of the period, Mr Mennell found that the stodginess of the food here compared with that in France was striking. Nearly every issue contained testimonials to Atora grated suet and Bird's Custard Powder. 'There's energy and warmth in hot Bird's Custard,' ran an advertisement forty years ago, 'also the material for sturdy growth.' In that same 1946 issue, a bleak ad for tinned sardines suggested that the middle classes were eating as joylessly as the poor: 'Oh, Tomkins, this is your evening out, is it not? Just lay the table for supper and put out the tin of Skippers. We'll open it ourselves.'

Things looked up when Florence White took over *Woman's Own* as cookery editor. She was one of the first journalists to espouse the cause of English regional cookery and was the driving force behind the founding of the English Folk Cookery Association. But, like folk-dancing, food was not really meant to give pleasure. Writing under her prim pseudonym of 'Mary Evelyn', with its hint of sensible woollen vests and no naughty French frou-frou, Florence preached utility. One of her articles on fish began: 'This food is cheap and very nourishing. It should appear on every table once or twice a week.' There was no suggestion that it was fun to eat.

What influence all this had on successive generations cannot be measured, but that close student of the Anglo-French scene André Simon, writing in 1954, wasn't hopeful that the end of wartime rationing would make the English dining-room more like the French. In Britain, he wrote, 'The housewife looks upon cooking as a chore and a bore; she prepares, without any pleasure, without any complaints, meals which are eaten without any pleasure, without any complaints if bad and without a word of praise if good. To the average French housewife, on the contrary, cooking is a hobby and a joy . . . she knows that she is cooking for people who take a keen interest in their meals.'

It's all a matter of attitudes really. Mr Mennell quotes a recipe for fish-balls from *Good Housekeeping* in the late 1960s which suggested that the reader should 'make up a packet of instant potato and combine with a packet of parsley sauce-mix. Flake and stir in salmon from a 7¼ oz can.' In 1979 a suggestion appeared in *Woman's Own* that 'classic fish-and-shrimp mousse is delicious but the recipe is a trifle long-winded. If you take a pack of frozen cod in shrimp sauce and liquidise it – you're halfway there!' Certainly not halfway to France nor to happiness.

All Manners of Food does not suggest that French manners are superior to our own but, in a speculative chapter on food dislikes, Stephen Mennell hints that we have more than our fair European share of faddiness. His quote from an Exeter teacher rings all too true. Her high school has regular exchange visits with a school in Rennes and she describes taking fifty teenagers, half of them English, half of them French for a traditional Devonshire cream tea in Bovey Tracey. 'The French children ate theirs with enjoyment; the English proved a nightmare with their various dislikes about the scones, the clotted cream and jam and demanding Coca-Cola instead of tea to drink.' Have we acquired over the years an incapacity to enjoy food, an immense deficiency of the natural appetites? Go, on alternate Sundays, to Boulogne and Dover for lunch and you may find the answer.

Part Three

PEOPLE AND
PLACES

1. Anatomy of a Banquet

Nobody does it quite so well, nobody does it so monotonously often, banqueting. 'It's very, very English,' a man said. 'I mean, you could organize a dinner dance for Sunday taxidermists and you'd get a full turn out, decorations and all!'

From the formal white-tied, turtle-soup-and-royalty occasion at Mansion House to the annual Ratepayers' dinner in the provincial Floral Hall, there's a deepseated national pleasure in dressing up and eating out. During the Blitz people even used to arrange *afternoon* banquets so that everyone could get back home safely before the bombing. The French, of course, know that you can't feed more than twelve people properly at any one time, but with us the food is of minimal importance. The occasion is all.

The profits from banqueting are far higher and more predictable than from an ordinary restaurant. One London banqueting house made a profit of £150,000 last year including a loss of £50,000 on its restaurant. 'Without our restaurant,' an executive told me, 'we shouldn't do as well on banqueting; it's a shop window for us, it enhances our prestige. But in the restaurant you're lucky to get a gross profit of 55 per cent – in banqueting it's 67 per cent.'

Although masonic banqueting is on the decline, the number of functions seem to be increasing. There are still enough professional organizations, social groups, business functions to keep banqueting rooms booked up months, even years in advance. To be sure of a Saturday night in a prestige hotel some groups may book two or three years ahead.

David McMillan is a banquet organiser who works for the Royal Society of Health and it was his idea back in 1962 to hold a dinner for the members and guests. The first function was given in the monster Connaught Rooms and from there they moved to the Hilton. In 1970 they chose to move to the Dorchester in Park Lane. Last year's function was at the end of September. The invitations to a possible 500 or 600 guests went out in early summer.

In previous years Mr P. Arthur Wells, the Society's Secretary, had selected the menu. But on this occasion they decided to choose the four courses with the help of an *ad hoc* committee. It turned out to be the perfect formula for gastronomic confusion. After a lot of impractical suggestions from the Society, Eugene Kaufeler, *maître chef des cuisines* of the Dorchester, provided four specimen menus which were cannibalized by the committee. The final choice, to cost £3.90, was:

> *La Crème de Volaille en Tasse*
> *Le Gratin de Sole Dorchester*
> *Le Contrefilet de Boeuf Bordelais*
> *Les Haricots Verts au Beurre*
> *Les Pommes Sablées*
> *L'Ananas Tout Paris*

M. Kaufeler, who has been at the Dorchester since 1939 and has cooked for something like 10 million guests in his day, was a little disappointed at the choice: 'You see, they now have a *cream* soup followed by fish in a creamy sauce. I would have preferred them to start with a clear soup.'

David Petrie, the Dorchester's Banqueting Manager, was not very enthusiastic either: 'I told Mr McMillan that having two creamy things to start the meal with was ridiculous, and he said, "Well, the committee have accepted this and if I go back and say you've got to change it there'll be murder."'

Masterminding the menu was only one of McMillan's problems. Most functions of this nature have a cabaret and, of course, a band: 'We have Claude Cavalotti. He performs exclusively at banquets and dinners as well, of course, as broadcasting on the Beeb – I mean he makes quite a point of it in his letters. Last year we had the Skating Meteors and El Condor. They did magic tricks with live birds and that sort of thing. I didn't go overboard about it, but it was a pleasant enough interlude.'

This year the Society decided to engage Margo Henderson who used to be with the Black and White Minstrel show. The cost of the cabaret and the band would work out at just over £200. There were to be three rooms for the reception. The Crystal Room for twenty VIP guests; the Silver Room for a lesser party of fifty, and the Gold Room for those who would have to buy their own drinks.

The planning was precise down to the last cruet. McMillan received from the Dorchester a month before the dinner a battle order listing the number of candelabras on each table, the flower arrangements, the price of the spotlights, the colour of the candles, the cost of the sandwiches for the band, the charge for the commissionaire (plus free dinner and beer) and the fact that a second cup of coffee was to be available *with plenty of Demerara sugar*. Two sheaves of flowers for presentation (in cellophane) were to be ready in the Crystal Room and Mr Arthur Whitehead had been booked as toastmaster for an inclusive fee of £16.50 including dinner and drinks. A few days before the dinner the twenty departments inside the hotel were circularized with the arrangements.

If success could depend on paper work then it was guaranteed.

Each dinner has its stars, its bit players and its extras. There's a front of house, all glitter and tinsel, and backstage the hard drudgery of cooking and washing up. A waiter who used to be on the halls said he enjoyed it just as much: 'You get dressed up to play your part, you know, "yes madam, no sir," all polite like, and you put on an act, don't you? When I come here at night I'm prepared to play a part – it would be nice to be Lord Muck or whoever takes the chair but I'm cast in the role of flunkey, so that's show business isn't it?'

All the key figures in the hotel side of the drama, the chefs, the head wine waiters, the banqueting managers are on the staff. But there is a hired troupe of extras whose loyalty is not absolute – the itinerant waiters who at £2.75 a night keep London banqueting going.

'A lot of them,' David Petrie tells me, 'are from abroad. Cypriots, Spanish, Portuguese, Cretan. In a world where you may do 15,000 covers one week and 2,000 the next no one can keep them permanently employed.' Most of them have only a smattering of English. Chef Kaufeler tells me with relish how on one occasion a Portuguese waiter began pouring bread sauce all over the bread rolls. Although the service upstairs may be amateur, down below the food is still prepared in the same way that it was when the Dorchester first opened its doors in 1931.

Most of Kaufeler's brigade have been with him for years He has a staff of 120 'white hats', 90 per cent of them British, the rest from the Continent. To work in these conditions (as hot almost as a ship's boiler room) requires a high degree of stamina and concentration. Already by four o'clock the kitchen staff are beginning the final countdown for the Royal Society's dinner. Malcolm Laird from Yorkshire, the chef saucier, is chopping vegetables, Geoffrey Hale is busy with the fish.

From all over London the 350 actors in this evening's drama are homing in on Park Lane. They are bidden for seven. Well before this time, the service men have arrived, the cloakroom attendants opened up, the wine butlers and cocktail waiters have begun laying out their drinks. If last year is anything to go by this will be a fairly abstemious night but banqueting can be a profitably boozy business.

One banqueting manager told me about a company which used to assemble its fifty top men for an epically drunken evening in London once a year. 'The liquor bill was always three times the cost of the food. It was a rather sinister occasion. There was no cabaret and towards the end of the evening people were expected to get up on their hind legs and spout about some particular subject. By then they were all as pissed as newts and it was all tape recorded for analysis by personality experts.'

Most functions involve a fairly substantial amount of drinking – lucrative for the banqueting house and lucrative often for the waiters. Because of the high level of casual labour employed there is a correspondingly low level of loyalty. Management go to great lengths to protect themselves and their customers from fiddling but as one banqueting man put it: 'It's a losing battle. Fiddling, I would say, happens in most banqueting houses in London.'

I asked what form it took. 'Well, nobody waters the spirits, that's considered crude, but there's overcharging and giving small measures. What guest is going to count his change or demand to know the price of a double Scotch?'

Many managements search their casual staff on arrival: 'You see they can smuggle in a bottle of whisky they've bought in a liquor mart cheaply and sell it over the bar for twice as much. We date-stamp our bottles but that doesn't help; they can empty their booze into our bottles.'

On the morning after a big function cellarmen can often be seen raking in the empty bottle baskets for what they call 'pirates', the bootleg bottles brought in from outside. Enterprising casual waiters naturally prefer a function where drinks are to be paid for in cash. As one waiter put it: 'Perhaps if we got paid a bit more decent there'd be less of the you-know-what-I-mean, but these chaps aren't going to quibble about a couple of bob, they're having a good night out, they've got the cash on them, why should they begrudge us a drink?'

When I ask David Petrie if he thinks the management of the Dorchester or their customers might be exposed to this kind of fiddling he chooses his words carefully: 'I refuse to accept that there's a racket *here*. I'm not going to say that it hasn't existed and I'm not going to say that everything is as 100 per cent as it should be. In my opinion I think a lot of us work the most appalling hours and people are not paid for the amount of labour and effort they put in. My view is that people in charge of vast quantities of drink which is easily convertible to cash should be paid a salary in accordance with the type of responsibility they're taking and this hotel is getting round to that view.'

Before the guests arrive I ask one of the wine waiters if he thinks he gets a reasonable wage – it works out to about £7 a day. 'We could do with more,' he says, 'but then so could everybody, I expect you could, too, sir. Opportunities for what, sir . . . fiddling? Nothing like that goes on here, sir, we'd be out quicker than that' – and he moves off with a tray of drinks to the Silver Room.

Suddenly the drama has begun. Unlike a theatre there's been no overture, no swish of the curtain and yet within minutes of the first guests arriving the evening is in orbit.

Closeted in the Crystal Room the Society's President, the Right Hon. the Lord Cohen of Birkenhead, greets the guest of honour Dr Roger Bannister, the Chairman of the Sports Council. But the bouquet of flowers for Mrs Bannister is not there. David McMillan dashes out to find out where it is. The banqueting manager calms him: 'On its way, sir, on its way.'

In the Gold Room the guests who have already paid £5.50 for their tickets are buying themselves gins and sherries. The members of the council, the executive vice-presidents and their ladies get free drinks as do their specially invited guests. The women's dresses make a vivid splash of colour against the penguin background of the men. There is a nervous ritual of greeting, recognizing, long-time-no-sees, two very old men are telling each other how well they look. The laughter is forced.

In the Ballroom itself the stage is prepared, the candles lit, the waiters bored. Tonight the Dorchester, tomorrow the Grosvenor, the day after that maybe the Hilton – it's just another chance to earn another £2.75. Before the mirror in the small banqueting office, headwaiter Leonardo Sebastian Ricardo Domenico Sanchi adjusts his white tie, flicks a speck from his lapels and clears his throat. He looks like a generalissimo about to lead his men into action. 'Right,' he says to no one in particular, 'Let's go!' and enters the Ballroom.

'Stand by your stations, Ballroom men,' – he has a built-in public address system that could crumble a bread roll at fifty yards. They call him the Dragon. His eyes sweep round the blue and white room, over the 36 crystal chandeliers, the 33 circular tables for 10 and the top table laid for 26. He surveys the pink linen, the gleaming candelabra, the bronze and yellow chrysanthemums, the glistening silver and his Pedro's army of hired waiters.

'Right, Juan! Where's Juan?' A half-hearted hand is raised. 'Let's have you then, you're on Table Four. Durati! Is Durati here? Has he gone to the bloody loo again?'

The waiters have as many names as the Marx brothers, one name for the wife, one for the Dorchester, another for the income tax. 'Is there a man called Maganori here,' asks the Dragon desperately. 'Or is it McGinnis?' Somehow by the time dinner is announced and the guests begin to stream into the Ballroom, order has been wrenched by the Dragon out of apathy. This doesn't surprise him particularly; he does it every night.

By now the waiters have clattered down the twenty-seven steps to the kitchen to queue to serve the first course. This is a world of whitewashed walls, lagged pipes, steam and heat. The waiters serving the top table are edged up front. At a signal, the tureens are handed out. Up the stairs into the service area where the soup is ladled on to plates. Out into the ballroom. The whole operation is completed in under three minutes.

If anything is the nub of the evening it's the speed with which the food can be transferred from the kitchen to the table. At the Dorchester the manoeuvre is clinical, precise and beautifully timed. But John Tone, an old hand in charge of the butter, is faintly patronizing about the new breed of Mediterranean waiter. 'They haven't got the stamina,' he says. 'Your old pre-war waiter, he could put on a good front. You ought to have seen us last Christmas, we even 'ad Harabs 'ere!' He wears a white mitten which somehow lends an air of hygiene to his fingers as they delve into iced water for butter pats.

In the Ballroom the wine waiters are moving about with bottles. The top table will drink Flambeau d'Alsace 'Hugel' at £1.60 a bottle with their fish and Châteauneuf du Pape at £2.25 a bottle with their beef. All the other guests must buy their own wine from a shortened list which the Dorchester uses on these occasions. The cheapest half bottle is a Graves at 95p. Nobody appears to be drinking the Dorchester's Krug Private Cuvée '64 at £17.55 a magnum.

Behind a screen the majestic silver-haired Master of Ceremonies, Mr Whitehead, who is yet to come into his own, dines in solitary state. He wears five medals on his scarlet-coated breast. He used to do all the British Weeks abroad he tells me. 'Milan, Paris, Copenhagen . . .' To him Cabinet Ministers, Tunkus and Shahs are two a penny. At sixty-nine he still has the kind of feudal presence that such an occasion demands and the time-honoured formulae: 'Your Grace, my Lord, your excellencies . . .'

Tonight's company are almost entirely untitled; the professional and semi-professional classes concerned with public health moving on now to the sole. Kaufeler has been handed the Society's printed Menu and Toast List. He raises an eyebrow. His *haricots verts au beurre* have become 'runner beans'. The elaborate dessert which his patissier Louis Bozzini spent all day creating has been put down bleakly as 'Pineapple and Strawberries'. The complicated and subtle *Gratin de Sole Dorchester* appears as poached sole, a bit like describing a Stradivarius as a fiddle.

As the meat follows the fish, the level of conversation in the Ballroom rises; perhaps the wine is loosening tongues. At 8.50 p.m. the pudding is served. In the service area dirty plates and cutlery are being washed up by a mainly Asian labour force. Waiters with agile fingers help themselves to leftovers. Mr Whitehead appears from behind his screen like the Great Levant to proclaim that the President will take wine with the Chef. Their gratitude is warm, says Lord Cohen, raising his glass. Kaufeler in his tall white toque raises his glass and bows politely. There is discreet applause.

At seven minutes past nine, as becomes members of a Royal Society, the Queen is toasted. With the coffee, the speeches, Lord Cohen takes nine minutes. Dr Bannister, he says, is a 'great advocate of *mens sana in corpore sano.*' Like Clapham feeding Dwyer, this will enable Dr Bannister to tell the one about the outfitter who advertised *mens and women's sana in corpore sano.*

There's an interval, a queue for the nose-powdering and the clearing-away of tables; then at 10.20, Cavalotti and his ten-man orchestra swing into the first medley. Down below, the casual waiters are being paid off, the guests drift back to their tables for more drinks and couples get up to dance in the slightly old-fashioned way that middle-aged people have.

When Margo Henderson arrives she wants the lighting turned down for her act: 'It might make me look a bit more like sixteen,' she says jokily. She has a powerful voice and goes down well imitating Jessie Matthews, Beryl Reid and Judy Garland. After the cabaret there is a mild exodus. Dr Bannister went early, his duty performed; others are feeling that they, too, might as well get along.

Cavalotti comes off the stand for a cigarette and tells me that he leads a busy life in the winter: 'Tonight I'm at the Dorchester and the Hilton – I've got a dinner dance there for the Westminster Bank. On Monday I shall be doing the Transport Ball and I've got a small band playing for the Footwear Association at the Hyde Park.'

The band seems to be doing well without him. I ask what sort of music they are playing: 'It's what we used to call society music,' he says, 'easy quicksteps, not too slow foxtrots, something they can jog along to.' Everybody is jogging now. David McMillan is mopping his brow, relaxed and happy. 'It's going wonderfully,' he says. 'I think it's the best dinner ever.' Out in the foyer Bernard Pazio the Polish cloakroom attendant has had a bad night: 'Good weather, no business,' he says. 'No coats, no tips.' He crumples a ticket and shrugs. A wine waiter tells me they've had a rotten night at the bar. 'Sober lot this lot, very quiet.'

At a quarter to midnight, there's the last waltz, a crocodile forms for *Auld Lang Syne*. Everyone appears to be sober. People tell me they've had a marvellous evening, most enjoyable.

In the emptying Ballroom someone has left a stole on a chair. The Dragon is locking his spirits cupboard, the band have folded their stands and slipped away. The last guests leave at twenty-nine minutes past one. 'A very nice evening indeed,' they are saying. One by one the lights are turned off. In the main foyer of the Dorchester the night maintenance men are painting a ceiling, outside Park Lane is almost deserted.

The bill when it comes will be £1,912.70. The Society has already made its provisional booking for 1973 and 1974. 'It would have been nicer,' says David McMillan sadly, 'if only more people had come.'

2. The Million-Word Epic

Alan Davidson answers the doorbell promptly. He has lived in the same early Victorian house in Chelsea with his American wife Jane for forty-one years on and off. Down the road he has an office where for the last sixteen years he has been assembling what his admirers believe will be the most comprehensive encyclopaedia of food ever published.

It's a bit of a joke among his friends that it may never be finished. 'Alan is such a perfectionist', one of them said recently, 'that he may be rearranging one last esoteric entry on his deathbed.' Death did come uncomfortably close in 1991 when a heart attack slowed things down a bit but the *Oxford Companion to Food* is back on course.

In his grey sweater, open-necked shirt and carpet slippers Alan might be mistaken for a poet or a composer. The ascetic face and the cultured voice give little away; certainly not a hint of Bearsden where he spent happy hours with his grandparents.

'My grandfather was a timber merchant. One branch of the family came from the Lowlands, one from the Highlands.' Although he was born in Northern Ireland where his father had been posted as a Tax Inspector it is the South Erskine Park childhood holidays that are most deeply imprinted on his memory. He and Jane still use grandma Merdy's baking tins and he still remembers her high teas. 'Shortly after five we would all sit down on high-backed mohair chairs and have a really lavish meal. The savoury dish might be fish custard or mince but every now and then it would be kippers.'

In 1988 Alan published a collection of essays which he called *A Kipper With My Tea*. High tea, Scots style, remains his favourite meal. He still has porridge for breakfast and retains strong ties with his ancestry. Alan's curiosity about food was fuelled by peripatetic adventures in the diplomatic trade. Armed with a double first in classics from Oxford he found little difficulty in gaining entry to the Foreign Service in 1948. 'I wanted to travel and I wanted to be a writer. I was attracted to the idea of public service as opposed to commercial activities.'

His first job was in Washington where he married Jane Macatee whose family lived in some style on Prospect Avenue in Georgetown – a street which was to provide the name for the publishing house they founded after Alan retired.

After postings to The Hague and Cairo the Davidsons found themselves in Tunis. 'The fish there were excellent but their names were puzzling.' Davidson promised his wife that he would furnish her with an explanatory list that she could use when she went to the market. When the greatest expert on Mediterranean fish, Professor Giorgio Boni, came to Tunis Alan learnt from him the rudiments of ichthyology from which sprang a booklet he called *Seafish of Tunisia and the Central Mediterranean*. A colleague who knew Elizabeth David sent her a copy and years later she persuaded her editor at Penguin, Jill Norman, to consider giving it a wider audience. Alan extended it and in 1972 it appeared as *Mediterranean Seafood*. A posting as Ambassador to Vientiane enabled him to write *Fish and Fish Dishes of Laos*. It was a fishy decade which yielded *Seafood of South East Asia* and in 1979 the authoritative *North Atlantic Seafood*. That was the year the Davidsons founded Prospect Books, a publishing imprint specializing in food history. Its journal, *Petits Propos Culinaire*, comes out three times a year and has just celebrated its fiftieth edition. *PPC*, as it's known to a small but select international readership, is dauntingly recondite. At times it can plunge into freefall down the steep slope to *Pseud's Corner*. Scholarly, eccentric, infinitely curious, *PPC* never fails to surprise. In the current issue even the letters section yields a rich harvest of mild barminess. A Brooklyn reader 'currently engaged in the admittedly dubious task of writing the history of ketchup' asks for help. A lecturer in

Illinois describes how a chance encounter with the Uighur tribe in Beijing has sparked off a quest for the origins of the bagel. From Andorra another reader reveals how she has become hooked on 'the question of holes made in bread in Uzbekistan'. There is a dissertation on what happens to an egg if you cook if for eighteen hours, an erudite account of cooking scenes in medieval calendars and a quizzical piece about the culinary activities of the old women frying eggs in the painting by Velazquez in the National Gallery of Scotland.

The pages of the *PPC* come dramatically to life once a year when 150 foodlovers descend on St Antony's College for the Oxford Food Symposium jointly inspired by historian Theodore Zeldin and Alan Davidson. 'It materialized in the air space surrounding the two of us, that's perhaps the best way of describing what happened. He stopped me in the corridor of St Antony's where I was temporarily a visiting Fellow. He said, "Alan, in what way do you propose to make manifest to the other members of the college your presence here and the reasons for it" – which floored me completely! He said, "You must hold a seminar, I will arrange it." That was 1981 and we've been going strong ever since.'

The *Symposia* are a magnet for scholars and food enthusiasts; there is nothing quite like them anywhere else and there will be nothing quite like the *Oxford Companion to Food*, even though it is now thirteen years overdue. 'The book was due to be handed over in 1983 but it's proved to be a bigger project than I or anybody foresaw.' Although there was an advance of £25,000, travel and the purchase of computers and software has largely swallowed that up – inflation didn't help either.

'I've been trying to make it global,' says Alan, 'in the sense that I'm devoting more space to little-known cuisines in parts of the world which are not famous for their food and less space to things which have been written about widely.'

The target figure is just under a million words. 'At the moment we have 960,000 words. There are just over 90,000 words allocated to fruit and about 88,000 to vegetables.' His own books have provided quite a lot of material; more has come from his comprehensive library. 'If somebody else has said it definitively I see no point in not quoting them. Jane and I have been pretty well all over the world collecting information and she is keeping an eye on the whole enterprise.'

The main helper is Helen Saberi, who not only lived in Afghanistan for ten years but married into an Afghan family. Prospect published her *Afghan Food & Cookery* in 1986.

'Afghanistan occurs in the pages more often than anyone might expect and that's true of Scotland too; it has a privileged place partly because Catherine Brown who has been helping me with the Scottish entries is a close friend of ours and because of my own Scottish connections. Indeed Jane once said to me why don't you rechristen the book the *Oxford Companion to food in Scotland and Afghanistan?*'

Perhaps the *Companion* will be handed over by the end of the year, perhaps not. When it does descend with a thump on the bookshop counters it will eclipse all previous works. I hope I shall be around to see it.

The Oxford Companion to Food was published on 14 October 1999, all 1.1 million words of it.

3. The Lure of the Market

Are you lucky enough to have a market where you live? I mean a real market selling local produce. Annette Morgan is very proud of hers – a theatre nurse, she lives with her art teacher husband in King's Lynn which the locals all refer to as Lynn.

'In fact,' she wrote to me this autumn, 'we have not one but two marketplaces – the Tuesday marketplace and the Saturday marketplace. The main market selling fresh produce from the Fens is held on Tuesday. In addition to the markets we have several good butchers and fishmongers within walking distance, some of them sporting royal coats of arms as they supply the Queen at nearby Sandringham.'

The Morgans used to live in London where Annette worked at Charing Cross Hospital and she's found, since moving to Norfolk, that her food bills have fallen remarkably. 'Why don't you come down and see for yourself?', she wrote. So on the rainiest day of October, I caught the 9.45 from King's Cross bound for the good food town of Lynn.

It was bucketing down when the train pulled in and Annette was there to meet me waving a very damp umbrella. With its Victorian Corn Exchange, seventeenth-century Customs House and its fine Georgian and Queen Anne houses Lynn is an architectural feast. 'We're lucky,' Annette said as we splashed through the rain, 'a lot of historic towns like this have had their hearts ripped out to make way for shopping centres: we were saved the worst excesses of developers.'

We made straight for the marketplace to Annette's favourite fruit and vegetable stall which is run by Fred and Vera Russell, two very active pensioners. How nostalgic to find carrots pulled straight from the ground with their greenery left intact and potatoes covered in black Fenland soil, not sanitized in see-through bar-coded bags.

Fred had three kinds of apples from Wisbech: Cox's Orange Pippins, Russets and Laxton Superb. There was a box of late tomatoes grown in nearby Terrington St Clements and the last of the runner beans along with cabbages and parsnips, green walnuts picked locally, celery and sprouts. There wasn't a thing on the stall imported from abroad and the prices were a revelation for someone used to supermarket pre-packs.

We toured the stalls and then visited Donaldson's the fishmonger in Norfolk Street and admired the local shrimps, bloaters, mussels, whelks from Wells-by-the-Sea and the lemon sole and herring. I bought a couple of dabs for my tea at the bargain price of 91p. Incidentally, when did you last see a bloater? If you can lay your hands on one don't hesitate. This herring smoked complete with its innards can be eaten raw or grilled and served with butter. If you remember the joys of bloater paste you'll know how good they can taste.

Annette had suggested that we might have a bite to eat in the Riverside restaurant which forms part of the town's art centre and with the rain still drenching us we made our way to the fourteenth-century warehouse on the banks of the River Ouse in which the complex has been created.

Inside, the old medieval beams and brickwork have been bared but not self-consciously so. The food is fresh and based not only on local ingredients but is largely sourced from the garden of the owners Michael and Sylvia Savage. Michael had left on our table a long list of the vegetables which he grows for the restaurant kitchen during the year: five kinds of lettuce, spring onions, three different varieties of radishes, leeks, garlic, kolhrabi, courgettes, three different kinds of beans, spinach, beetroot and garden peas.

We sat at a table overlooking the river and, it being a cold day, I plumped for the vegetable soup and then had fish pie with, naturally, vegetables from the garden. The restaurant is elegant but not ostentatious; there's a light £4.50 lunch and more ambitious dishes on the a la carte menu. As we lunched, the ferryman in bright yellow oilskins set off from the far side of the river. The rain beating against the windows and the charcoal black clouds scudding across the Fens made a dramatic backdrop.

Had I the time I would have visited the industrious Melanie Knibbs who, twelve years ago, started making wonderful jams in her Lynn kitchen. They contain nothing but fruit and sugar. Lots of fruit: strawberry, raspberry, Victoria plum, blackcurrant and blackberry and apple. She also makes five different styles of marmalade and bakes excellent cakes and sponges. At Christmas time she adds mincemeat to her repertoire.

She sells her homemade produce which includes a range of very popular chutneys on Thursdays at Fakenham market and on Saturdays at Swaffham market. Norfolk is better off than most counties when it comes to open-air markets; you'll find them at Thetford, Watton, North Walsham and, of course, at Norwich there's one of the finest food markets in the British Isles. And that doesn't include the fifteen or so WI markets held in different villages and towns in Norfolk.

4. Heaven on Earth

Paphos is noted both for its magnificent polychrome mosaics and its succulent peanuts. The mosaics, revealed by a farmer's plough in 1962, have been dated to the third century AD, and the peanuts, lightly salted and baked, are a revelation.

Cyprus is full of such surprises. Oranges, lemons, grapes and grapefruits I expected, but not a plain full of banana trees, their hanging green hands wrapped in blue plastic bags against the unlikely event of a frost. Dwarf cyclamens, mauve and white, grow from rocky outcrops round the House of Theseus; along the road leading to the new cement hotel apartments purple bougainvillaea is in flower.

Mountainous like Crete and Corsica, Cyprus has all the Mediterranean virtues: vines, olive trees, almost constant sunshine. It has also, since 1974, had the Turks occupying the northern part of the island. You no longer ask for Turkish coffee, and Turkish Delight has become a bitter sweet.

On the flight out, I sit next to a merchant who tells me he lost a million when the Turks commandeered his properties in Nicosia. He has just come back from Bath, where he's been buying a miraculous piece of machinery which will give tough old bits of meat a spurious tenderness they never had on the hook. 'It flakes the meat into small pieces, like this' – he tears a bit the size of a microchip off the corner of his paper. 'Then it's all pressed together again into steaks and chops.'

'Or kebabs?'

'Yes,' he says, 'anything.' It looks as if I'll just arrive in time – before all the *kleftiko* and *kappamas* become minced into a re-formed, chewy, tenderized, flavour-enhanced burger. But in the villages and the tourist tavernas high-tech food has not yet arrived. The food is still freshly prepared. Goat and lamb, red mullet, bream, squid, cuttlefish and prawns and an abundance of garlic and olive oil.

Lunching in Limassol with Neo Rhodas, the manager of the government's Vine Products Commission, we have a *meze* made from fish caught that morning. The *meze* (pronounced 'metzay') is the nearest approach to the Chinese manner of serving food you'll find – a succession of hot and cold dishes, served at intervals in appetizingly underwhelming quantities. There is grilled white fish, small fried cutlets, cuttlefish with onions, *psari plaki* (fish with tomato sauce), *taramasalata*, octopus in garlic and tomato, *tachinosalata* (a blend of sesame, garlic, black olives, lemon juice and parsley) and a range of white wines made mainly from the local xynisteri grapes. They are quaffable, and rugged enough to cope with any amount of strong and pickled food.

In 1965 Professor Branas came from France to advise the Cypriots on how to renew their old vineyards with vines of better quality and higher yield. The experiments which began twenty-five years ago in phylloxera-free Cyprus are beginning to move wine into the class it needs to be in to compete in Britain with cheap wines from the rest of Europe.

In the 2,800-foot-high village of Panayia, which is sur-rounded by eight square miles of vines, all sorts of new experimental varieties have been planted. George Genetuliou of the Vine Commission takes us there to meet the president of the community, Panayiotis Georghiades, and the village elders, who have been making wine for their own domestic consumption for centuries. Andreas Marouchos, a former forest officer, is our interpreter. He tells me that the village is hoping to acquire a winery to stimulate production. It will cost £330,000, and will, they hope, end the less profitable tradition whereby all the annual output of four and a half million kilos of grapes was trucked down to the four big wineries in Limassol.

After a while we get back in the car and move a mile or so

higher up the hillside to the monastery of Chrysorroyiatissa, where Abbot Dionysios, a keen oenologist, has laid on lunch. Along with 300,000 other Greek Cypriots, he became a refugee after the Turkish invasion. In 1971 he had become the Director of the Centre for the Preservation of Manuscripts and Icons in the monastery of St Spyridon. When he fled, he left behind the most valuable religious library in Cyprus. His present refuge is on the slopes of a mountain called Royia. The view is spectacular. Below is a green and fertile valley dotted with villages; higher up is the dark pine and cedar forest of Stavros-tis-Psokas, full of wild sheep, rhododendrons, myrtle and beech. At the foot of Mount Royia are the monastery orchards of cherries, figs, apples and pears – and, of course, vines. Abbot Dionysios is also building a winery; if all goes well, he may even get into the export business.

We adjourn to the terrace for lunch. The food arrives: skewered lamb, a smoked sausage called *loukanika*, pickled quails' eggs and *kapari*, the small branches of the wild caper bush. There is *haloumi*, too, goat's cheese and other delights. When the Abbot entertained Speaker Thomas in these idyllic surroundings, he surveyed the panorama below and made a prophecy. 'Abbot,' he said, 'I think when you arrive in Heaven you're going to be greatly disappointed!'

5. A Great Crusader for Common Sense

Like many other readers of this magazine, I was deeply saddened by the death of Sheila Hutchins who in the course of her long and distinguished career as a writer did more than most to keep alive the best traditions of British cookery. She was great fun to be with and never put up with nonsense. The last trip we went on together was to Jersey for one of the annual food festivals and she livened up the event no end. In the early days she was cookery correspondent of that great newspaper the liberal and Liberal *News Chronicle* but I suppose she will be remembered more for her long service with the *Daily Express*, years which produced some of her best journalism.

Of all her books the one I still read and re-read with great pleasure is *English Recipes* which included traditional dishes from the whole of Britain which she skilfully adapted for modern appetites and modern kitchens.

The book was inspired by her husband Austin who not only found all the eighteenth- and nineteenth-century engravings which adorn it, 'but made me clarify my ideas, reduced a mass of dishevelled manuscript to a logical form, generally egged me on and also compiled the bibliography.' This joint work of love is now, alas, twenty-two years after its publication, out of print but if you are combing secondhand bookshops look out for a copy, it's a great joy.

What Sheila and her husband achieved in *English Recipes* was to remind us of the heritage of good things that the war had almost made us forget about for ever. 'Many of our best dishes', Sheila wrote, 'have disappeared already, others have been spoiled by cooks who have tried to make them without the proper ingredients.'

She reminded us that in the eighteenth century we ate more and we ate better than people in the rest of Europe. 'There were all kinds of soft cheeses now forgotten, home-brewed ales, delicate puddings.' Those were the days when oysters were cheap enough to use as stuffing for boiled fowl and legs of mutton, and cooks scoured the countryside for morels and truffles.

By the time she came to write *English Recipes* Sheila had acquired a working library of early cookery books and one of the startling discoveries she made was that among the old recipes were, perhaps, a score of first-rate sauces which were no longer being used. 'There was currant sauce for roast pork, a sorrel sauce for roast duckling, celery sauce for turkey and one made with cucumbers for roast mutton which is equally delicious, as well as that excellent sauce made with fresh-grated horseradish which we still serve with roast beef but have forgotten how to serve with fish although it goes very well with it.'

Nowadays when we find the same processed food from one end of the country to the other it's salutary to be reminded that regional specialities flourished in the days of the stage coach. 'Gentlemen used to travel down to Weymouth for the red mullet, to Christchurch for salmon, Cookham for fried chicken, Melton Mowbray for pork pies, Richmond for eels, Scarborough for cod and Worcester for lampreys.'

So where did our enthusiasm for good food go? Why have we embraced bland cheeses, tasteless bread, soups whose only flavour is that of modified starch and chickens as dull as wadding. I once discussed this subject with Sheila and we both agreed that something had gone wrong somewhere with the national gastronomic psyche. Sheila put it down to prudery. She felt that many people felt safer with food that has almost no flavour. She put it very well in her introduction to *English Recipes*. 'We are still riddled with guilt about eating, for all our new abandonment to the pleasures of garlic. One can still come sometimes on those hotel dining rooms where the meal is taken in whispered undertones, where a thick silence reigns while everyone chews daintily with the front teeth.'

In the, sadly, too short time that Sheila wrote for *Saga Magazine* she constantly encouraged the joys of cooking and eating and reminded us that food was fun and not something to get uptight about. Along with Jane Grigson and Margaret Costa she celebrated all that was best in our native cuisine and loudly deplored the excesses of processing which have cheapened and adulterated so much that was once worth eating.

But let us not be too miserable. Things are improving in all sorts of ways. I spent this last summer making a series of television programmes about the Scottish larder and was pleasantly surprised to find that local produce is being marketed more energetically than ever before. When I first went to the Isle of Barra, for instance, there wasn't a cockle to be had in any of the hotels. Now cockles in garlic butter are on every menu. There's more seafood available, too, more emphasis on good baking and home-made jams. In the village of Clatt in Aberdeenshire one Sunday afternoon I had a tea which Sheila Hutchins would have raved about. There was farm butter, farm crowdie, home-baked cakes, scones, pancakes and oatcakes and people queuing at the door of the local village hall to enjoy it. The wives of Clatt got together some five years ago and decided to do teas at the weekend to earn a bit of extra money. Now people in cars come from thirty miles away for afternoon tea.

It proves what I have always believed and I know that Sheila Hutchins passionately believed the same thing – if you provide good food then people will beat a path to your door. It was Sheila's great contribution to our national life that she made the enjoyment of good food sound both logical and sensible. I hope that before long her *English Recipes* will be republished. As I said, if you can find a copy you won't be disappointed – it's Sheila at her best.

6. Reestit and Muggies

The first time I went to Shetland I primed myself by getting hold of *The Shetland Cookery Book* by Margaret Stout. Shetlanders, it seemed, were fond of dishes with stark Viking names like flackies, krolls, krampies, vivda, hoonska, stooins and pramm. But when I got there they didn't offer me Hakka Muggies (fish stomach filled with liver, oatmeal and seasoning) but prawn cocktail. Instead of Slot (cod's roe floured and shaped into balls) I had boil-in-the-bag chicken supreme.

I went back last summer and, although I didn't find any of those old traditional things, there seemed to be more places offering good, fresh food – lots of fish straight out of the sea and vegetables out of the ground. 'If you want to meet a really good cook,' said Suzanne Gibbs, senior producer at Radio Shetland, 'go and see Rhoda Bulter – she's a grand person.' And a poet, too. On Saturday I bought her collected poems and on Sunday morning I called at the council house in Goodlad Crescent where she lives.

There was a warm smell of simmering soup and roasting coming from the kitchen. Rhoda has written some satirical verses about all the processed stuff the shops in Lerwick are full of: 'Dis biscuit an fancy cake at's klertit ower wi coloured craem . . . dir things at's nedder fysh or flesh!'

Her heart is in her childhood in the days before oil came. 'Oil didn't do a great deal of good to Shetland, other than to make people realize just what was slipping through their fingers – like their dialect and their diet. But I think the young wives are getting very interested in the old ways.'

Quite a few traditions still survive. 'Like the way we work with our fish and mutton, the same as it's always been, because it's a very good way of working with it. Now that the deep-freezes are in, a great deal of meat is eaten fresh, but the unique taste of the "reestit" is still very popular.' You take a leg or shoulder of mutton and put it in pickle. 'Just coarse salt and water; you know when it's reached the proper strength because a potato or an egg will float in it. The joints are pickled for about three weeks – you've got to make sure the salt penetrates right to the bone. Then you hang it up to drip, and dry it in a room with a peat fire until it's rock-hard.'

Reestit mutton will keep for years. 'O my! Whaat wid I gie eenoo for tattie soup wi reestit mutton' one of Rhoda's poems ends. 'You boil the mutton, skim off the fat and add potatoes, onion, turnip and cabbage, maybe some carrots. That soup is delicious; as they say nowadays, it's something else.'

Fish livers are hard to come by now, but there were scores of different ways of using them. 'Except a privately owned boat goes to the fishin' we don't get the livers. The fish are all gutted at sea and they just dump the insides. But if you get a large cod head and stuff it with fish livers and boil it, that's gorgeous. Or you could make what we call krappin – livers mixed with oatmeal and flour until it becomes a dough and put in a floured cloth and boiled. Then you can slice it down and eat it hot. Then there's muggies, that's the word for the stomach. Fill the inside of a fish with livers and roast it over an open fire.'

The Shetlanders threw nothing away. 'We always used to eat the inside of an animal – what we called faas. You would clean all the organs, and then make savoury or sweet puddings. If you added onions and dried fruit and then put this into the skin and boiled it, you could eat it hot, or fry it or grill it when it was cold. Then you could add treacle and spices instead of onion and you'd have a sweet pudding. And there was liver pudding: sheep's liver and minced heart and any other meat you could get, and that was like a meat loaf full of onions.'

In those days the sheep fed on seaweed when the summer grass was finished. 'Every house had milking cattle, and of course they made their own butter and kirn milk, a sort of cottage cheese but very hard. We sliced it and ate it with rhubarb:

> O foo aften did I lick me lips as a waatched da
>   flesh hing idda reest;
> Enjoy me slice a kirn mylk wi rhubarb jam, or
>   a plate a beest.'

Then there was the whey, or blaand, a great thirst-quencher, especially when it began to get really sour. 'In Iceland today,' said Rhoda, 'they have a great thing going with this blaand. They keep it till it's fizzy.' But few Shetlanders remember the days when 'you hed nae fizzy lemonade or Pepsi-Cola oota cans'.

You need a glossary to understand some of Rhoda's more phonetic poems, but in 'Gjaan for da Airrents' (Going for the Errands) she describes the unrewarding supermarket round:

> We waak aboot an help wirsels ta things wir
>   niver waantin;
> At niver seems ta setisfee, an laves wis
>   still black fantin [hungry].

7. Bad Day for Brown Shrimps and Black Pudding

I don't know what images Lancashire conjures up for you. At the top of my list George Formby, Eccles cake, Gracie Fields and the famous Hot Pot would be jostling for first place. I went to Lancashire recently, my first extended visit for a good few years, and was once again bowled over by the extrovert warmth of everyone you meet.

If you want to get an idea of what people eat the best place to head for is not the nearest supermarket but to the food market if there's still one in existence. There's a grand one in Blackburn still but I made for Wigan where I had a rendezvous with local food historian and domestic science teacher Helen Pollard.

I got there about five years too late. As in many another town the planners had ripped out the grimy heart of the place and put up one of those nondescript constructions which enable you to contemplate the plumbing wreathing round the stomach of the place like yards of metal intestines.

I met Helen at a stall selling goose eggs so large they would have made a breakfast for a brace of hungry miners if there'd been any coal miners left. I suppose there must be geese in the south of England but I haven't seen a goose egg down there for years. 'Have one boiled,' said the large and buxom woman selling them, 'it'll set you up for the rest of the day along with a couple of potato cakes.'

Then we moved on to the stalls displaying tripe, elder, pigs' feet, lamb trotters and bacon ribs. We had a long chat with the woman on the tripe stall; with characteristic Lancashire honesty she admitted that she preferred the way the French dress it.

'Ours is bleached,' she said, 'that's the way people want it, all white looking. But it's got no taste. It'll just soak up the taste of whatever you cook with it. Now, in France their tripe isn't bleached at all and it's really delicious.'

In the fish market we found another manifestation of English prejudice. I was hoping for a feed of shrimps; Morecambe Bay and Southport aren't all that far away. But there were no shrimps to be seen. Plenty of azo-dyed kippers and those wretchedly meretricious Pacific sticks – cheap, white minced fish, full of polyphosphates, monosodium glutamate and coloured to look like crab.

Where were the little brown shrimps? 'We haven't had any for ten months,' said the fishmongeress, 'the Dutch and the Belgians are prepared to pay three times more for them than we are so that's where they're going. Couldn't sell them here at that price!'

I got the impression that the younger generation, seduced by burgers and hotdogs, were not at all keen on clothcap food like winkles and tripe. An impression confirmed later in the day when I went to a factory at Heath Charnock just outside Chorley where they make some of the finest black puddings in the world. The testimonials to their worth were glistening in cabinets all around manager Richard Thornley's office. He's a third generation pudding maker and the product wins trophies and gold medals year after year in France and Belgium.

'The funny thing is,' said Richard, 'we don't do as well at exhibitions in Bolton as we do in France.' Black pudding fanciers are aggressively loyal to their suppliers. People who buy Bury pudding wouldn't be seen in public dining off a Chorley pudding. Boudin noir, as the French call them, are simply pigs' blood sausages. The ingredients, apart from the blood and barley, are kept as a closely guarded family secret.

On the food front, business is getting more difficult by the day. Richard's customers want him to make products as cheaply as possible. He wants to make them as good and as wholesome as possible. He pointed to a ham with 20 per cent added water. 'For the price people are prepared to pay, that's what they get. Ham shouldn't have all that water in it but there you are.'

It's the same with sausages. To keep prices down manufacturers are forced to fill the skins with a slurry of gristle, bone, fat and unmentionables. This 'mechanically recovered meat' as it's known is cheap and rather nasty. But then if you want cheap sausages that's what you'll wind up with. Thornley's are diversifying into pizzas these days; the mark-ups are higher than on black puddings. Another old historic food on the way out?

The following day I went to Goosnargh to visit John and Ruth Kirkham at Beesley Farm. Ruth's grandmother made cheese; so did her mother. The milk comes from John's small Friesian herd of thirty cows. Every day of the year Ruth makes three 45lb cheeses and connoisseurs reckon they are the finest unpasteurized Lancashire cheese to be had. So Randolph Hodgson of Neal's Yard in Covent Garden exports them to New York.

Ruth hasn't had a holiday since she married twenty-four years ago but this summer she's planning a fortnight in Switzerland. John won't be going. 'Someone has to milk the cows,' he said; while Ruth is away the little dairy will be repainted for her return.

Lancashire cheese is as pale as cream and when properly matured has a decided tang to it. It's crumbly and not at all like the softer cheese they make from pasteurized milk in the big automated creameries. This is two-day curd cheese, not the single factory cheese which lacks the flavour and bite of a hand-made work of art like Ruth's. It needs maturing for at least three months.

I took away a 6.75lb cheese which I'm going to keep in a cool place for at least six months. It should be eating well come Christmas. Sadly none of the Kirkhams' children are interested in farming. When John retires Ruth's expertise will be gone. Another casualty on the food front; another link with the past over and done with.

8. *Arabella Boxer*

In her mid-fifties Arabella Boxer is a serene and elegant grandmother. She has won awards for her books and for twenty-two years was *Vogue*'s resident food writer. In her London home she is now taking stock. 'I am having a sabbatical; I don't want to be restricted by a regular column. There are other things – I'm learning Japanese fairly intensively.'

Just out is her *Book of English Food* which she describes as a rediscovery of British food from before the war. The recipes are based on the food served in the huge country houses which right up to 1939 maintained platoons of servants and took their raw materials from the bounty of estates which sprawled across the countryside for miles.

A year or so before Arabella was born, her father, Lord Doune, on assuming the Earldom of Moray, inherited just such a place. Darnaway in Findhorn country is a vast granite mansion built in 1810 on the site of an earlier castle in which Mary Queen of Scots had held court and which for a time belonged to James IV.

Arabella recalls her childhood in Darnaway with mixed feelings. It was certainly not a place which her American mother warmed to. 'It was so huge my mother used to say it took her ten minutes to get from her sitting room out of doors by which time the sun had disappeared and it was raining.'

And the food in this stately pile? 'My father was very particular about food and it had to be just perfect. My mother found it all a terrible bore. We had three farms on the estate, an eleven-acre walled kitchen garden with greenhouses, a salmon river and grouse moors so we were almost self-supporting. My father hated cream and sauces so everything was very simple.

Every Sunday without fail we had roast beef. My father carved, the butler was in attendance and a footman. For the next few days we ate the beef cold and very rare. Salmon was always simply poached and we ate a lot of game and salads.'

It was wholesome food. 'There was nothing one could find disgusting about it but it wasn't any fun. We had the same cook always, a Mrs Jones from Liverpool. She was very cross and bad-tempered and even more so when the war came and Darnaway became a military hospital and she had to cook for a hundred.'

And there was no question of asking for special treats. 'Because we were never allowed in the kitchen nobody ever asked what we liked. Often I was given the same things again and again that I really hated, like oxtail soup that used to make me absolutely sick.'

Arabella's mother, Barbara, was later to write about the problems of being an American chatelaine in a historic Scottish castle. 'The running sore was a feud between the nanny, a fiery farmer's daughter from Crieff, and the cook. The butler and the cook were also locked in permanent battle, each department making things as difficult as possible for the other by endless little mean tricks.'

The cook would, on a whim, decide she needed 40lb of raspberries to make jam, particularly if that presented problems for the gardener. The earl's culinary eccentricities fuelled discontent. He alienated the grieve by proclaiming that the farm butter was inedible and insisted that an alternative supply should be imported from England. The cook's jams he found inferior and insisted on having Tiptree preserves on the table.

While her mother found the scale of the rooms and the social proprieties of castle life oppressive, Arabella does remember sunny days and childhood treats.

'The garden produced lots of lovely and unusual things like white raspberries, yellow tomatoes, nectarines, figs and white flesh peaches which were more delicious than anything I can buy today. We all had summer birthdays and the gardeners always managed to produce the first of something: the first raspberries or the first hothouse grapes. So that was always a treat but food didn't seem important to us really.'

Looking back on life in Darnaway Arabella is wistful about the ordinary pleasures of childhood which status and wealth seemed to preclude. 'There was none of that nice thing that happens with most children where you're in and out of the kitchen, your mother's cooking, you help make the pastry. It wasn't like that; food wasn't fun. I don't think any of us enjoyed it – being grand.'

When her father died and the Moray inheritance passed to another member of the family Arabella left Darnaway and went to live for three years in the Borders in the great Georgian house of Mellerstain designed by William and Robert Adam.

'A neighbouring family happened to have a daughter who was my age and they felt she was lonely so I went to live with them. The food was totally different; very rich. I remember a pudding with layers of flaky pastry with whipped cream and strawberries in the middle. My father would have fainted with horror.'

When the war was over Arabella spent four joyful summers in America with her mother. 'We'd stay first in New York and then we'd go up to Maine where my grandparents had a summer house on the water. My mother has this theory that only Americans know how to have fun. We were spoilt and we had a wonderful time. It wasn't until then that I realized what fun food could be – strawberry ice cream with real strawberries, Rice Krispies, tons of fruit, things that seemed positively delicious.'

When she was fifteen Arabella spent a year living in Paris learning French. 'I started to cook a bit and none of my friends knew how to cook so they were most impressed. It must have been intuitive. I had never seen anyone cook anything. Even when we lived in London after my father died one only went into the kitchen at Christmas time to wish the cook Happy Christmas.'

Coming from the Darnaway cuisine of endless roast beef everything seemed wonderful. 'I remember when I had my first steak I thought that was just incredible. One had had so little experience of food that I was the opposite of blasé. I just thought that plain roast chicken was the best thing anyone could want ever!'

She still believes that good ingredients should be left to exhibit their own virtues: 'I think the only thing I don't really like is haute cuisine. French grand food, I'm a bit like my father, I don't like too many sauces.'

British food, she feels, has lost out in postwar years to the lure of the Mediterranean. After years of austerity and rationing Elizabeth David released the national yearning for sunshine and novelty. 'We were starved of interesting food and of foreign travel and we embraced the Mediterranean with joy. Today it's north Italian food that dominates the scene. All this is intrinsically good and enjoyable in the extreme when eaten in Italy but it does seem slightly ridiculous that pesto should have become a national dish.'

She finds it sad that we don't seem to value our own culinary inheritance – hence the new book, part memoir, part social history, which she hopes will turn us back to good Scottish breakfasts, English teas and puddings and pies, bread stuffing, stews and soups.

But there is a problem. 'A lot of our sort of food calls for much more precision and timing than a dish of pasta or a stir-fry. Mediterranean food is more casual and adaptable. But if you're cooking game it really is a matter of minutes whether it's overdone or not and to make it really good you ought to have the bread sauce, game chips, the gravy, the trimmings. Even something as simple and delicious as a fish pie takes a long time to make.'

Which is why supermarket meals have become so popular perhaps? 'I realize that a lot of people are working very hard and probably hate cooking but for me these Marks & Spencer meals stand for everything I don't like. I find them expensive and worst of all monotonous. I never want to eat something exactly the same twice running. If you make something yourself each time it's different. With these things, each time they're the same. Monotonous.'

When it comes to cooking for herself Arabella goes for simple food and infinite variety. 'What I usually try to do is have raw food in the middle of the day – a salad, or, if it's very cold, soup. I don't eat much meat and I don't eat a lot of fish but I always eat fish when I go out. Because of the book I've been cooking a lot of British food but I have the feeling that I shall soon go back to cooking Middle Eastern things or Italian or whatever takes my fancy. Occasionally I'll cook something faintly Chinese or Indian.'

After she left Mellerstain House Arabella didn't set foot in her native Scotland for forty years. But Darnaway with its tensions still dominates her memories.

'Recently I've got to know my cousins who now live in the castle and they're so incredibly nice that I've been back twice now and I love it. But I don't want to go there a lot because it's quite . . . disturbing. You walk into a room and all these memories come back. Echoes of childhood floating around. It's very . . . odd.'

9. Privilege Preserved

When I arrived for lunch at Cliveden recently Holiday, the butler, was hovering on the gravel. 'Who shall I say is calling?' he seemed to be saying. Dressed like Jeeves, with a stick-up collar all too reminiscent of the arch-appeaser Neville Chamberlain, he looked the very epitome of the kind of functionary who would have opened the door of your carriage in the days when the Astors held open house.

'Mr Sinclair is making a phone call in the *porte cochère*,' said Holiday, bending slightly from the waist, 'and will be with you directly.' John Sinclair, late of Eton, the Savoy, Claridges and the luxurious Lancaster in Paris, heir to the Viscountcy of Thurso and now general manager of Cliveden, is the perfect manager for the ultimate country house hotel.

The company which employs him has spent over £2 million installing the comforts that people prepared to spend up to £350 a night for bed and breakfast seem to need. 'When you start something like this,' says John, 'you are so far from normal hotel-keeping that you have nothing to measure it by,' but he hopes he has recreated an Edwardian feel. Guests will not be discouraged from dressing for dinner; valets and ladies' maids will unpack your luggage, turn your taps on and unwrap your special Cliveden soap. There are liveried footmen on duty and breakfast, served in the eighteenth-century rococo panelled room lifted from Château d'Asnières by that Leviathan of wealth Lord Astor, will be as sumptuous as anything offered to Lawrence of Arabia and Ribbentrop in the days when Nancy Astor held sway.

John Webber, one of the most creative young English chefs, has been brought from Gidleigh Park to run the kitchens. He intends to present a lightened version of a traditional English country-house cuisine. His omelette Arnold Bennett is already more than halfway there. There are plenty of accounts of life at Cliveden, when a staff of 100 ran the house and 50 gardeners tended the 375 acres. Henry James stayed frequently and was so impressed that he gave the place a fulsome testimonial: 'Of all the great things the English have invented, the most perfect, the only one they have mastered completely in all its details, is the well-appointed, well-administered, well-filled country house.'

There was, of course, no difficulty in filling it. Half the nobility, and the ignoble too, vied with each other for a free weekend. Cliveden was oiled by a limitless supply of money from successive owners like the Dukes of Sutherland and Westminster, the Astors and a limitless supply of exploitable hands and feet ready to fetch and carry the scuttles of coal and the pitchers of boiling water. A small railway ran round the basement to promote efficiency.

There is nothing like that today, but now the twenty-five bedrooms all have their own bathrooms, and the staff ratio (two to each bedroom) will be one of the highest in Europe. Until recently, Cliveden was leased by The National Trust to Stanford University, an arrangement which may have helped Anglo-American understanding as the Astors intended but which didn't do much for the fabric, or the fixtures and fittings.

Cliveden is now more sumptuous and more sparkling than ever. The £1 million Sargent portrait of Lady Astor looks down approvingly in the entrance hall on a blazing log fire; parlourmaids flick dusters over objects of virtu and the first guests seem slightly overwhelmed by the elegance, and the fact that they are there at all.

There is no doubt that it has been most tastefully renovated, and an air of privilege and exclusiveness has been most care-fully cultivated. But should it have been done at all? I only ask because when the National Trust was incorporated by Act of Parliament in 1907 its specific function was to preserve buildings and land for public access by all. The forty-five-year lease given to the hotel group which operates Cliveden restricts public admission to the building. They will be barred from all but three rooms, and these will only be open for inspection on two afternoons a week for a limited period of the year.

'The National Trust', says its Cliveden brochure, 'preserves houses for your enjoyment.' How much better if the Trust had followed the example of the Spanish government. When it began converting palaces, castles, monasteries and great country houses into hotels or *paradors* it was decreed from the start that the scale of charges should be such that no member of the public would be debarred from enjoying a meal or a night's sleep.

In becoming a party to the creation of Cliveden, the most expensive country-house hotel in Britain, the Trust is adopting a posture which would not have been approved by its Victorian founders. The Trust was founded for the people, not just for people with American Express cards.

10. The Ballymaloe Experience

To arrive at the wisteria-hung Georgian house of Ballymaloe is to be swept up immediately into the heart of an extended family all of whose activities centre on the provision and promotion of the best of Irish food. At the centre of this hurricane of enterprise is a grey-haired and attractive grandmother called Myrtle Allen, the doyenne of Irish cookery, who has not only created what many believe to be the finest and least pretentious restaurant in Eire but has almost singlehanded brought about a revival of real food which has had international repercussions.

When I arrived on the Friday Myrtle had flour on her hands but off came the apron and I was plunged at once into what one might describe as the Ballymaloe experience. 'If you like,' she said, 'we might lunch at the cookery school and meet the staff and the students, then I want to take you to meet my butcher, Mr Cuddigan, and if we've time we'll call in at a corn mill I thought you'd like to see. Tomorrow we're going to dine with a group of country-house hoteliers at Kanturk, then on Sunday I've invited all sorts of food producers and chefs for lunch – about twenty of them and . . .'

Myrtle was determined that I should see everything from the herb gardens of her own house to the good local produce grown by her neighbours. But always we came back to the house of Ballymaloe itself, parts of which date from the fourteenth century. It is the core of a network of inter-related enterprises all of which have grown from Myrtle's deep interest in cooking.

She was born in 1924 near Cork, the daughter of a distinguished architect. Running a restaurant couldn't have been further from her thoughts when she married a young farmer called Ivan Allen. 'I had begun to train as an architect,' she told me, 'and I took classes in cooking and dressmaking which seemed quite a good idea for somebody of my age. At the same time I started a love affair with Ivan and, of course, when we got married cooking seemed more important than architecture.'

In 1948 Ivan bought the farmlands of Ballymaloe and the house which has become the best-known country hotel in Ireland. 'We were very happy here and this is where we brought up our family.' Myrtle, who has a restless curiosity and yen to be involved in everything around her, found herself caught up in the young farmers' movement. 'I retired from that as I approached forty but by then I was writing a cookery column in *The Farmer's Journal*. Ivan and I had always talked about opening a restaurant because the food in this part of the country is so good, so I thought, well, let's have a go. We set out on an absolute shoestring – put a bit of clean wallpaper up, bought some tables and got blue linen cloths. I knew a bit about cooking and giving a dinner party and that was about it.'

The Allens put an advertisement in the *Cork Examiner*, 'Dine in a country house, was all it said and it gave our phone number. Well, the phone didn't ring at all. Then one day I was going down the drive to do a bit of shopping in Cork and a car came up towards the house and the driver said, ' "Is this the new restaurant?" I said yes, do you want to make a reservation? He said, "No, but I think you might be interested in my wines." So we had a wine merchant before we had a customer.'

To drum up business the Allens gave a launching party. 'None of the people who came wanted to try our dinner. We were charging 21/- and I think they thought we were too expensive. There was something very relaxing and leisurely about those early days. At the beginning, we were very quiet. I was doing what I wanted to do. Our income came from farming; I knew I mustn't *lose* any money but I didn't have to make a vast profit.'

It was this financial security that allowed Myrtle to create a restaurant serving the very finest local food without having to make any commercial compromises. 'If I'd had to make money it would have been scampi and steak and chips every day because that's what people wanted back in 1964. If we had four for dinner or ten it didn't matter. Then one day we picked up the *Irish Times* and they were reporting the Egon Ronay guide which had put us in and they said we were a good restaurant which might become famous. Of course, after that people were prepared to eat what I was offering.'

The style of the food has changed little since then. It hinges on using the best local ingredients and cooking them in such a manner that the natural tastes and flavours are enhanced. All kinds of bread are baked daily, the fish and seafood comes straight from the boats at nearby Ballycotton. There are fine Irish cheeses, lots of butter and cream, of course, for this is rich dairy country. Let me make your mouth water with what you might be offered – salmon soup, summer turkey with marjoram, plaice in herb butter, calves' liver flamed in whiskey, carrageen moss pudding, beef with stout, steak and oyster pie, mussels in mayonnaise and, of course, the famous Ballymaloe Irish Stew which Myrtle, ambassadress of good food, has cooked as a guest in kitchens from Beverly Hills to Hong Kong.

In the early days their own farm supplied a lot of the produce that appeared in the Ballymaloe restaurant. 'We had our own pigs, cows, sheep, chickens and geese – now we have only sheep. Soon after we started a young couple came to the door from Kenmare – they had sea urchins, mussels, clams and crabs and we were able to do a shellfish buffet on Fridays, and we still do that.'

Over the years Myrtle has trained scores of young chefs who have gone on to win honours elsewhere. She has an enviable knack for detecting talent in others and encouraging the pursuit of excellence. When she took me to lunch at the cookery school I met students from all over the world. Like the restaurant, it came about more by coincidence than by design.

'I started it in the wintertime when we weren't busy and it was difficult to know how to get enough money to pay the wages every week. Then my daughter-in-law, Darina, who had come to cook in the kitchen here and married my son Timothy, started helping me to demonstrate cookery. The next thing was that my youngest daughter, Fern, thought she'd like to learn to cook, so we devised a three-month course for her in the winter because she couldn't get into any of the cookery schools in London – they were all booked up. We got six or seven other people to do it with her and from then on Darina built the cookery school up and now she and Timothy run it full-time.'

Besides the highly successful school which now has an international reputation, almost everyone in the Allen family is involved in some aspect of the Ballymaloe food business. 'My daughter, Wendy, runs the kitchen shop, Fern is in charge of the café at the art gallery in Cork, another son, Rory, manages the 400-acre farmlands. Yasmin is setting up a small company making country relishes, Wendy's husband, Jim, looks after the wine, Rory's wife, Hazel, supervises the gardens.' And soon, no doubt, the nineteen grandchildren will be entering into the spirit of Ballymaloe.

There are twenty chefs working in the Ballymaloe kitchen and altogether the Allens employ about 120 people during the height of the summer tourist season. For five years Myrtle was involved in running a restaurant in Paris, La Ferme Irlandaise, which became a showplace for the best of Irish produce. In the quarter of a century that Ballymaloe House has been in existence all sorts of other country house hotels have sprung into being; food producers have multiplied and Ireland (where once a good meal was mainly rashers and eggs) is now firmly on the European good food map.

Even the local butcher in Cloyne has been inspired to dig in his heels against the bureaucracy of Brussels and keep to the old ways of pasturing and hanging his meat. Myrtle gets all her meat from him these days. 'I have a standing order for beef and lamb. I always aim for an oxtail every week for soup and a tongue and the Ballymaloe order is structured into his business. A wonderful thing has evolved over the years in this part of Cork. I've been able to encourage anybody with good free-range poultry to supply us and they know now that we will take so many ducks, so many chickens, so many geese right through the year and they plan their production programme to my needs.'

For some time now Myrtle has been actively campaigning to protect small Irish food producers from EC legislation which might put them out of business. She is vice-president of the European Community of Chefs and once a month she and her fellow chefs in Ireland meet together to examine new produce and new suppliers. 'We have a great chat and we exchange information and if you're in trouble with some technical problem you very often find someone can resolve it. We already have quite an influence on Irish food production and I hope eventually we'll influence European legislation.'

Myrtle looks back with nostalgia to the days when you took fish from the sea, gathered blackberries, ate cream and butter with no thought of what effect it might have on your health. 'In my childhood the quality of the food was very good. We had potatoes in their skins, watercress for vitamin C, eggs, milk, soda bread, spring water. Now we've become afraid of food – we're indulging in what I call negative health. We walk less and less. If I wanted to go to Midleton, six miles away, I had a bicycle and I was completely independent. Now my grandchildren can't go unless there's somebody to drive them.'

But Myrtle is a born fighter. Recently she and her farming neighbours, many of whom run guesthouses, effectively spiked the plans of a big pharmaceutical company which wanted to build a factory and pump its noxious effluents into Youghal Bay. 'There were to be sixty jobs but, of course, it would have threatened the beauty and the amenity of the whole coastline. Sanity won, I'm glad to say.'

Last year Myrtle and Darina, who is now a television celebrity with her own cookery series on the 'box', took over the food column in the *Irish Times*. Myrtle shows no sign of winding down or lightening her hectic schedule. Will she go on until she drops?

'I'm dropping all the time,' she laughs. 'I'd like to hand over as much as I can bit by bit. The basis of the whole place is the farm – that's what we've all grown from but the most important business is Ballymaloe House and if that doesn't continue to function properly then the other satellite businesses could be in trouble. We all bounce off each other. We're still working on plans for the future. But there's always more to be done. And now, if you'll excuse me, I'm wanted in the kitchen – there's a little problem come up.'

11. Joyous Return of an Old Friend

Over the years there's been one book on my shelves that has become more dog-eared than the others. *Food in England* was published in 1954 and, having attained classic status, is now happily in print again. Its author, historian Dorothy Hartley, had already written eight volumes on the social history of the British Isles when she decided to compile this riveting account of the way we have fed ourselves down the centuries.

She writes of fuels and fireplaces, of the rituals of country life, of dairy produce, fruits, herbs and vegetables, of sheep on the hills and autumn partridge in the woods. 'Please consider this book', she writes, 'an old-fashioned kitchen, not impressive, but a warm, friendly place, where one can come in any time and have a chat with the cook.'

The cook in this case has an almost visionary sense of the past and when she wrote *Food in England* was old enough to recall the vanished age before the advent of the microwave, the freezer and the ready meal. In the countryside every dairy farm made butter and cheese and what came to the table was dictated by the seasons. This brought variety to the kitchen not monotony – 'it is we who level out the year into monotony by demanding the same food all the year round!'

Dorothy Hartley's first memories were of a kitchen in a stone-floored cottage in the Yorkshire dales; on the table a basin of mutton broth with a long-boned chop in it. 'I remember, too, being carried high on the farmhand's shoulder and feeling him drop down and rise up as he picked white mushrooms out of the wet grass. Then there was a country rectory in the shires between Nottingham and Leicestershire: 'A lovely old house with every medieval inconvenience. The nearest shop was five miles away and we had no car. A butcher called once a week, a grocer once a fortnight.'

Being both cook and historian, Dorothy Hartley weaves her formidable scholarship into the tapestry of daily life. She knows why the invention of the internal combustion engine spelt the end of individual localized cheeses: 'Milk collecting by motor became easy, so the makers in large cheese centres took over the small local trade and closed down the local cheese-making, and in about fifty years over fifty different types of English cheese had ceased to exist.' The cheese presses were sold off and the farmers' daughters, instead of toiling in the dairy at home, motored down with the milk lorry to the factory where, well-paid, they made cheeses on an industrial scale.

Dorothy Hartley, as historian/housekeeper, laments the way in which people were driven off the land by the Industrial Revolution and cut off from their natural food supply. They were compelled for the first time to buy food and what they were able to buy on their low wages was vastly inferior to the seasonal plenty they had left behind. Not only were country folk often paid in kind but they were able to grow a lot of their own food. A pig was kept, poultry and often a cow and a hive of bees.

There was a simplicity about rural life, a sense of fitness which we have lost. Leafing through this gazetteer of good things is to be reminded not only of vanished skills but the whole repertoire of the ordinary kitchen which has been displaced by the ready meals on the supermarket shelves.

Dorothy Hartley writes of rabbits cooked Dorset fashion and grayling flavoured with thyme; of cider singing low and sweetly in the barrel, of pickled winkles and damson cheese, Norfolk Biffins and Tonbridge brawn. In these pages you can read your way through a thousand years of cooking, growing hungrier as you go. The author is at her best when recalling her own memories of the way things were. In spring, blue-veined Wensleydale cheese, in winter, Stilton, sedate in a white napkin. 'The mutton was fat, the cakes full of eggs and in September we made wonderful wines, jams and preserves.'

In our contemporary landscape of Little Chefs and Happy Eaters there is perhaps no place for the individuality of a Yorkshire woman called Betsy Tatterstall who kept between the wars a little house famous all over the north for its shrimp teas. In the flagstoned yard there were three round wooden tables covered with white cloths. When you had settled Betsy would bring out a pot of tea, two big plates of thin bread and butter – brown and white – a big green plate of watercress and a big pink plate of shrimps. That was the signal to tuck in.

After a decent interval Betsy came out again with a white apron over her black gown to replenish the teapot and see if you wanted any more bread and butter. Dorothy Hartley recalled that there was 'something very conversational' about a shrimp tea. 'Presently you wiped up and sat back and Betsy carried a bowl of bewhiskered debris to the hens and you bought some fresh eggs and a jar of potted shrimps to take away with you.'

I doubt if Betsy would have survived in our hygienic age. The Environmental Health Officers would have stopped her selling eggs in case they had salmonella and they would have closed her kitchen down – it would almost certainly not have complied with the regulations. As for the fishmonger who supplied the shrimps, his shop is probably a mobile phone emporium.

Food In England is by no means a lament for lost treats; it celebrates the past with great joy and enthusiasm and I'm glad it's back in print.

12. A Taste of Cumbria

I'm told that the place of pilgrimage for Japanese tourists visiting Britain these days is not the Tower of London or Stratford but the Lake District where they dash to Beatrix Potter's home to immerse themselves in the world of Squirrel Nutkin, Jemima Puddleduck and Timmy Tiptoes. I went to Cumbria a few weeks ago not in search of flopsy bunnies or daffodils but on the good food trail. How much of Cumbria's traditional regional food had survived into the 1990s? That was my mission.

I got off to a cracking start in the little village of Lane End where Richard Woodall is carrying on a family business of bacon curing founded in 1828.

'I'm the seventh generation,' he told me as we stood in the old-fashioned shop where some of the finest bacon and ham in England is sold. 'And there behind the counter is the eighth generation, my young niece. We've always been involved in farming and bacon-making.'

Woodall's send their produce by mail all over the country and their hams travel the world. 'We used to supply the old White Star line and there were, sadly, scores of our finest hams which went down with the *Titanic*. Today we supply Concorde, so you could say we've plumbed the depths and the heights.'

Unlike so much gungy supermarket bacon Woodall's rashers don't have even an extra drop of water in them. 'If you produce something "right" people will buy it. Our bacon is cured for a fortnight, hams for a month and it's what we call a dry cure,' he explains. They rub saltpetre, brown sugar, treacle, salt and sometimes Newcastle Brown into their home-reared pork – the largest hams are left to mature for twelve months. It is, they are convinced, the only way to achieve real flavour.

'Of course you lose a lot of weight in the process. In the big bacon factories where they inject brine into their meat they can convert 20lb of pork into 23lb overnight. We're in the business of extracting moisture – we may start with 20lb of meat and finish up with only 14lb.'

At Woodall's they cure 200 sides of bacon a week. The family raise their own pigs, all of whom have access to fresh air and abundant straw. Richard took me up to the loft where the hams, after being washed and dried, are hung up to age. As well as curing traditional Cumberland hams, so popular at Christmas, the Woodalls have pioneered air-dried ham not dissimilar to those produced in Parma and Bayonne which are sliced paper-thin and eaten raw. The Cumbria Mature Royal Ham is based on a recipe dating from 1843.

Not far away is a much newer enterprise but again one in which integrity and honesty of purpose inform the whole process. At Skellerah Farm in Corney a former wine merchant, Harry Fellows, is smoking a wide variety of local produce in the old-fashioned way. 'We set out to "do the job reet" as the local saying has it. Most smoking these days is done in stainless steel automatically controlled kilns which recirculate the smoke and blast it at the product. That hardens the outside but you don't get any penetration – it's purely cosmetic. Our method is very labour intensive.'

Harry is proud of the way they tackle the job. 'We try to get the very best from fields and farms and from the quayside. We cart the best oak from Eskdale, the most aromatic juniper from Coniston and then we are very patient with our smoking.' It takes about three weeks just to cure a leg of mutton in salt, herbs and spices but the meat has been a long time growing. It comes from the famous Herdwick sheep whose distinctive fleece shades from grey to a dark chocolate brown. 'The Herdwick is a grazer of the high fells. It takes at least two growths of spring grass, two summer suns on their backs and two testing winters for this slow-maturing animal to gain the weight, character and taste we need.'

After his years in the wine trade Harry likens the smoking of meat to the maturing of wine. 'You've got to let Nature play her part in curing. In some ways it's like letting a fine claret come of age ready to drink. As a matter of interest, a mutton ham weighing 10lb in its raw state will yield about 4–4½lb of sliced meat!'

Herdwick Macon still holds pride of place in the catalogue of Ashdown Smokers food. Trout, salmon, chicken, wild venison, Ulverston beef, even garlic is given the smokehouse treatment and, like Woodall's hams and bacon, it finds its way to every corner of Britain.

On my first night in the Lake District we talked of the famous Windermere char, an arcane member of the salmon family about the size of a small trout which darts about the bottom of Lake Windermere. They were featured on a Taste of Cumbria menu presented at the elegant Linthwaite House Hotel at Bowness. Chef Ian Bravey prepared quenelles of Hawkshead trout and char accompanied by a saffron sauce as one of his starters. There were other local delicacies – Morecambe Bay shrimps, locally procured venison marinated with a sauce of wild mushrooms and Cumbrian ale, loin of Lakeland lamb and fillets of Solway salmon.

Cumbria likes to think of itself as not only the most beautiful nook of England but its chief gourmet area. Locals talk proudly of their Kendal mint cake, Cumberland rum butter, Silloth shrimps, Lyth valley damsons, Flookburgh flukes, Penrith fudge and, of course, the famous gingerbread.

Just before leaving I went to Grasmere to the old school by the church lychgate where in 1855 Sarah Nelson set up shop to make her gingerbread.

What was its secret? They wouldn't tell me but I do know that William Wordsworth went crazy for the gingerbread his sister Dorothy made. In their house at Rydal Mount you can see the spice cupboard where Dorothy kept her precious ginger to make the Poet Laureate his favourite treat. They are both buried a few yards away in the village churchyard. There is no record of the great man writing a sonnet in praise of gingerbread – he really should have.

After much research I've unearthed a recipe for the gingerbread that Dorothy might have baked – in her day it was made not with wheat flour but with oatmeal. You take ½lb fine oatmeal, ¼lb butter, ½lb sugar, 1 tablespoon of syrup, 1 teaspoonful of ginger, ½ teaspoon of cream of tartar and bicarbonate of soda. Mix the dry ingredients together and beat in the melted butter or fat, sugar and syrup to bind it very dryly. Press into a tin and bake and do not turn out until quite cold.

13. Don't Spoil the Soil

I was taking part in a chat show the other day in which various members of the panel were lamenting the way in which the taste of food had declined in postwar years. Asked why they thought this was, some very conflicting answers emerged. Someone blamed the supermarkets for restricting choice to the kind of produce that sold in large quantities. Another guest said it was to do with chemical farming – too many sprays and fertilisers.

When, asked the chairman, did the rot set in? Most people felt it started with intensive farming and the spread of those inhumane battery sheds. That was where the salmonella came from. And how could you have a tasty chicken when it was fed on fishmeal and ground-up chicken feathers? There may be something in all that but if a rot did set in it was long before that.

When, for instance, do you think these words were written: 'The decline of the English cheese is one of the best examples of how commercial values have ruined good taste and discrimination . . . English cheeses have vanished with English cooking.' Would you believe me if I said more than fifty years ago? The writer went on to lament the lack of inherited knowledge necessary to produce a really good piece of Cheddar. 'The proud Englishman', he wrote, 'prefers pieces of foreign stuff like soap wrapped up in silver paper.'

These are the words of one of the finest lovers of the countryside who ever lived. He was in the bucolic tradition of William Cobbett and his theme was, to quote his own words, 'the relationship between man and nature, its fruitfulness and the disastrous consequences of disturbing it.'

John Massingham was born in 1888 when shire horses pulled the ploughs and corn sheaves were tied by hand. He died in the age of the tractor and the prairie farm. Massingham wrote about many aspects of the countryside and he was passionately concerned about the well-being of the land. He was preoccupied with organic farming in the days when most farmers were abandoning muck and mystery in favour of the liquid hoe. 'Our modern food', he wrote in 1942, 'is bad because it is de-natured out of its wholeness – it is, as we say, without knowing what we mean, unwholesome.'

Splendid stuff to write at the height of the Second World War when everyone was digging for victory and toiling in their allotments. A year before he died in 1952 he called for us to make peace with nature, to work *with* the land and not try to dominate it with artificial fertilizers, insecticides and disinfectants.

The best of Massingham's writing has been collected in an anthology called *A Mirror of England* and you will find so much common sense there that it will warm your heart. More than forty years ago he was trying to persuade us to appreciate our native apples and I am glad he is not around today to watch the way in which the government is starving our national apple collection of support.

'The England of today', wrote Massingham in 1948, is unworthy of her apples because its economic system has victimized them. We waste millions of apples yearly for the good reason that our money-system regards the importation of inferior foreign apples as more profitable than the cultivation of our own.'

How true those words ring in 1990. When did you last eat a ribbed Gravenstein, a Newton Wonder, a scarlet John Standish, an Allington Pippin, a Beauty of Bath or a Baddow Pippin? And yet these were only half a dozen of the apples that Massingham had in his apple-house in the autumn of 1948 and most of them he had grown himself.

Like Lady Eve Balfour, the founder of the Soil Association

who died this year at the age of ninety-one, John Massingham knew instinctively that a sick soil means sick plants, sick beasts and sick men. For both of them ill-treating the land and its creatures was a recipe for disaster. Nobody listened to either of them, nobody, that is, who had any power in the land. We turned to more and more intensive production and sowed the seeds of our present discontent – polluted rivers and depleted soil.

But now the tide seems to be turning. I was heartened in Scotland the other day to talk to two enthusiasts from Edinburgh University's School of Agriculture who are working on a joint project with the Safeway supermarket chain, the European Community and the Scottish Development Agency. £600,000 has been raised for a two-year experiment in organic farming where the rivers Tay and Earn meet in Perthshire. In 1985 there were only 5,000 acres under organic cultivation in Britain – today the figure has risen to 35,000 acres.

The Soil Association hopes that by the end of the century 20 per cent of our land will be farmed organically. Realists say that we will be lucky if we achieve 2 per cent. But at last we are on our way to a saner way of growing our food. 'To support ourselves by organic methods', John Massingham wrote in *The Wisdom of the Fields*, 'would lead us out of the economic wilderness by opening vast new fields of employment in the home market.' I do not know how true that rings today but morally and spiritually Massingham must be right. Unless the land is in good heart the soul of the nation dies.

14. The Kitchen Standard

If you met Katie Stewart for the first time you'd be hard put to place her. She has the lean ranginess of a games mistress. The upper class accent has an unmistakable Scottish edge; indeed you might well pigeonhole her as the head of an Aberdonian girls' school, lacking only chalk in one hand and a hockey stick in the other. But Katie, as her millions of fans know, is a mistress not of the classroom but of the stove. For twenty years now she has been cookery editor of *Woman's Journal* and for twelve of those years she was food correspondent of *The Times*. Although she has lived in the south of England for much of her life, her cultural links are with the north-east.

'My father came from Macduff and after school went down to Aberdeen to do medicine. My mother's family owned a cattle mart; she was a domestic science student in Aberdeen and that's where they met. Father came south, built a surgery and sat there waiting for the customers to come in. I was born down there and must have been about five when my brother and I were sent back to Aberdeen to avoid the bombs.'

There was a grandmother in Aberfoyle and childhood memories of Scotch broth and good simple roasts. 'My mother was a very good baker but her cooking was fairly repetitive. She was cooking economically the way she knew; nothing was ever wasted in our house. You could almost tell the day of the week from the food that appeared on the table. Sunday was a roast with maybe an apple pudding; Monday was cold meat and stovies, even the potato peelings went out to the chickens. The food was good and wholesome; mother cooked mince terribly well too – 'I've never been as good at cooking mince as she was but then maybe the meat was better in those days.

We used to have white puddings. Mealie Jimmies, with mince and mashed tatties.'

When she was growing up, cooking was not at the front of her mind. 'I was a very outdoor child, I loved riding and chasing around with the boys – I was never domesticated. I think my father looked at me and said to himself: "I've got to do something about this girl!" He said to me: "Katie, I'm sending you to domestic science school where you'll learn to cook and sew and make some man a useful wife!" And it wasn't meant unkindly. I did find a man but I don't know that I made him happy – we split up unfortunately very soon afterwards; our son Andrew is thirty.'

After the domestic science course in Aberdeen, Katie went south and took a diploma course at Westminster Catering College. 'By then food had become an obsession. After Westminster, I went to the Cordon Bleu school in Paris. That was after being a nanny to a wealthy French family. I was in Paris in the early Fifties and it was beautiful, few tourists, very different from today.'

It wasn't to journalism Katie now turned but to the commercial world of food. 'I wanted to work in industry, that was for me the thing. So I went to America and got offered a job with Nestlé in White Plains, New York state. I was there two years doing product development – stock cubes, drinks, chocolates, cheese. America was like nowhere I'd ever seen. Here were immigrants who'd come to a country and who had hung on to their food culture so there were all sorts of new tastes to enjoy. I wrote letters to my mother trying to describe cheesecake which I thought was fantastic. I'd never seen pizza before and lasagne was new to me. I'd never seen a supermarket or used a cake mix. It was terribly exciting. I came back to a Britain still the same as the one I'd left two years before. There were no jobs, nothing in industry at all. It was a shock. In the States I'd worked in a test kitchen with eight other cooks and we were all busy testing new products; great competition and excitement.'

Katie marked time for what seemed ages and then, just by chance, she met Hugh Cudlipp's wife, Eileen Ashcroft. 'She was impressed that I'd been to America and offered me a job on *Woman's Mirror*. I was cookery editor for about eight years in the 1960s until it folded. At the same time *The Times* started a woman's page and they offered me a column; I think I got £15 an article.'

Consistently over the years Katie has provided the nation with good home-cooking recipes presented in a clear and simple style. She's never said or written a pretentious line in her life. 'Maybe because I don't have the sort of brain that thinks up the amazing ideas you see these days on television and in magazines. I tend to be very practical; I only print anything I like and that's simple to do. I don't like a recipe that's got too many bits in it. I'm all for taking time but I'm very conscious I'm writing for people who may not have all day to spend in the kitchen.'

A passionate cook herself, Katie is depressed by the way in which TV commercials often present cookery as drudgery. The pressures to feed the family on ready meals are producing what she sees as a new generation deskilled by the food industry.

This year she has particularly enjoyed watching Rick Stein cooking on TV. 'He was wonderful; he brought sense back into food. That's the only programme I've ever watched where my mouth watered as he prepared his food. And I loved him for himself; he was so articulate, such a generous and nice person. Floyd? I treat him with amusement. I wouldn't want to get working with Floyd because he might be a bit difficult. Delia? I've known Delia for years and I think she does a good job in her own way. Everybody's very horrid about Delia. Sometimes I don't think her methods are quite right but she's brought cooking and food to millions of people, she's good.'

When Katie began writing about food thirty-five years ago, she shone among a very small field. Now life is fiercely competitive. 'You've got to be a star on television to sell a book. My books don't last more than a couple of years in print now.'

In the early 1970s there was her *Cooking with Katie* series
for Grampian. 'I loved it. In those days you did it in one go,
there wasn't the business of stopping and re-filming; it was
much more hairy. I once brought some biscuits out of the
oven and they were burnt so we scrapped the programme and
started all over again.'

What does a skilled cook and food lover run up for herself
at the end of a hard working day in the photographer's studio?
'I would bake a potato for myself and I'd cook pasta. I'd do
lots of soups; I love soup and I'm very good at it. Lentil soups
I love very much with apple and bacon; spinach and nutmeg is
good and carrot and tomato, celery and Stilton. If it's for
myself, I suppose it's got to be fairly quick.'

Katie has written a dozen books but talking to her you get
the feeling that the continuous search for new recipes which
the world of books and magazines demands is sometimes self-
defeating. 'If you're a food writer and you've got a regular
column you've got to keep on coming up with more ideas.
People always say to me: "How do you do it?" I find that once
you've got a recipe right and you like it, it becomes irritating
when you have to come up with something else. Sometimes
you give a really good dish a few different ingredients and a
new title but it's hard work inventing new recipes.

'I'm quite careful about testing my recipes because I've got
a reputation for being accurate and clear.'

So what will the doyenne of Scottish cookery writers be
having for Christmas dinner tomorrow? 'Well, I've bought a
bronze turkey from Heal Farm in Devon, where Anne Petch
rears her animals in the most humane way possible. Like many
other people I am becoming increasingly concerned about how
our food is grown and processed and for Christmas I'm putting
my money where my mouth is. I'll be stuffing the bird with
oatmeal because that's one of my really favourite ingredients.

'We'll have roast potato, bread sauce and all the trimmings
and, along with that, the main vegetable is going to be leeks in
old-fashioned white sauce with grated nutmeg. There'll be

Christmas pudding – I've got a quick recipe that really works. Then there'll be cheeses and fruit compote for those who don't want pudding. We'll probably drink a fairly big Australian red wine and there'll be calvados with the coffee. Nothing elaborate, just good simple food. That's the best, isn't it?'

15. The Glow on the Pudding

It was completely predictable that the best fish and chips I have
had in years were to be found in Yorkshire. I had discovered
the Gainsboro' in Hull years ago, fish straight from the docks
served lavishly in crisp batter with lots of chips and bread and
butter and tea. Harry Ramsden's is, of course, a legend – they
even run coach tours to it. Bryan's Fish Restaurant in Heading-
ley is in the same league; don't miss it.

Married to an East Riding woman, I had known for a long
time what to expect when asked out to 'tea' by one of her
farming relatives. Tea? Were your ears attuned to the wave-
length of oak, you would hear the table groan under the weight
of a Yorkshire tea: cakes, pies, tarts, joints, puddings. So it was
when we went to have tea with Walter and Betty Walker in
their farmhouse in the Dales. The Walkers cure their own
pork, and the hams hang maturing like stage props from the
sixteenth-century beams in the kitchen. Everything spread
before us was home baked, a cornucopia of good things: simnel
cake, Sally Lunns, almond and cherry loaf, strawberry pie, Cut
and Come Again Cake, Yorkshire parkin, farmhouse loaf, apple
tart and Wensleydale cheese to go with it. 'Apple pie without
cheese,' they say in the Dales, 'is like a kiss without a squeeze.'

Why is it that they are such good bakers in Yorkshire? All
those coalfields, cheap fuels for ovens? Certainly, it is a pudding
that is at the heart of Sunday dinner and, as miners know, it is
best with rabbit gravy.

'If it ain't got some rabbit gravy,' a miner tells us, 'it's not
Yorkshire pudding.' Pudding served, not as a mean little cake
on the side of the plate as they do down South, but as a
triumphant opening batsman. 'They used to say to the kids: "If

you don't eat all your Yorkshire pudding up, you don't get no meat." Eat your pudding up, you didn't want no meat! If you didn't eat it up, it were the same, you don't get no meat.'

There has always been a tradition in Yorkshire of making the most of everything; hence the delight in offal. Take tripe, stewed with onions or eaten with the fingers off a stall. Dewsbury is the English Caen of tripe. Twenty years ago, there were six tripe-dressers in Dewsbury, now only Ron Hey is left. He sells about a ton of tripe a week to other butchers, and three days a week his market stall is besieged by fanciers of elder, cowheel and the milky honeycomb.

Tripe, Rons says, is nutritional and a good buy into the bargain. Dressing tripe is, for those who haven't stumbled upon the art before, a malodorous industry. If the wind is in the right direction, you will have no trouble in finding Ron's Ideal Tripe Works. Our secretary stays outside the door, a hankie clamped over her nose. Inside, Ron, in a white coat and wellies, assisted by three lads, is turning cow's stomach into the famous Dewsbury delicacy. He picks up what looks like a blanket remnant: 'This is the stomach of a beast; first you've got to remove the lining.' The lads are scraping with brushes, combing it clean. Scalding and scraping are followed by boiling, and boiling cow's stomach calls for strong stomachs indeed – and skill. 'It's got to be not too tough, not too tender. You get cattle that's been killed at home and been fed on barley, they take only two hours' boiling. You get an old cow tripe, ten or twelve years old, that wants five hours' boiling – but it can all be made nice.'

Making it nice is Ron's business. It is flung into a spinner to soften it up and is bleached whiter than white. Although most people go for the honeycomb, Ron thinks they are wrong: 'The best part is the plain; the seams are inclined to be fatty.' Ron is contemptuous of the tripe turned out in factories. 'Dewsbury's always been noted for putting a good end quality on. In other towns, tripe dressing has just died a sudden death. These big firms, they get a lot of staff and they couldn't care less; when it's five o'clock they knock off. Even if it wants another hour's boiling, come five o'clock it's got to come out.'

Although much of the wealth of Britain was produced in Yorkshire, the profits have never been conspicuously apparent. Red meat was a luxury few could afford. When an animal was killed, nothing was thrown away; not even the blood, the base for that other Yorkshire delicacy, black pudding. Black puddings are found in both Germany and France, but the Yorkshire breed are noted for the richness imparted to them by pork fat. King of the pudding-makers is Albert Hirst of Barnsley.

Every weekday morning, he and his assistants, Walter and George, who have been working with him for forty years, produce 450 pounds of black puddings. 'I call it the caviare of the North,' he says cheerily, surveying the blood-soaked scene, the yards of intestines being filled and twisted into four-ounce puddings. 'To me it really is something. I mean, what could you wish for better than blood, flour, onions, seasoning?'

George is filling the skins, Walter is tying them. 'When Walter gets tired, they just change ends. Walter does the filling and George the tying. When eggs were cheaper, we used to think nothing of throwing four or five dozen into it. We do it the hard way, no machinery.'

After they have been boiled, the puddings, looking like a gut caught in some terminal agony, are brought into the hanging room for polishing: 'There you are,' says Albert with pride, 'real Yorkshire puddings just like Yorkshire men – honest, true and stalwart.' Albert covers the palms of his hands with vegetable oil. 'Now to give them a really good polish. If you remember, in the army a soldier wasn't smart unless he had a pair of smart boots on; well, it's the same with black pudding. Without that polish it can't be black pudding. It has to have a glow; the glow in everything counts.'

The older people say that the glow is going out of life. Nowadays, with housewives out at work all day, the kitchen has become just a place where you heat up food out of tins. Retired miners lament the passing of a way of life which, although sparse, was never spartan: 'There was no such thing as going to a shop and buying a loaf of bread in them days. When I were going to school, everyone made their own bread. The bread today is all dough, concertina bread I call it, you could play a tune with it. I still can't see why we can't have better snap than it is. In the old days, it was all fresh what you had at dinner time. The puddings were fresh, the cakes were fresh and everything else.'

Although convenience foods fill every larder, there are many Yorkshire women who still take pride in their cooking skills; women like Pat Spruce who lives in the mining area of Walton, near Wakefield, and makes Yorkshire pudding, not from a packet mix, but in the traditional way, out of flour, salt, eggs, milk and water: 'The beating is the main thing so that the air goes in and makes it light. You don't want a piece of leather when it comes out of the oven.' Mrs Spruce puts her tin in the oven with a little dripping and waits until it is blue-hot: 'Then you bring it out and put the mixture in. This one's going to be a savoury pudding, so I have the sage and onion already mixed to go in.'

As carefully as she makes them, Mrs Spruce doesn't think they can be as good today as they were in her mother's time. 'Even with all our coalfields in Yorkshire, the council houses have all had the coal ovens taken out, and electricity is not the same. You can get them crisp, but they're not as crisp and nice as they used to be.'

As the miner said, snap isn't what it was, even in Yorkshire.

16. The Happy Face of Farming

Sarah Ward is wearing a woolly hat, wellies and a dung-hued waterproof. At Maidstone cattle market she's unloading three bullocks, a steer and two heifers, for the Monday morning auction. She also has thirty Suffolk cross-hoggets in the sale and she explains the finer points of their conformation with educated fingers. 'If you just press here you'll feel any surplus fat; it's lean lamb people want these days. My grandfather wouldn't have approved at all!'

Sarah's great-grandfather would have been equally dismissive too. For generations now, the family has farmed 600 acres in the Darent Valley, land which has been under the plough since Roman times. The first records date from the eleventh century, when the four manors of Horton were sequestered from the Saxons who held them, and given to a Norman knight called De Ros. He built himself a small flintstone castle and the five-foot-thick walls now form part of the sitting-room of Court Lodge farmhouse. There have been medieval and Georgian additions. Izaak Walton came to fish in the river that flows through the walled garden.

Sarah shows me the Norman dovecot, the picturesque stable block built to designs approved by Prince Albert. Geese and hens peck through the stackyard, horses are being watered; it's the kind of place that the Disney Organization might build if it were going to create an olde English rural theme-park. Hard to believe, until you see the suburban semis on the hill, that you're only twenty miles from Charing Cross.

Although this is no self-conscious showplace, one can't help feeling that Sarah Ward is more idealistic than most. She runs the place in partnership with her father, who at seventy-eight still puts in a full day's work. If they had given up mixed farming maybe they would have more money in the bank, but not, you feel, so much satisfaction. 'The farm is both home and work,' she explains. 'To a great extent it's a labour of love. We may have to simplify in the future because you can't farm in the traditional way without people, and people must be paid a proper wage to do it.'

At the moment the farm supports 400 breeding ewes, fed on kale in the winter and on grass leys in the summer. This week they are sowing spring barley and durum wheat; there will be potatoes, oats, peas and fruit in the fullness of the year, and twenty-six acres of hops, which have been grown in this part of the country since the sixteenth century. 'I don't think people have any idea', says Sarah, 'of the work that goes on every day just to keep the place ticking over. People come and see sheep feeding on grass, but they don't realize that it probably cost £250 an acre to sow.'

Sarah's philosophy of farming is both hard-headed and soft-hearted. 'We have to give customers what they want. If it's lean meat, then we must produce lean meat, but you must do things with compassion.' She shows me the barn where the ewes and their young lambs are moving about contentedly in deep straw. 'These are six-week-old Easter lambs. They have a very secure life while they're here. They're fed with home-grown food and mother's milk. The cattle are also fed naturally on home-grown maize, corn and "chat" potatoes. Unless your animals are happy they won't be healthy. I wouldn't like to have animals unless they were happy.'

At the end of the war there were forty hands working the farm full time; now there are only eight. Six years ago, Sarah decided to turn the redundant cattleyard into workshops, where craftsmen are now doing their free-enterprise thing – repairing violins, restoring furniture, making garden seats. When she opens the old wooden door of the oasthouse, hi-fi booms out; that's been turned into a recording studio.

'I think we're going to have to be as flexible as we can in

the future. That's easy for us because we have so many options, but one worries about hill farmers in Wales or the North whose only income is from livestock. People are eating less meat.' Sarah is saddened when she sees meat in shops which has not been properly matured. She grows potatoes more for their flavour than their profitability and is not a great believer in antibiotics or the overuse of chemicals. A hundred years ago her great-grandfather was denounced in the nearby parish church for interfering with the hand of Providence – he had been among the first to spray his hops against aphis and fungi. Sarah has thought seriously of moving into organic farming. 'It would be quite easy for us; we've got cattle, and cattle give you muck. Having stock is good for the ground.'

What she does hope to do is involve members of the public in the activities of the farm. She has open days. 'I think you have to take people into your confidence, explain what farming is about. I'd like people to see the farm as part of the pattern of their own lives as well as our own.' She reminds me that when Cobbett was riding round England he complained about farmers who were spending too much money improving their houses, while farmeresses were beginning to play the piano instead of making butter. We're still complaining, I suppose, not about the way farmers relax but about their obsession with chemical warfare. Sarah Ward's 600 acres represent the happier face of farming, and it hasn't yet put the family in the poorhouse.

17. Crubeens in Cork

We went to Cork to find good food. A perverse choice, perhaps, to go to a part of Ireland noted in history mainly for starvation and famine. It was to find food, after the failure of the potato crop in the 1840s, that hundreds of families left Cork. They sailed downriver in what came to be known as 'coffin' ships; weakened by disease and hunger, only a minority survived the voyage to America. The legacy of hardship and want remained for generations. When it came to cooking, a Victorian writer remarked, the peasant woman in Ireland knew nothing beyond the boiling of a potato, bread was scarcely ever seen, ovens were unknown. It took most of your time to find enough food to put on your table for the large families which the Church encouraged. It was a tiring round which left no time for superfluous elegances; empty bellies wanted food, not frills. Although Ireland hasn't overnight become a garden bursting with fruit and vegetables, there is more variety to be had in the Cork market than ever before.

The days when the safest bet in the dining-room of a commercial hotel in Galway or Limerick was rashers and eggs are over as well, thanks to a new generation of hoteliers, many of them local enthusiasts who are making the best of the good raw materials to hand. Typical of them is Declan Ryan, whom we filmed at Arbutus Lodge, an unpretentious hotel overlooking the River Lee in the centre of Cork. Declan's family owned the hotel and, when he finished school, they sent him to Hendon Catering College. After two years, he went to London's Russell Hotel as a management trainee. It was in the days when Raymond Zarb was presiding over the kitchen: 'Look,' said Zarb, 'you'll never make a hotel manager, but I could make a chef out of you.' That was in the early Sixties. After a spell at the Russell, Declan was about to set off to work in a German restaurant when he got a frantic SOS from his father; there was a busy time in the hotel, could he come back and help out in the kitchen? 'I came home,' says Declan, 'and I'm still here.'

When he isn't busy at Arbutus, Declan Ryan takes working holidays in the great European restaurants: 'I began by spending some time in the Rijnhotel at Rotterdam, and since then I've worked with Bill Lacy in London and at the Troisgros in Roanne. The problem is, where can you go after that? At that level, you can't find anything better, only something different.'

Declan's own cooking qualifies outstandingly for the last category. Lifting some of the Cork specialities into the realms of haute cuisine, he has married his French training to an Irish background.

In Cork market are to be found two simple foods which Declan has invested with an added dimension. 'Drisheen is a Cork speciality; it's a sausage made from sheep's blood which once used to contain tansy, a herb which grows by the roadside in Ireland. We grow it in the garden. I serve the drisheen with a tansy sauce to get back the old taste, and all the businessmen flock to eat it.' All you do with the drisheen is bring it to the boil and simmer it for about ten minutes. 'When it's cooked, we remove the skin and put it on a bed of buttered white bread and then cover it with tansy sauce. My favourite time for eating it is Sunday breakfast, but most people would have it for tea.'

At Arbutus Lodge, there is nettle soup in spring when the shoots are young, fresh perch from the rivers, and Irish brown bread; an irresistible temptation when placed hot on your side plate. Then there's crubeens – pig's feet. But, at Arbutus, they're educated feet that have been to a French finishing school. You pickle them in brine for twenty-four hours, then bandage them in a splint so that they don't lose their shape. After you have cooked them for six hours in a bouillon of carrots, onions, white wine, wine vinegar, crushed peppercorns and a sprig of lovage, they are left to grow cold in their own jelly. Then you roll the feet in melted butter, robe them in spiced breadcrumbs, grill them and serve with vinaigrette sauce.

'The most famous place for crubeens after a hard night's drinking used to be at Katie Barrie's. She was one of Cork's greatest characters, a woman renowned in song. The place was a favourite haunt of the law fraternity for some reason. She cooked her crubeens in a pot which was always on the stove and was reputed never to have been emptied or washed since the day it went on, forty years previously. I'm afraid Katie was famous for crubeens, not hygiene.'

Declan serves his salmon with sorrel sauce and his *gnocchi verdi* are made from spinach fresh from the garden. The menu is international, with Irish overtones, and, in Ireland, the overtones can be surprising. Take the aptly named Gladys Buttimer, whom we found buttering eggs in a way that is unique to County Cork. She says it improves the flavour and keeps the eggs fresh for at least a couple of months: 'The secret is to rub the melted butter on the shells while the eggs are still warm. It seals the pores up and keeps all the goodness in, instead of letting it all escape.'

Old men can still be seen taking their milk churns to the co-operative creamery in little carts pulled by donkeys, and many of them remember hard times and long days: 'I started work at ten. In the summertime you had to be out of your bed at half-four in the morning to drive the cows in to be milked, and, by the time you'd been to the creamery in Kanturk in the evening and washed the churns out and landed home, the clock was striking ten: all for four bob a week!' The grass is lush and green in Ireland and the Friesians produce prodigious quantities of summer milk. A lot of it ends up in the super £6 million creamery at Ballineen which, each year, converts 50 million gallons of milk into 11,000 tons of cheddar and 10,000 tons of skimmed-milk powder. And being Ireland, it converts unwanted milk-sugar into alcohol as well. The bulk of the cheese goes to England, a country with which Ireland has had a tragic, and often bitter, relationship since the twelfth century.

Invaded and repressed, Ireland has never been subdued. After Cromwell's iron settlement, only half a million Irish survived. Power passed into the hands of a Protestant oligarchy, and tens of thousands of Catholic families emigrated. The big houses became Protestant strongholds. Longueville House, a superb Georgian residence at Mallow, did not return into Catholic hands until the 1930s, when the O'Callaghans, whose family had been in the area for generations, were able to buy it. Today, Longueville and its 500 acres are run as both farm and hotel – all part of the highly profitable country-house revolution in tourist-conscious Ireland.

Most of the food eaten at Longueville is home-produced. Not only is Michael O'Callaghan's flock of prize-winning sheep able to provide lamb almost all the year round, but there is a ten-acre kitchen garden, growing asparagus, vines, fruit, courgettes, carrots – everything a cook could ask for. There is fresh trout and salmon from the Blackwater, which flows through the grounds, and everything on the menu is fresh.

The burden of running the hotel falls on Jane O'Callaghan, a vivacious, talkative, enthusiastic woman, who started from less than scratch: 'All I had was a sort of bride's course in Dublin; you know, how to do a dinner for four.' Now her flair for cooking well and simply has won her a place in all the guides. Thirty years ago, when I made my first visit to Ireland, the food was nothing to write home about. Today, the *Good Food Guide* is able to produce a special Irish section. As Jane O'Callaghan explained: 'We've become aware of what people want. We have the best produce in the world, and we want people to enjoy it with us.'

18. Green Gurus

They hit London last week like a pair of New Age missionaries. Paul, the evangelist of organic wine; John, the chef-guru who presides over a magic garden which is astonishing even in the Eden of California.

It is a dazzling double act full of pithy one-liners.

'All of us cast a vote every time we choose what we buy to eat,' says John, stirring a pan of polenta.

'Working in harmony and with respect for the human spirit,' says Paul, 'we are committed to sharing information about the enjoyment of food and wine in a lifestyle of moderation and responsibility.'

He hasn't made that up on the spur of the moment. It is part of the Fetzer Mission Statement which is inscribed on the back of every Fetzer executive's visiting card.

Paul Dolan, winemaker and president of Fetzer vineyards, and John Ash, culinary director of its Valley Oaks food and wine centre, are in Britain promoting their wine and their vision of life.

In November, Ash will return to cook a meal in Ken McCulloch's new Malmaison in Glasgow. In the meantime he is busy in the penthouse apartment of a Chelsea tower block running up a light lunch for a small party of food writers invited to taste the fruits of Fetzer's labours.

While Ash constructs a salad of greens, root vegetables and tempura soft-shelled crab, puts the finishing touches to a fresh apple-herb vichyssoise and peers in the oven to see how his rolled soufflé with leeks and cheese is progressing, Dolan casts aside his crutches and sits down to expound his philosophy. He has not been struck down on the road to Damascus, but is suffering from a broken leg sustained on a downhill run in the snows above Lake Tahoe.

His is a message of hope and inspiration. 'Anything can be done if you have the conviction and the will to do it,' he says. What has been done so far, 120 miles north of San Francisco in Mendocino County, is astonishing enough. Already Fetzer has 1,400 acres of vineyards which are either certified organic or halfway there. All the stems and seeds from Fetzer's annual crushing of 20,000 tons of grapes go into compost.

The company, the tenth-largest winemaker in the US, makes two million cases of wine a year and the sun shines from every facet of its environmentally and ecologically correct corporate body. Dolan, an apostle of natural farming, tells us that having banished chemicals from the land, he ultimately expects to free himself from the national grid and lead Fetzer on to the shining uplands of solar power.

In Britain, where the organic is regarded as fit only for sandalled nutters, to hear a highly successful businessman talking green could truly be described as inspirational. But Dolan is no nutter. His family has been in the wine business for generations. After getting a degree in business and finance at the university of Santa Clara, Dolan went on to study oenology at California State in Fresno and joined Fetzer as head winemaker at the age of twenty-seven. Since then, he has been instrumental in moving the company to the forefront of the industry both in quality and integrity.

It was back in 1985 that they started experimenting with a five-acre biodynamic garden. It was a time when children began to be told at school that wine was a drug and the Fetzer family felt that was wrong. Jim Fetzer believed wine was a food which should be sold alongside carrots rather than hard liquor, and it was he who coined the phrase 'from the earth to the table' to remind consumers of the natural origins of what they eat and drink.

Despite being planted on waterlogged clay left idle because it was too heavy to grow grapes, the new organic garden flourished. Companion plants were chosen to attract harmful insects' natural enemies, spraying was with soap and compost provided free heat. The Fetzer winemakers soon found that table grapes planted in the new garden tasted better than grapes grown with chemicals. Today, more than a hundred varieties of fruit, vegetables, herbs and edible flowers are flourishing. This summer they will be growing 54 varieties of tomato, 85 kinds of apple and 28 different lettuces. It was the success of the garden produce that moved Fetzer inevitably to extend the organic growing concepts into its vineyards.

Dolan says: 'I'm convinced that by 2000 California will have become entirely organic. The 200 farmers growing for us are very sympathetic to the idea. Grapes are the easiest crop in the world to grow organically. If you can maintain a diversity of bug life you can do very well indeed. The greatest challenge is to convince people to make the change.'

He believes that in the long run natural farming is less expensive. 'The initial investment in equipment, such as compost spreading machines, weeding machines and seeders for cover crops can be recouped within two years. But it is not so much about money as the future. We were worried not only about polluting our water resources with pesticides and insecticides but about the unknown dangers chemical farming posed for future generations.'

If you are going to farm organically, California is certainly the place to do it. The climate in Mendocino County, with its cold winters and dry summers, is a gardener's dream, and the Fetzer experiment has paid off handsomely.

Although the ethos of Fetzer's food and wine centre is not vegetarian, the cooking school and culinary research centre presided over by John Ash emphasizes the delights of the plant kingdom. He has developed a cuisine based on fresh seasonal produce and his enthusiastic support for local organic farmers has created scores of cottage industries supplying the restaurants, markets and speciality shops of the sunshine state.

Ash agrees that it might not be so easy to be a vegetarian

elsewhere in the world, particularly Scotland in the winter. He still eats meat, indeed he has written a book called *American Game Cooking*, but he now keeps flesh at the back of his mind.

'Many of the great cuisines of the world were based on using vegetarian sources. Meat was always a luxury.' And that is a word he frequently uses about his plants. 'Grilled mushrooms have all the character and complexity of steak. They are even robust enough to pair with red wines.'

But not any mushroom will do: 'A lot of people believe that a clever cook can do wonders with any piece of junk. Absolutely not! The mark of a great cook is one who spends more time choosing ingredients than cooking them.'

With his light and delightful lunch we drank small amounts of some of Dolan's favourite Fetzer wines. An oaky fumé blanc and an extraordinarily flowery Gewürztraminer with the vichyssoise – Fetzer is the largest producer in the United States of this easy-to-appreciate varietal. Their chardonnay is a bestseller too and they hope to export substantial quantities of their new merlot and zinfandel to Europe.

'Fetzer,' says Dolan, 'has a unique story to tell. Our cooking school offers life enhancement classes teaching adults and children how to grow organically because that's the only sane way ahead. If we go on using chemicals as we do then we will destroy the world.'

If Dolan is an evangelist of wine then Ash is equally messianic about food. Next month, chefs from all over America will descend on Valley Oaks with their sleeping bags for a three-day seminar on the future of food. Ash says: 'Chefs are one of the most important groups in any country. If we insist on the finest ingredients then we can influence growers and producers to provide those ingredients. Once you have tasted the kind of peppers, tomatoes, potatoes, beans and salads we are growing at Fetzer you wouldn't want anything less good.'

In the States, chefs are experimenting with a wider spectrum of salad greens. Instead of the bland and watery iceberg lettuce they seek out red butter, lollo rossa, bitter radicchio and red oakleaf. They want their spinach, mustard, kale, chard, arugula and turnip greens fresh picked and they get them. Could it happen here? Ash has certainly been making converts among British chefs in the last few days.

As a taste of what is to come Dolan brought over some bottles of Fetzer's new Bonterra wines. If this is the way the whole of winegrowing California is going, then they are going to have a strong influence on the viticultural techniques not only of other New World countries such as Australia and New Zealand but perhaps in the south of England too. In the New Age world of Fetzer, money seems to be taking second place to social responsibilty and that is a move which any food and wine lover must applaud.

19. Stylish Table Talk

Margaret Costa told me once how, after she'd written a piece for *Gourmet* magazine about the Connaught, a party of Americans flew in to Heathrow, rang up and asked for an exact replica of the meal, down to the wine she had drunk and the table she had sat at. Thus they hoped to buy satisfaction at second hand. Such people would derive little satisfaction from the books of Margaret Frances Kennedy Fisher, who has always believed that eating is not some kind of optional extra, like going to the opera, but a fundamental of the human condition.

Daughter of a newspaperman, she grew up in California and after UCLA spent three years at Dijon University. In 1937, at the age of twenty-nine, she published her first collection of essays, *Serve it Forth*. In 1941 came *Consider the Oyster*, a year later *How to Cook a Wolf*; then *The Gastronomical Me* and, after the war, *An Alphabet for Gourmets*, all now in paperback (in one volume: *The Art of Eating*). Altogether there have been fifteen books recording her life and travels all over the world. Much in love, and much married, she has lived in France, Switzerland, Mexico and Italy, and now is anchored back on the West Coast.

She has that sensitivity and toughness which mark Lillian Hellman and Dorothy Parker. Auden said of her: 'I do not know anyone in the United States today who writes better prose.' That prose is as clean as wholemeal bread, as fresh as fish in lime juice. MFK is the kind of person in whom others confide; a good listener with a socially observant eye as keen as her crystal-clear palate.

Where others diminish the pleasures of eating by making them obsessionally pre-eminent, she puts them in their proper place: eating and drinking in her compassionate scheme of things is no more or less important than loving and living. Her rail journey from Vevey to Milan with her dying husband Chexbres in 1939, although it centres upon the dining car, is not about food but fascism. On the train a political prisoner breaks a window and destroys himself on the jagged glass. 'There in the train, hurrying across the ripe fields, we knew for a few minutes that we had not escaped. We knew no knife of glass, no distillate of hatred, could keep the pain of war outside. I felt illimitably old, there in the train, knowing that escape was not peace, ever.'

She describes with awe going to her first restaurant, running a kitchen in Provence, travelling on a freighter in 1932 from Marseilles to Los Angeles, eating alone in the Grande Salle of the Gare de Lyon, cooking in Switzerland and Illinois, tasting her first voluptuous oysters at Miss Huntingdon's School for Girls, cooking perch on Lac Léman, inventing the perfect meal for the flowering of mutual desire: 'Good Scotch and water for him, and a very dry Martini for me. A hot soup made of equal parts of clam juice, chicken broth and dry white wine. A light curry of shrimps or crayfish tails. Rice for the curry and a bland green salad. A dessert based on chilled cooked fruits. By preference a moderately dry champagne.'

MFK is a very human being, as they say in California. She knows that without conversation food is nothing; there must be appreciation and love: 'I have in public places watched women suddenly turn a tableful of human beings into scowling tigers and hyenas with their quiet, ferocious nagging, and I have shuddered especially at the signs of pure criminality that then veil children's eyes as they bolt down their poisoned food and flee.'

She does not care for early meals followed by an evening in which time is killed by cards. 'If time, so fleeting, must like humans die, let it be filled with good food and good talk. For my own meals I like simplicity above all. I like leisure. I like mutual ease.' What she dislikes is the elevation of food by

Foodies to an edible version of the Porsche; fantasy fulfilment with knife and fork. Mrs Fisher is gently withering about those who use food as a social passport: 'They subscribe to *Gourmet*, they belong to local food-and-wine groups and bring back packages of musty filé powder from New Orleans and order snails from a former maître d'hôtel who lives next to the airport in Lisbon. They serve the proper wines at the proper temperature, and over everything lies a weight of uncomfortable caution. That is what spreads such faint but inescapable vapours of timidity and insecurity over the fine plates and glasses.'

Tired of the same old question 'How can you write about something so trivial as food?', MFK in these pages affirms that there is no virtue in denying the appetites of hunger: 'We must eat. If, in the face of that dread fact, we can find other nourishment and tolerance and compassion for it, we'll be no less full of human dignity. There is a communion of more than our bodies when bread is broken and wine drunk. And that is my answer, when people ask me: "Why do you write about hunger, and not wars or love?"'

20. The Staples of Ireland

Living off the land in some remote and peaceful place is very chic at the moment. Adam (LSE and sometime radical activist) delves and grows *mange-tout* and garlic; Eve (part-time potter and nuclear physicist) spins wool gathered from fences and makes their chunky ethnic garb.

This week, we went to the remote and peaceful extremities of western Ireland, where living off the land has always been a necessity. Under the shadow of Mount Gabriel, poverty, handed down like a curse from generation to generation, forced you to be self-sufficient.

We set up the cameras on Mizen Head, the very last bit of homeland that many a departing family saw in the hungry 1840s. Now in this part of the world there are not many people, but plenty of unroofed cottages and tumbledown cabins. Even in the best years, when the potatoes did not entirely fail, the living was always tenuous, the food basic.

Take Irish stew; there is nothing elegant or delicate about that. Like all food produced out of privation, it is filling and fitting. Mrs Cotter, elderly now and living with her husband, showed us how her mother made it and how she still makes it herself. Those versed in the complexities of 'colour supplement' cookery may feel this isn't a real Irish stew at all ('What, no bouquet garni?'), but Mrs Cotter is real enough. 'I chop up bacon and beef. Then I chop up carrots, parsnips, onions and turnips, and add salt and pepper. I let it simmer for 2½ hours and then it's ready.'

The staple of food in Ireland has always been the potato. Before the famines, whole families were raised on potatoes and buttermilk, and a writer of the time compared the diet favourably with the English labourer's bread and cheese. 'I have no doubt', he wrote, 'that a bellyful of potatoes is much better than half a bellyful of bread and cheese.'

We went to see Nellie O'Driscoll, who lives on Long Island. Her children go to school on a neighbouring island, so, for much of the year, she lives alone with her dog and a few hens. Nellie has no electricity or piped water, but she has a quarter-acre potato patch which feeds herself and the animals. One of her everyday meals is bacon, cabbage and potatoes. But now the children are home and she is making their favourite pudding. Bill McCartney and Finbarr O'Reagan, two fishermen neighbours, have given her some carrageen. You can buy carrageen expensively packaged in health-food shops, but here it is free. After it has been picked, it has to be laid out on the rocks: 'You must let it stay there for about a week. It needs a lot of rain to bleach it white, otherwise it's no good at all.' Then you tease all the rootlets off and boil it and strain it and let it set. 'It's lovely when you get used to it; you can't do without it. You could make it every day and you'd never get tired of it.' Carrageen is good for the digestion, rich in minerals and vitamins. In the glow of the oil lamp by the peat fire, the children ladle wild raspberry jelly on to this gelatinous pudding from the sea.

There are other free gifts from the sea, too. John Hughes, who lives by the shore, shows us what he does with a salmon if one gives itself up: 'You never use a knife on it, or let any metal touch the flesh. First of all, we have to remove his head.' Expert fingers twist the head from the body. 'And now you work your finger in there and take out his gut. Wipe him clean and dry him with a cloth. We're going to boil him today and we've got an old pot that's been on the same fire since about 1926. We've still got it, and it boils as good as ever. We don't use fresh water; you want sea water to get the original flavour.'

The coastal waters were once thick with sails. The bay at Barley Cove was a swaying forest of masts. Huge windjammers, fast grain ships from Australia, whalers and banana boats sheltered here from the Atlantic gales or took on stores for voyages lasting months. To provision the ships, butchers would be sent out all over the countryside to buy and dress meat, and that pushed prices way out of the reach of the peasantry.

The Irish are deeply obsessed with their past; even in song. There are laments which celebrate the heroes of 'the troubles' which led to the south's independence, and songs which go even farther back, to the lean five years of famine when over a million men, women and children starved to death. We went to Skibbereen, one of the areas hit hardest when, in 1846, the potato fields were blackened with blight and the entire harvest rotted. There had been disease in the fields before, and, already, malnutrition and near-starvation were common – but now there was no food at all. Charity was dispensed from a building which still stands; too little and too late. The soup was a mere drop in a sea of famine.

The streets of Skibbereen were littered with bodies, fever raged, and so common was death that corpses were no longer buried in individual graves, but in pits. There was not a loaf of bread or a pound of meal in the town, and even had there been, the starving could not have bought it, for they were penniless. Visitors reported entering cabins and finding entire families dying of hunger. So weakened were the living that they lacked the strength to bury their dead. There was a general movement of people down to the ports, hoping to find a ship to take them to America or England, where food would be easier to find. Not a strand of seaweed was left on the shores to the west of Skibbereen; all of it had been eaten.

Men in their cups talk of this great tragedy as if it had happened within living memory. And to be in your cups in the west is not all that difficult or expensive. When the Celtic twilight turns to darkness, the west of Ireland turns to '*poitin*'. In Connemara alone, it is estimated that there are 200 illicit stills bubbling away, and the poteen industry is worth £1 million a year. The Earl of Kingston tried to wipe out the trade in the 1830s: ''Tis but a short step', he said, 'from drinking poteen to talking politics.'

The Irish have been distilling and talking politics ever since, but they are careful not to reveal their sources of supply. There is a move afoot to have poteen legalized and made as respectable as other craft industries, like weaving or basket-making. Poteen, clear as mountain dew, tends to be handed discreetly to you in bottles labelled, libellously, 'Lucozade' or 'Cork Dry Gin'. It is an ardent spirit, long on fire and short on age. 'Like a torchlight procession going down your throat,' someone said. Others rate it highly as a lumbago rub. 'If I told you how to get it,' said a man elliptically, in a pub, 'which I couldn't do anyway, in the first place, but if I did, just perhaps, every *garda* in west Cork would be after me, and anyway, nobody round here knows where they make it. They might be making it and, then again, they might not!' Just before we left, a man on a bicycle brought us a sample in a bottle labelled 'white rum'. 'For God's sakes,' said a man on the Aer Lingus flight back to London, 'be terribly careful you don't drop that bottle. It could burn a hole in the bottom of the plane.'

21. Honey From a Weed

In July I went to the very south of Italy to record an interview for Radio 4 with Patience Gray. I was anticipating some kind of unpolluted terrain where peasants cherished the land in the old traditional ways. From a distance it does look a bit like that. But as you drive past the gnarled olive trees and the deep-rooted vines you see, by the roadside, what at first sight might be construed as some device to scare birds away. The empty plastic bottles hang like dead men from the branches of trees and are meant to scare people away – these fields have been sprayed with toxic chemicals, they say. Trespass at your peril.

The land in this part of Apulia is rich in chemicals. When we go to the market we find vegetables which have been reared with pesticides, fungicides and artificial fertilizers. The sea is corrupted too; those who eat raw shellfish frequently end up in the hepatitis ward of the nearest hospital. For the last eighteen years Patience Gray and the sculptor Norman Mommens have tried to create a more wholesome environment on the small farm of Spigolizzi set on a hill in the Basso Salento. Although Patience translated the *Larousse Gastronomique* and, in 1957, co-authored the out-of-print classic *Plats du Jour*, she is far more concerned with people than with food. Her award-winning book *Honey From a Weed* contains recipes but it's not, she insists, a cookery book. It is an account of her life with Norman, first of all in a mountain village above Carrara, then in Vendrell near Tarragona, in Apallona on Naxos and latterly in Apulia where they grow as much of what they need as they can, not with chemicals but with natural compost.

They make their own wine and their own olive oil. The *salsa di pomodori* has been prepared from their own tomatoes

320

and in the tree above the open air table where they take their meals the figs are ripening. Climb the steps to the barrel-vaulted roof and your eye encompasses a complete circle of the Ionian Sea. Only cicadas disturb the peace of this almost empty landscape. There is no piped water at Spigolizzi, no electricity, no troublous telephone. Visitors, surveying the cool room where Patience writes, the studio in which Norman carves his stone, sometimes think they've stumbled on paradise. Norman, who is a realist, has been known to observe that hell might be more convenient.

In spring and autumn Patience wanders over the hill looking for herbs and wild plants. It was a line of William Cowper's that provided the title for her book: 'they whom Truth and Wisdom lead, Can gather Honey from a Weed'. She became interested in weeds on Naxos – wild chicory, dandelions, comfrey, wood sorrel, fennel, angelica, which appears in February, and purslane, which springs up in late summer. 'The food that suddenly presents itself, like the wild asparagus in March, is what we have been looking forward to and longing for. Every season arouses an anticipation.'

In the heat of summer – it was pushing a hundred Fahrenheit the day we arrived – Patience rises at five in the morning to prepare the day's food. When she is cooking she has guests very much in mind. 'Food properly imagined and prepared can make people feel better. I try to imagine the state in which people are. If they're terribly nervous I take a great deal of trouble in providing some pasta or something like that to calm them down. The question one must ask is what do people need in the way of food? The answer comes with what is available at the moment. It's got nothing to do with what might be in a tin.'

In *Honey From a Weed* Patience outlined a philosophy of living which has been almost entirely lost these days, even in the wilderness of Apulia. It relies on a sensitive appreciation of the way in which the produce of the land can be transformed into an occasion for both nourishment and rejoicing; poverty rather than wealth, she has come to realize, gives the good things of life their true significance.

But Spigolizzi, you feel, is a time-warp of sanity in a world corrupted by the cash advantages of chemical farming. While Patience Gray draws inspiration from the countryside it's clear that most of the locals have decamped to the nearest large village or town in search of the amenities which TV commercials suggest they might be missing out on. In a region whose culture is rooted in the cultivation of the olive and the vine, the *cucina americana*, the fitted kitchen with its all-electric machinery, is the ultimate goal for every young couple. Patience and Norman, with not a five-watt bulb between them, are regarded as eccentric and their alternative life as an aberration. But not by everyone. Some youngsters have come out from the towns to see the way they live and are impressed. At Spigolizzi they are growing food to be eaten not to be processed and denatured. Counter-revolutions have sprung from lesser examples than this.

22. Monkey Business

When the Cathay restaurant opened in Singapore in the 1950s, it was the ultimate in opulence. The cuisine was mainly Cantonese, but there were a few wild extravagances. The most exotic item among the starters was Himalayan Bear Paw Soaked in Honey. We naturally ordered it. 'Sorry,' said the waiter, 'Bear Paw off.' As we were among the first diners on the restaurant's first night, we thought this strange. Each time we went back to the Cathay, we ritually ordered Bear Paw. Each time it was off. We came to the conclusion it had never been on – a chimera in the manager's mind.

I was reminded of this by a recent report in *Newsweek* that rich Americans who can afford to eat what is called over there 'gourmet' food are getting tired of fresh salmon and watercress salad. One Washington restaurateur regularly features kangaroo bourguignon, alligator scaloppine and moose nose. If you have a jaded palate, anything can be produced – lion, antelope, hippo and camel are all being farmed for the table.

Did they really eat these things, or is someone pulling my leg? I remain deeply sceptical when I hear about bizarre meals. Reports reach me from time to time that someone met somebody who actually ate live monkey brains while dining with millionaires in the Far East. It is always millionaires and always the Far East. That's where the story was born – in March 1952, to be precise. I know: I was there.

It was at the height of what the British, in their patronizing way, referred to as 'the Emergency'. It was in fact a very nasty war in which a lot of people were being killed, and it had brought that campaigning columnist Arthur Helliwell to Singapore to see how 'our boys' were getting on. Arthur is gone, but the story he wrote for the *People* lives on in folk memory.

When Arthur arrived in what he was to dub 'Snob City' he was taken out for a meal in a Chinese restaurant, where he was intrigued, old investigative journalist that he was, by a circular hole in the centre of the table. The explanation he was given suspended his disbelief. It was a gem of a story, which sent him racing back to his typewriter in the Raffles Hotel. The piece which appeared the following Sunday contrasted the appalling privations of our lads in the green hell of the Malayan jungle with 'the old-school-tie boors and bores' who were 'wallowing in fantastic luxury, sipping gin slings until midnight'. But it was the opening paragraph of Arthur's colourful dispatch that outraged Decent Folk back home.

'In his Arabian Nights palace out at Queen Astrid Park tonight,' thundered Arthur, 'one of Singapore's many Chinese multimillionaires is giving a party to celebrate the birth of a son. The *pièce de résistance* at the twenty-course banquet will be – forgive me if I put you off your Sunday morning bacon and egg – *live monkey's brains*. They are said to increase virility.'

Arthur went on to describe, with righteous indignation, how the guests would sit round a table with a small hole cut in the middle: 'Beneath will squat a little Chinese boy with a basketful of live monkeys. At intervals he will push one of them through the hole until the top of its head is showing. Then the host will slice neatly through the skull with one swing of a razor-sharp knife – and everyone will dip into the still warm brains with long silver spoons.'

The documentation was vividly gruesome. The *People* was deluged with protests from outraged animal lovers. On 6 April, rallying to Arthur's support, the paper claimed it had found a journalist in London who had indeed been a witness to a monkey-brain banquet. 'So much', said the *People*, 'for the screams of denial and protest from Singapore. Will Malayan papers please copy.' The name of the journalist who had attended this bizarre feast was never revealed.

The story had been syndicated all over the world and was, unfortunately for the *People*, reprinted in the *Straits Times* in Singapore. There was only one Chinese millionaire living in Queen Astrid Park and he promptly sued the *People* for defamation. His damages were substantial.

One of the journalists who had pulled Arthur's leg told me that their spur-of-the-moment joke had been honed to perfection: 'We told him they *cracked* the skull, but I like the "razor-sharp knife" – a good touch, that. And long silver spoons was good, too – we told him they used chopsticks.'

And the real purpose of the sinister Hole in the Table? It is for *ke-tze*, or steamboat, as the old-school-tie boors used to call it – just big enough to take a charcoal-heated chafing-dish filled with broth. Everyone sits round, provided with side dishes of chicken, prawn, liver, abalone and vegetables which are cooked and enjoyed communally. Chopsticks are used – not long silver spoons.

23. East End – West End

I don't suppose you could find in the whole of London two eating establishments more unlike each other than Wilton's, in the heart of clubland, and Harry Joyce's eel-and-pie shop in Tower Bridge Road, SE1.

Both specialize in fish, both are run by Cockneys born within the sound of Bow Bells, but socially they are poles apart; a polarity of wealth more than taste. Oysters, once the handmaiden of poverty in the East End, are now the West End's most expensive luxury – food for the few.

And a well-heeled few at that. Mr Marks – nobody seems to know his first name – has presided over Wilton's oyster bar for as long as his aristocratic customers can remember. He arrived there from the Jewish East End as a waiter; now, ninety next year, he is in benevolent, if autocratic, charge.

The walls are hung with photographs of the famous; the Snowdons smile and wave above the lobsters, the Royal Family pose between the ice buckets. Dukes come here to eat lobster; princes slip in unobtrusively for a couple of dozen Colchesters and a bottle of bubbly.

Mr Marks still starts his day with a dozen oysters and a glass or two of champagne: 'What's good enough for the rich is good for me.' And only the best is good enough.

Bill Potter, an oyster trader at Billingsgate whose wife must be the only woman left in the East End still putting oysters in her steak and kidney puddings, tells us that Mr Marks insists on prime quality produce: 'That's a really top-class place, Wilton's. Mr Marks will accept nothing but the very, very best and if it comes anything under his standard, he'll send it back – and quick!'

Mr Marks tells me, as we wait for the camera to be set up, that fish is not the only thing he sends back if he is not satisfied. Only the other day, a marquess was refused admittance because he was wearing a sweater. 'I sent him back to the Cavendish, where he was staying, to put on a jacket and tie. I have the cream de la cream coming here, and things have got to be nice. I'm not going to mention names, but it's the cream de la cream.'

When Marks, as the patrons address him, came to Wilton's, oysters were 3/6d a dozen; today, they are £5 a dozen. Although there still seems to be a lot of money around in the West End, Mr Marks detects hard times ahead. 'In my young days, I used to sell a tin of caviar a day. Do you know how long it takes me to sell two kilos now?' A pregnant pause, as Mr Marks looks inquiringly round the gilded restaurant with its discreet alcoves and subdued lighting: '*Nearly a month!*'

While cameraman David Jackson reloads his Arriflex, a waiter deftly reloads my glass with Krug.

One of the points BBC producer Andrew Snell wants to make in this programme is that, over the years, the everyday foods of the East End have become the luxuries of the West End.

Even jellied eels, which now have to be airfreighted in from as far away as New Zealand, are becoming a luxury. At one time, the apprentices of London revolted because they complained they were being fed too much salmon, Oysters, as Sam Weller once remarked, went naturally with poverty, but Mr Marks does not recall that time. 'Working people never ate oysters, they were fighting for their existence with bread and butter. There was never any bloody oysters in the East End. The poor people were poor in those bloody days.'

Mr Marks is a great believer in the health-giving properties of the oyster. 'They've got beautiful vitamins, nutriment and everything. You take the doctors: when their patients was queer, they all flew to oysters. When there was an illness of royalty, I used to run to Buckingham Palace with oysters. Even on a Sunday, I used to go to Marlborough House with oysters if they weren't well.'

Can anybody eat at Wilton's? I ask Mr Marks if he would welcome a couple of Cockneys who, perhaps, had had a win on the horses and fancied a feed of oysters: 'No, no, no, no, no! Money doesn't affect me. This is a certain place, and you've got to keep it up to a certain pitch. I wouldn't like to see a feller come 'ere with long hair and no coat or vest on, or some even with no tie on. No, this wouldn't be Wilton's; that sort of thing would spoil my reputation.'

As we pack up our equipment, an emissary of the Aga Khan – a secretary, perhaps, or a bodyguard – arrives. We form the impression that he is worried in case we have planted a bomb.

We have been to Billingsgate to meet Lou Hart, Sid Gibbard, Manny Abrahams and Bill Potter, and find out what they think real East End food is. They talk of the old days – hot-potato stalls, chestnut and muffin men, boiled beef and carrots with pease pudding, fish and chips. But it always comes back to eels:

'I'd say jellied eels, without any doubt at all.'

'Every other pub had its jellied eel stall, and the kids in the charabancs on their way back from Southend would enjoy jellied eels along with their parents.'

But there is an even firmer favourite. 'I'd say pies and mash if you can find them.'

'But can you find 'em these days? Most of the pie shops are in old property and when they rebuild them they don't want the shops any more. They don't want what the East Ender wants.'

We go down to the oldest pie-and-mash shop in London – Harry Joyce's in Tower Bridge Road. Harry was born over the shop sixty years ago, but, like Billingsgate market itself, his shop, so the rumour goes, is due for demolition. Perhaps it will emerge from the rubble as a boutique, selling Get Well cards, or finger-lickin' Kentucky Chicken, or as a Hamburger Heaven.

Wilton's has deep-pile carpeting; Harry Joyce sprinkles sawdust on his floor. There is a counter where you collect your food, and pews with scrubbed wooden tables where you can eat it. Whatever you have – pie and mash or stewed eels – it is liberally dowsed with what Harry calls 'liquor' – a bright green sauce made of flour and dried parsley.

He charges 20p for a huge, steaming plateful of pie and mashed potatoes, the price of half an oyster at Wilton's. There is no cover charge, no tipping, no wine list, no service, but a steady stream of patrons comes and goes.

Harry's busiest times are Fridays and Saturdays from one until two. He makes his own meat pies on the premises and bakes them in a coal oven. Even if the shop is not pulled down to make a wider road for the lorries that thunder past, there will be no one to take Harry's place. 'The family aren't interested. There's nobody really. People don't want to come and work here; it's too many hours, isn't it? It's a cockney meal and it's still cheap.'

After the pubs have closed at three o'clock, three blokes and a bird come in. They want to know whether we're the 'effin' BBC' or the 'effin' ITV'. They collect their pie and mash and sit down unerringly in the pew where all our recording gear is. They object loudly to what one of them describes, not inaccurately, as 'all this poncin' about'. 'Turn those effin' lights off!'

I have been handcrafting a few well-chosen words, seated and annoying no one, in a pew at the back of the shop. Andrew explains about the opening sequence. He says that there is this rather nice close-up of a single flower growing in a garden and then you pull back to reveal rooftops stretching into the mid-distance. On the soundtrack there will be Harry Champion singing that song about the houses in between: ''Cos it reely is a wery pretty gardin, and 'Ackney to the east may be seen; and by clingin' to the chimbley, you could see across to Wembley, if it wasn't for *the houses in between*.' That is the title of the programme.

Andrew says the blitz knocked down a lot of houses and now there are tower flats, and although the old community spirit is dying, it still survives. We are going to interview Tubby Isaacs who runs a jellied eel stall in Aldgate; and one of the few fishmongers who is still smoking haddock in his own backyard.

The party in the window is getting stroppier by the minute. I suggest we wait until they have gone before trying to do any more.

'Don't worry,' says Andrew, 'I'll have a word with them.' I remember thinking that it would be a good idea if he removed his spectacles at this stage. I return to my thoughts. 'A lot of the houses in between,' I propose to say, standing in the steam from Harry's pies, 'have disappeared in postwar years, giving place to high-rise flats, but the old community feeling has survived . . .'

Up in the front of the shop, the old community feeling erupts violently. I cannot hear what Andrew is saying, but suddenly his glasses fly through the air and he is felled to the ground. I wonder would Mr Marks have sent them home for ties at this stage?

A leg of the tripod is smashed; Marion, our researcher, goes off to research the nearest phone. Fists and arms flail. We seem to be unpopular. By the time the police arrive, the aggro pie-party has gone.

I take up my stance against the counter to do my bit about the old community feeling surviving. Andrew polishes his glasses reflectively.

I'm sure this sort of thing does not happen at Wilton's.

24. The Most Persuasive
Bag Lady

Caroline Walker was the most persuasive bag lady who ever burst into *The Food Programme* office. She was an instinctive communicator and she found out early on in her battle to improve the food we eat that talking about diet in academic terms was, for a non-scientific audience, a total turn-off.

As a scientist and nutritionist herself, she spoke with an authority that commanded respect from her colleagues. At the London School of Hygiene, her postgraduate work had centred on food and poverty. When she moved to the Dunn Clinical Nutrition Centre at Cambridge, as a research scientist specializing in nutrition in the community, she began to realize that it was time to speak out against our appalling diet of over-processed food.

Her technique was devastatingly simple. When invited to speak at a conference she would leave the statistics to others. Mounting the platform with a shopping bag, she would begin to pull out the heavily advertised rubbish that was masquerading as good food and through ridicule and laughter make the point that much of the nation's legacy of ill-health came from these very packets and tins.

On radio, television and in the press she waged war on the profit-hungry food manufacturers and the politicians who defended what she saw as the unacceptable face of food processing. As a council member of the Coronary Prevention Group she fought for more informative labelling on food.

In 1984 she took the struggle into the House of Commons and fed Jonathan Aitken MP not only with a damaging set of facts about the rubbish we eat, but a pair of socks and a pound of sausages. Aitken made her point with great style. 'We know more about what's in these socks', he said, 'than in this string of sausages.'

Caroline used her props to campaign against the adulteration of fish fingers with water, to anatomize the sugar-rich 'soups' and the awful slices of British bread. There were plenty of triumphs along the way. Batchelor's were so embarrassed by the slide she used in lectures revealing that their asparagus soup was dyed with Brilliant Blue FCF (banned in seventeen European countries) that in self-defence they eventually replaced it with a less controversial dye.

While at the Dunn Centre, Caroline became secretary of the subcommittee which, under the chairmanship of Professor Philip James, produced the National Advisory Committee on Nutrition Education's report. This suggested that the Government should reduce the excessive amount of fat and sugar in processed food. The NACNE report struck at the very core of the food manufacturing industry, but the industry being such a powerful lobby in Whitehall, the Government were unwilling to accept the NACNE recommendations.

Angered by what she regarded as an attempt to conceal the truth from the public, Caroline leaked the contents of the report, and the details of the wheeling and dealing behind its compilation, to *Sunday Times* journalist Geoffrey Cannon. NACNE became public knowledge. Interest in the facts it revealed was so keen that Caroline went on to write a bestselling book called *The Food Scandal* (with Geoffrey Cannon, whom she eventually married).

Four years ago, Caroline learnt she had cancer. She died on 22 September at the tragically early age of thirty-eight. Although she, and other campaigners who joined her, had done a lot to improve public awareness of the need for a healthier supply of food, she knew that the battle was still in its early stages. Just before she died Caroline Walker recorded an interview for *The Food Programme* in which she looked back on what had been achieved and forward to what remained to be accomplished.

What particularly saddened her about food and health in Britain was the way in which decisions are made about food policy. 'Far too many are left to middle-aged, middle-class men who don't cook and don't go shopping. When I go to conferences with sacks full of food I can absolutely guarantee that afterwards some man will come up to me and say, "This is fascinating, where do you get this stuff?" And I can't believe it. I say: "Where do you *think* I got it! In a shop!" They've got no idea what's on sale.'

Caroline Walker felt strongly that we had over-medicalized food, turned it into nutrition tables and arguments about cholesterol. 'I think we're coming to a period which will be very exciting and I'm sorry I won't be around to see it. One of the great steps forward that can now be made is to join together the aims of environmentalists, nutritionists like myself, cookery writers, scientists . . . to try to work towards a common goal.'

25. Where Hops will Grow

It must have been the sheer cornucopia of Kent and Sussex that put us off going there before – how could you put all that fruit and fish and meat in one half-hour programme? Rich pastures, woodland bursting with produce. Fought over and fought for, farmed and tilled since Domesday, invaded by Normans in boats and Londoners in coaches, it has somehow managed to retain a rural identity.

Oast houses rise marooned among the bungalows, but there are still acres of apples and orchards full of cherries, pears, plums and damsons. Kentish honey, fuggles and golding hops, Bramleys and Laxton Superbs, Southdown and Romney Marsh lamb, Dover soles – even the beaches yield unusual delicacies. Seakale is a succulent and rare vegetable which Jim Smith has been encouraging in his windswept shingle garden near Pevensey for years. The seeds are planted in autumn and the roots go down six and eight feet. When the shoots appear in the New Year, they are covered up with pebbles until the spring so that they appear blanched, surprised and white.

'They say it's the cabbage family, and all cabbages come from the sea, I've been told. Whether that's right or wrong I can't say,' said Jim.

There are fishing-boats pulled up on the steeply shelving shingle, and, fenced round, is a bit of old beach where Jim cultivates his kale. In the old days, when it grew unpredictably wild, if you found some you kept quiet about it: 'There was a bit here, perhaps, and a bit there, way over yonder, and the old men would creep out and get a feed, and one wouldn't tell the other one where he'd got his bit. There was a Dr Coombes reckoned it has got a lot of iron in it, and if you cut it with a steel knife the blade goes dark with the iron.'

The kale can be eaten raw with cheese, just like celery, but Jim's wife serves it hot on Christmas Day with the turkey. It tastes like a cross between asparagus, celery and cauliflower; firm and sea-fresh.

Even the wretched Ribbentrop, when he was Hitler's ambassador in London, enjoyed Jim's kale: 'His daughter was at Bexhill Ladies' School, and he came over to visit her and stayed the night at the Cooden Beach hotel. The chef wanted seakale for his dinner, so the wife and I had to cut Ribbentrop some and take it over.'

Within sound of the sea are some of the finest sheep in the world. Before the war, nearly half a million of them roamed the Downs and the salt marshes of Romney, Dymchurch and Dungeness. When Ribbentrop went home and the Germans reached the Channel ports, the pick of the long-wooled Romneys and the delicate-fleshed Southdowns were evacuated. An old shepherd recalled the government officials arriving at his farm: 'They put the broad arrow on all the best sheep and we had to sort them all, and they were sent to Scotland, where it was safe.' During the war, the marshes were sown with peas, but now most of the land is back to grass: 'It's exceptional grass. Some of the old pastures will carry ten ewes to an acre, a feat which is unheard of in other parts. On this farm you've got three fields that are real fattening fields. I think it's how the sea left the silt. When the tide went back, it left it better in some places than others; that's what happened.'

And it eats well, too, as any shepherd will tell you: 'It wouldn't worry me if I'd been shearing all day that I got to eat lamb. It does some older shepherds, though; they would never eat mutton while they were lambing – it would put them off. Myself, I don't think you can beat Romney Marsh lamb two or three months old, you know.' They eat it with mint sauce and peas, perhaps, or broad beans, and, later in the year, scarlet runners, and polish it off with what they call 'well pudding' or 'pound pudding'.

The names are obscured by time. Is it pound pudding because you put a pound of everything in, or 'pond pudding' because it creates a rich reservoir of juice? What you do is chop up fresh beef suet and mix it with flour to a paste. Then you line a bowl with it and fill it with brown sugar and currants and boil it for three or four hours and ladle cream all over it.

Good fresh food can still be found all along the south coast, particularly shellfish, shrimps, haddock and plaice, and Londoners on a day trip to Margate, Hastings or Brighton still go for fish and chips. It was the hopfields of Kent that gave East End families their only holiday of the year.

In the old days, when everything from soft fruit to hops had to be picked by hand, between 30,000 and 40,000 Cockneys would descend on the hop gardens in the first week of September. Few can regret the passing of an age which offered hard work in the country as a holiday from hard work in the town, but David and Louise Hart of Bermondsey have been hopping for seventy-six years now, and they will go on doing it for as long as the machines are kept at bay.

'We used to come down with mum from London Bridge. The farmer would book a train and you had to be there at two or three in the morning, and then he'd be there with a big old wagon at Paddock Wood or Selling, or wherever the farm was, to pick you up, and you'd chuck all your boxes on and you'd arrived. Now they come in motors. In the old days, we had about 150 women out here all with their baskets. We used to take a bit of grub up the field with us, bread and cheese, make a pot of tea.

'We mucked in together in those days, slept on straw. But the spirit's not 'ere now. You're not out in the garden all picking together. They're all spread out, some at the machine shops, some here, some there. Now we come down and we miss one another. This year, we come down and found another couple had gone. They'll come down one year and we'll be gone. But not yet. They say to me, "You want to go abroad." I say no, I want to go 'opping. I said, "Never in your life", I won't go up in an aeroplane. This is the place to be. Walk up a country lane, marvellous. We're not frightened of getting mugged down here. Country air. Look at the age they live: eighty, eighty-six, ninety. Blimey, they never go, 'arf of 'em.'

In those days of cheap beer, the hop-pickers always had a barrel handy. 'If they didn't have their beer, they would do no work.' In recent years, brewers have demanded new varieties of hop. Tastes have changed, just as they have for cider.

The old cider orchards have been grubbed up and replanted with more profitable cash crops, or replaced by apples that look well, keep well, and sell well, shrink-wrapped on the supermarket shelves. Just as there are independent brewers like Shepherd Neame of Faversham who still survive, so there are one or two independent cider makers – like Bob Luck of Goudhurst, who can remember making his first cider back in 1935.

'There was a severe frost, and none of the valleys grew apples; the oak and ash trees all went black. But I found out where I could get some apples and I started taking it out at a shilling a gallon to the local farmers. I gradually got into selling in public houses and free houses, and we built up from there.'

Apples are brought in from the orchards and pulped to release the aroma from the skins. The pomace, as it is called, is built up into 'cheeses', using wattle panels. It is important that the right balance is achieved, the bitter apples complementing the sweet, the tannin and acid levels just right.

'This is not sweet carbonated cider suitable for young girls and children; it is serious cider for sipping thoughtfully. There are still old people in the pubs of Kent who can remember the days when a real drop of cider could put grown men under the table in next to no time: 'There was troops in wartime used to come in here, and, if we ran out of beer, they'd get on the cider. God bugger! I seen 'em chucked up in them lorries like dead sheep, drunk as lords. They was the days they were.'

26. Unbeatable at any Price

Remember Ralph Nader and those early campaigns against dangerous cars? For the last fifteen years, Dr Michael Jacobson, a Nader disciple, has been campaigning equally effectively against potentially carcinogenic food practices. Most additives, he is convinced, are not safe in any quantity.

He was in London recently to address two conferences on additives, one organized by FACT, the Food Additives Campaign Team, and the other by the Health Education Council. His theme: how public information and consumer pressure can promote the production and consumption of foods as free from dangerous chemicals as possible.

By training a chemist and biologist, Jacobson took a PhD in microbiology at the Massachusetts Institute of Technology before founding the Center for Science in the Public Interest in 1971. CSPI has been lobbying to such purpose on Capitol Hill that it has forced the US government to recognize that not all food is good food. Partly as a result of CSPI's intense campaigning, the US Department of Agriculture began in 1980 to urge Americans to change to a diet lower in fat, sugar and salt.

Jacobson has a mop of hair, like Einstein's, a Groucho moustache and electric reserves of energy. He is a stylish communicator, turns out books, pamphlets and technical papers with ferocious regularity and is not without a sense of humour. Six years ago, he and Ralph Nader opened a 'Junk Food Hall of Shame' in Washington and put on display all the objects of their scorn, shelves of branded goods high in sugar and price and low in nutritional value.

CSPI, which now has 70,000 subscribers, has organized

National Food Days and nutrition campaigns, and challenged many common misconceptions about food. At one stage it took on the Campbell Soup Company and what it regarded as an inaccurate and insupportable statement that 'soup is good food'. When Dr Jacobson came to *The Food Programme* studio he was reeling under his first impressions of the British food scene. He'd been surprised, he told me, to find organically grown fruit and vegetables on sale in Safeway: 'Believe me, I'm going to go back and say "Safeway, you tell me you can't have organically grown food on sale in your supermarkets in the States but in England you do. Why don't we deserve such foods also?"'

One of the main problems facing a campaigner like Jacobson is the now richly ingrained belief that all food must be fun – easy to eat or drink, easy to chew and bland as possible. 'Everywhere we are beckoned by junkie foods. There are vending machines everywhere that offer candy and soda pop. You go to supermarkets and there's just aisle after aisle of junk – avenues fifty feet long with soft drinks on both sides.'

On the other hand, there is a growing awareness that wanting to eat more healthily is no longer an aberration of weirdos. 'When I started in the early Seventies, anybody who advocated wholemeal bread, yoghurt or brown rice was immediately labelled a faddist and derided. Now all the Burger Kings and Wendies have wonderful salad bars, and you can actually get a fresh vegetable at a fast-food restaurant. The death rate due to heart disease has gone down by about a third in the last twenty years – a remarkable change. We still have a high rate, about as high as Britain, but much lower than it was. But we're still being offered far too much garbage, much of it tailored to the taste of children.'

When Michael Jacobson began investigating the activities of the major food companies he found as much difficulty as Nader had found with the automobile industry of Detroit. 'Companies are, by their very nature, secretive. They gain nothing by divulging information, and we go to great lengths to get information, either by demanding that the government require them to put more information on the label or put pressure on them to release information.'

He is convinced that the battle for information is an easier one to win in the States than here: 'You have an Official Secrets Act that enables the Government to keep key information secret from the public. In the United States we don't have to rely on our government's word that a product is safe. We have access to every shred of information that goes into the decision-making process on a food additive. For you in Britain, getting rid of the Official Secrets Act would be a key step forward.'

Jacobson believes that every victory has to be fought for. 'Companies that are making millions and millions of dollars on a product that is not healthful are not going to change their products voluntarily. They have a winning formula – they want not only to keep selling the product but to sell even more of it. And that's where the resistance is going to come from.'

It is the supermarkets, perhaps, which hold the key to better and healthier food. 'They don't care what they sell,' says Jacobson. 'If healthy food sells, they'll sell that; if it's junk food that sells, they'll sell that. Fortunately, some of the natural foods are more profitable than the processed foods, so they have an incentive to sell those healthier things.' In this country more and more people concerned with the nation's health are hoping the incentives will soon prove overwhelming.

27. Bye-bye Beigel, hallo Wondabun

After the first programme in the BBC2 series *A Taste of Britain* – the one about the asparagus of Evesham, the lamperns of the River Severn, Hereford beef and food, home-brewed Worcester beer – I had a letter from a viewer in Twickenham. 'How refreshing', she wrote, 'to get the old lump in the throat seeing our wonderful English countryside and hearing normal, sensible Englishmen talking with pride about the country and produce. In this day and age, I am sure this programme was like a shot in the arm to every patriotic Englishman who wants to see our country great again.'

I wonder what she thought of yesterday's instalment which was mainly about our dependence on imported flavours and the debt we owe to all the immigrants who have settled here. The programme was centred on London because it was up the Thames that most of the imports of Empire came and most of the refugees arrived.

Take tea. There's nothing more British than that, is there? The world centre of tea trading is London and yet, like many of the other raw materials which have become a part of our way of eating and drinking, we are completely dependent on foreigners to produce it for us. We founded high tea on those dried leaves from India and Ceylon; we survived the Blitz with its help; we have been comforted by it in the evening and moved by it in the morning. We re-exported the habit all over the world and we still use the dregs to tell fortunes, fertilize roses and clean our carpets.

Even older than tea are all the other 'English' tastes which come from even farther away. By that process of acquisition which we were better at than anybody else in the nineteenth century, we eventually seized almost complete command of the sources of all the good things we needed in the kitchen.

You could even make out a case to prove that it was our desire for pepper and spices that led to the creation of the British Empire. The spice trade, originally in Arab hands, passed to Venice, thence to the Portuguese, the Dutch and, finally, to the merchants of London. We took control of the roots and leaves, the dried seeds and pieces of bark, the fragrant and lucrative spices.

At the beginning of the twentieth century, practically every country exporting spices was marked red on the map, but our delight in them was much older – it dated back to the days when a sea voyage to the spice islands was more hazardous than space travel, and the fruits of those journeys found their way only to the tables of the wealthy. Even pepper, as spice merchant John Hodson told us, is a part of our social history, and of the language: 'We still talk about peppercorn rent, but, in those days, peppercorns were a luxury, very expensive and probably worth the equivalent of £10 or £15 today – so a peppercorn rent really meant something substantial. Even a pound of nutmegs was worth three sheep or half a cow.'

Today, we have a vast and very British cuisine founded on these exotic imports. What, for instance, is more traditionally Scottish than gingerbread? But the first shipload on which we founded our ginger snaps, ginger jam, ginger beer, was not imported from Jamaica until 1585. Cinnamon toast, apple tart with cloves, nutmeg on bread and butter pudding, mixed spice in mincemeat, aniseed balls, mace in pork sausages, vanilla ice cream, pimento in pickles: all are old and familiar tastes, but none indigenous.

And how English is that typically winter dish – oxtail stew? Like many other favourites, it owes its presence here to intolerance in Europe. Nearly 50,000 Huguenots arrived in the seventeenth century from La Rochelle and Nantes to settle round Spitalfields. Tradition says that, living near the tanneries, these poor families, mainly weavers, were able to get hold of the tails of beasts for nothing, because Londoners didn't fancy them. Hence oxtail stew and oxtail soup.

Later, persecution brought new foods to the East End. Between 1881 and 1905, over a million Jews left Russia and Eastern Europe to escape poverty and pogroms; about 100,000 made their way to Britain, and the majority sailed up the Thames and settled in Whitechapel. Their advent had, perhaps, more of an effect on art and literature than it did on food, but the most famous restaurant in the East End, Blooms, is a kosher one, and you can still buy such Jewish delicacies as latkes and beigels in Wentworth Street. But for how long?

Although Kossoff's bakery still makes challahs – the 'best bread' eaten on the Sabbath – it may be only a matter of time before the special skill involved in the plaiting of the bread is completely lost. David Kossoff has handed the business over to his son now. He arrived at the age of seventeen, as a refugee from Kiev, in the days when the East End was dominated by the Jewish community. Now, the Jews are giving way to Asians, and the old traditions are dying out:

'You can't get the labour, that's the main thing. And you can't get the people that can do this work. Plaiting a challah cannot be done by a machine. When it's three strings, anybody can do it, but when it comes to five, six and even eight strings, then you've got to have really good men to plait it. Other bakers try to make it, but they can't.'

Mr Kossoff remembers the first Jewish bakers' strike: 'They were asking for an eleven-hour day, and the strike went on for six weeks until they won. I've got a photo upstairs where you can see about 50, 60 bakers – the union used to have 300 members, but now there isn't any at all. There's nobody to be a union member.'

According to Mr Kossoff, the new generation will never know what they are missing; bread and cakes made by the machines lack the finesse and flavour of the handmade product.

There is no enthusiasm in machines: 'We had a baker, and, for Friday, we make a special batter cake which we usually use for Saturday morning for coffee. And that man was the only man who could make it.

'He used to stay the night in our flat so that he should be able to get up at three o'clock in the morning and make the dough. He used to have all the doors and windows shut: there shouldn't be no draught. And when his cake came out, it was like an artist makes a painting. That was the way.'

Forty bakers now dwindled to a pair. Soon, there will be no one to bake the beigels, let alone stand in the street selling them. As Jewish food shops close, so Indian businesses take their place; the challah has been replaced by curry, rye bread by rice. Despite the number of Jewish immigrants who settled in Britain, their influence on gentile eating habits was surprisingly marginal. But one small community who made their home in Limehouse have recruited themselves, and spread so rapidly, that they have altered the dining habits of the British out of all proportion to their numbers.

Even the smallest town now has at least one Chinese restaurant, and the Hong Kong Cantonese, by their industry, their total disregard for working hours and their sharp observation of what the British are prepared to eat after an evening in the pub, has given them (along with the Indians and Pakistanis) a near-monopoly of the late-night restaurant trade in many hitherto undercatered areas. Visit a small seaside town on the south coast at 10.30 on a wet winter's night and, were it not for the Golden Duck or the Taj Mahal, you would go to bed hungry.

Our grateful acceptance of Asian food has even been commercialized by British manufacturers – you won't find platzels or gefilte fish on every supermarket shelf, but you certainly will find packs of processed curry and rice and boil-in-a-bag Chinese meals. It is our ability to eat almost anything that has made the fast-food business so cosmopolitan. You can still take away fish and chips, but look at the imported novelties that are eroding their monopoly: Kentucky fried chicken, hamburger heavens, hotdogs, pancakes and pizzas.

Behind much of the changing taste of Britain is the powerful and pervasive influence of the USA. What America eats today, we eat tomorrow, monosodium glutamate and all. We have gained a specious new wonderland of what the more cynical American consumers have dubbed so accurately 'junk' food – food with eye appeal, lots of colour, lots of flavour and little or no nutrition. But we are losing the individually made delights which, in the past, have made the taste of Britain a very varied one. As, one by one, the small family bakeries close, the field will be left to the giants.

Perhaps it is only a matter of time before beigels will be gone for ever, along with simnel cake, Chelsea buns and the hundred and one things that bakers used to bake – all to be replaced by a nationally marketed whiter-than-white Wonda-bun. A forecast not as fanciful as you may think.

28. Food for Love

It was entirely appropriate that the Jane Grigson article published in the *Observer Magazine*, the day before she died should have rescued the hamburger from the debased fat-saturated thing it has become in fairgrounds and seaside resorts.

'Do you like baked beans?' she asked this January when I visited the Wiltshire farmhouse where she had lived for so many happy years with Geoffrey and their daughter Sophie. She was in the middle of researching her series which restored honesty to food hijacked by the High Street franchises. The beans were, of course, home-baked and cooked perfectly.

For Jane, concepts like *haute cuisine* or posh food didn't exist; there was good food and the rest was not worth eating. She wrote equally enthusiastically of everyday dishes and unusual treats. Her contempt for meretricious factory food surfaced in the *Observer* when we conducted a series of comparative tastings of products from the supermarket shelves. When we sipped our way through instant coffee, she pronounced most of the samples to be nasty and disgusting. The canned vegetable soups stung her to complain that they seemed to have no connection at all with real food. This was not elitist arrogance but outrage at an industry which was adulterating food and drink so perversely that all the goodness and the taste and flavour were processed out. Vegetable soup, she exclaimed with anger, should be one of the great gastronomic delights of life, not a plastic pot full of modified starch and monosodium glutamate.

In 1974, in *English Food*, she pointed out how increasingly difficult it was becoming to buy the raw materials from which good meals could be prepared. 'Tomatoes have no taste. The finest-flavoured potatoes are not available in shops. Vegetables and fruit are seldom fresh. Cheeses are imprisoned in plastic wrappings. Words such as "fresh" and "home-made" have been borrowed by commerce to tell lies.'

She wrote encouraging letters to independent producers, publicized their work in her articles and fought valiantly for an improvement in the quality of our food. At a Guild of Food Writers meeting in November 1988 attended by the Minister of Agriculture, she attacked him for buttressing an industry which made its profits by serving the population with inferior food. 'I do not understand', she said, 'why we are not on the streets demonstrating. We demonstrate against the bomb while our bread has been ruined and our foods have been stuffed full of very slow poison.'

This was before disease in the poultry flocks had forced the Government to warn the nation not to eat raw eggs. After that Christmas, the first in her lifetime when it was no longer considered safe to make almond icing or boil an egg lightly, she sat down and reflected on her four decades of food writing. 'I never thought', she wrote in the Guild magazine, 'that I would end up being forced into polemical food journalism as I have been during the last six months. It was one thing to crack away at the producers of watery tomatoes. Being frightened about what one can safely give a child to eat is something else. Having to avoid mayonnaise, scrambled eggs and omelettes, having to remove the peel of apples and potatoes when a young family comes to stay, is appalling. There one has to take a stand. Knowing what we know, how can we be silent?'

Jane's voice is silent now but her life's work will go on shining like a beacon of integrity. When she began to write for the *Observer Magazine* in 1968 she felt that she knew nothing abut cookery beyond the research she had done for her much-acclaimed first book *Charcuterie and French Pork Cookery*. It was her poet-naturalist husband Geoffrey, she always said, who came to her rescue. 'I knew a certain amount about painting, literature, the civilization and history of Europe. My first subject was the strawberry. Right, he said, we'll find out what the strawberry has meant to people, what they have done to it, how they have developed it and so on. Somehow we got through. I cooked recipes over and over again until he was satisfied.'

And that's how Jane wrote right up to her death on 12 March. 'It was', she said, 'a way of expressing joy in the life we led.' Food, she believed, touched every aspect of experience, nothing was irrelevant. Whether writing about the regional dishes of France, where she and her family spent part of the year, or about the kipper, Bible cake and parkin of the North-East where she was brought up, she deployed her curiosity, her scholarship and her sensual delight in the pleasure of food with evangelical skill. Raised in a country which has consistently ignored food, she took great pleasure in according it a rightful prominence in the daily round. 'One of my most vivid memories of the Three Choirs Festival,' she recalled in *Fish Cookery*, 'is not the music but the spectacle of a whole boiled salmon consumed at a luncheon party. It came from the Severn or Wye and tasted marvellous.'

The creative ease with which she related cookery to life beyond the kitchen turned everything she wrote into a voyage of cultural discovery. It says a lot about the values of the society in which we live that her uncompromising stand for good food went conspicuously unmarked by public recognition.

29. *Coming Singing from the Sands*

If you set out on a tour of Wales, armed with a *Good Food Guide*, you might be forgiven for thinking that it is something of a gastronomic disaster area and, in Hampstead terms, you would be right. The incidence of pâté making in Penarth is relatively low; few kitchens in the Gower valleys are hung with garlic; olive oil is still something strictly for the ear.

But, if eating out is not much of a treat, what about eating in? According to that seminal work, *British Tastes* by D. Elliston Allen, the Welsh, like the Scots, have a poorly developed tradition of eating fresh fruit and vegetables, and have the heaviest consumption in Britain of quick-frozen foods. They eat the most canned meat, a great deal of canned salmon and canned peaches, and drink all the canned milk and cream they can afford. The sales of sweetened condensed milk are the highest in the country and milk puddings a firm favourite.

But, with their great love of milk and a preference for mild and milk-white cheeses like Caerphilly, there are other more interesting traditions. When we went to film in South Wales, we found one of the most ancient forms of cooking in Europe and we found it only just in time. Like the Scots, the Welsh founded their cooking on the open fire. There were no ovens, so practically everything consumed was either simmered in a pot or cooked on a flat iron griddle: the Welsh call them bakestones. The Welsh *bara brith* is common to all the Celtic countries. In Ireland, it is called barm brack, in Scotland, it appears as the Selkirk bannock and, in Brittany, as a *Morlaix brioche*. And the same with that other Celtic speciality which

349

the Welsh call *crempogs*, the Bretons *crêpes*, the Scots crumpets or pancakes – all conditioned by the open hearth.

The same tradition of making broth occurs in both Wales and Scotland. You simmer your meat for hours in a mixture of vegetables and then eat it, gaining the advantage both of a soup and a stew. In Wales, they call this broth *cawl*, and we found Ann Jones making it in her farmhouse from leeks, potatoes, carrots, swedes, cabbages and (again the Celtic influence) oatmeal.

The open hearth warmed the kitchen, dried the clothes on wet days, provided endless kettles of boiling water, had an oven at the side for the weekly baking of bread and a chain to hang a bakestone on, for making *bara crai*, the unleavened bread made from flour and salt and buttermilk and eaten hot and crisp with lots of salty farmhouse butter.

A few weeks after we were in Mrs Jones's kitchen, the old hearth was bricked up, and a shining new Rayburn Rhapsody took its place. And as that was the last open hearth in Wales, if you want to see one now, you'll have to go to a folk museum. The Rayburn will certainly make life easier and will cook even more efficiently but, despite the arrival of gas and electricity and all the miracles of processing, many Welsh men and women will tell you that food no longer tastes the same. As one fisherman put it, talking of *cawl*: 'It was a beautiful smell. It were all on the table with big basins, with a big spoon, you know. And then we were mopping it up and a bit of rice pudding after it. Oh, smashin'! You can't get that food today; they don't cook the same.'

True, or just an old man's nostalgia? There is nostalgia in plenty in the Gower Peninsular where the ancient cockle-beds have been almost abandoned. Some put it down to the increase in the flocks of oyster-catchers, others to the movement of the sandbanks, some to pollution. In the past, in times of depression, the cocklebeds were a godsend, but now there are not sufficient cockles for anyone to make a living. The cockleless future almost brings tears to the eyes of Rosie

Matthews, who has lived all her seventy-seven years in the village of Crofty. She still sells cockles regularly in Swansea but not local ones. Although they are as popular a feed as ever in South Wales, they now have to be imported from Boston and King's Lynn.

Rosie bakes a cockle pie for us – a layer of bacon, a layer of cockles, a layer of boiled and pulped onions, but they are not Crofty cockles: 'It's a sad place, not only Crofty, but Penclawdd and the neighbouring villages as well: we're desolate. There are no cars: nothing on the roads going for the cockles. Quiet. Nothing. Well, I remember it used to be a pleasure to hear the youngsters singing coming in from the sands, bringing their loads of cockles. Happy. But not now.'

Another peculiarly South Wales delicacy is still there for the taking, but, as with the cockles, although the processing takes place in Wales, the raw materials come from far away. Only a few local women still pick *bara lawr*, the red seaweed, Porphyra. They wash it, boil it, and then fry it up with oatmeal and eat it with bacon for breakfast.

The closing of the railways hit local collection of seaweed and, in a time when people expect regular working hours, a job which, because of the movement of the tides, had to start one hour later each day, lost its appeal. The Porphyra comes now from Cumberland and Cornwall, Stranraer and Dunbar. Cliff Roberts's family have been processing laverbread for four generations and the demand for it is as keen as ever in the area bounded by Carmarthen on the west and Newport on the east. It was always very popular in the mining valleys because of its high iron content – laverbread is said to contain fifty-two minerals. Some find it laxative, others will not eat it when there's an 'r' in the month. The secret, according to Mr Roberts, lies in the blending.

'The person making it would have his own particular blend, people get accustomed to eating your product and this is where the art comes in. And, of course, you have to be careful to get the sand out.' The seaweed is washed four times, boiled for six hours with three pounds of salt to every hundredweight, minced and then allowed to set in its own gelatine.

It is a black, shiny, spinachy-looking product with a strong sea tang. 'Not unlike a cowpat,' as one Welshman put it. I will not grieve if I never taste it again.

There is an even older tradition which survives only in Wales. Coracles have been used for salmon and sea-trout fishing on the Teifi, Towy and Taf for over 2,000 years. Some of them nowadays are made of fibreglass, not wattles and cowhide as in Roman times, but their continued use is being challenged by anglers. In the middle of the nineteenth century, there were 300 coracle fishermen on one river alone; today, there are only 19 men left in Wales with a licence to fish from a coracle.

Fishing from one of these frail, basin-shaped craft is an art you almost have to be born with; certainly, it is a family business. Two coracles drift downstream, a twenty-foot net paid out between them. The fishermen control the net with one hand and their own progress with a paddle in the other. It looks simple and the salmon and trout seem easy to catch – which is why the rod-and-line lobby is so opposed to the coraclemen.

It looks as if the coracle, which many nationalists see as being as symbolically Welsh as the language itself, might be doomed to the dust of the folk museum, too. In fact, working for a programme like *A Taste of Britain* is rather like always arriving at the theatre just as the curtain is going down. We just caught the last few minutes of Ann Jones's bakestone, we interviewed the last of the coracle men, we filmed the last handful of cockle gatherers.

I am no disciple of the school which believes that the artificial fostering of old traditions can keep them alive. But, when there is so genuine a regard for the way things *used* to taste, it is sad to watch them disappear, one by one. It is usually a complicated set of circumstances which kills an old tradition. The Yarmouth bloater failed with the disappearance of the herring shoals but, had the shoals survived, would there have been the men to catch them and the women to gut them?

Two years ago, filming in Orkney, I noticed how critically poised some marginal foods can be. We went to the last surviving water-mill in the islands – a working museum-piece where local barley was still being ground, profitably and professionally. It was also the only mill in Scotland where bere is ground. Bere, from which beremeal is made, is a species of barley grown only in the far north of Scotland, and then only on a very small scale. From it, you can make beremeal porridge or beremeal bannocks. If the mill closes, then the cultivation of bere will cease, too, because there is nowhere else for it to be ground. And so farewell to yet another ancient taste.

In a crofting township in the Hebrides the other day, I stood in the grocer's behind a young housewife whose bill came to £7. Apart from a bag of potatoes, everything she bought was processed: canned soup, stew, peaches, peas, cream, biscuits, crisps, Pepsi-Cola, cereals, jam, even tinned rice pudding. And yet her grandmother would have made porridge from oatmeal, broth from butcher's meat, have baked her own scones and cakes. There would have been fish fresh from the sea, potatoes and turnips from the croft, fresh cream from the cow. There would have been times, too, when the family went hungry; it was not an idyllic way of life.

But, it seems to me, it was a more satisfactory one. Nowadays, picking seaweed, gathering cockles, planting and digging is something most of us have lost the taste for. Why break your back when there's light work in the toy factory round the corner? Why spend hours making a stew when you can get something filling out of a tin or packet? We have gained much more leisure this generation, but at the same time we have disinherited ourselves and our children irreversibly from a whole range of wholesome, simple food.

30. A Restaurant with Rooms

This May, Sonia and Patrick Stevenson celebrated their twenty-second year running the Horn of Plenty, a restaurant with rooms in Devon. The formula is simple: Sonia cooks the kind of food Patrick likes to eat. Over the years her good food has drawn visitors from all around the world. It is fresh, seasonal and, wherever possible, local. It can be sophisticated in the very best sense of that word but it is never pretentious. It is country cuisine with classical foundations, although Sonia Stevenson might laugh at such a description, for, like many of the best cooks in the land, she is self-taught. She didn't even come from a family who derived great pleasure at the table.

'My background was Scottish. Spending money on food was not considered all that desirable. My mother taught me how to make scones and porridge without sugar and that was about it!'

Her father was principal of the Northern College of Music and Sonia found herself at the age of nineteen studying the violin in London. It was there that she met Patrick Stevenson, a singer. 'He was twice my age. He'd lived in lodgings for years and was never out of restaurants. He loved music and food and I learnt to cook because I wanted to cook for him.'

The early days of their marriage were gastronomically pragmatic. Patrick remembers with great clarity the menu for the first week after they had returned from their honeymoon.

'On the first night we had sausages and mash with champagne. On the second night we had sausages and mash with white wine; third night was red wine; fourth night it was beer – Fremlins No. 3 I seem to recall. So I said, what about a spot of roast beef for a change?'

The Royal College of Music was just down the road from Barkers, which had an excellent food hall. The following day Sonia approached their master butcher and asked for a leg of beef. She still doubles up with mirth at the memory of it.

'He asked me how many I wanted the beef for. Two, I said, and he gave me a very strange look. But from then on he took me under his wing and he would suggest things like hare or wild duck or shoulder of lamb and show me how I should carve it. He never knew he was teaching a future cook. We did have the most tremendous fun.'

Patrick was her hungry Svengali and he introduced her to the pleasures of good food. 'I couldn't cook myself,' he says, 'but I knew what I liked. We used to go to restaurants where the food was excellent, so gradually Sonia came to know what the classic dishes should taste like.'

She regards those days of dining out as the most formative in her life. 'Patrick would take me to a restaurant and say, "They do a marvellous coq au vin here." And I would go home and say I wonder if I can do that? So I learnt my cooking from knowing what it should taste like before I tried to do it myself.'

She found Patrick to be an inspiring teacher. 'He can draw more out of anybody, make them do things they never knew they could. He's the most wonderful encourager and his palate is incredible.'

Still studying the violin, Sonia was now beginning to graduate at the stove. 'Once you have the feel of food it's like painting, you just cook. I wish that people would stop getting recipe books out and just following the instructions slavishly. You need to know your raw materials and perhaps you do need books to begin with, but once you've got your basic techniques it should come from the mind and the heart.'

The cooking at home began to get so good that Patrick, ten years into their marriage, felt that they would see more of each other if they opened a restaurant together. In one of his pre-musical incarnations he had been a railway cadet, and as a rather unusual gentleman fireman shovelling his way in steam trains through the south of England he had fallen in love with Devon. The Stevensons found a stolid Georgian house over-looking the Tamar which had once belonged to the captain of the Devon copper and arsenic mine whose eviscerated excava-tions can still be seen down in the valley.

Sonia went to Mère Brazier at Col de la Luère to learn how to make quenelles. She and Patrick quickly organized their sources of supply: venison from the Plym forest, salmon from the Tamar and early morning visits to the Plymouth Barbican to see the night's catch being landed and auctioned – John Dory, monkfish, brill, squid, sea bass, scallops, eel, lobster and crayfish.

'We set out with all these raw materials', says Patrick, 'to make the kind of dishes we intended to go on serving and we have done just that. It's not to everyone's taste of course. My only sadness is that we can't sell more English dishes. We have a splendid recipe for a steak and kidney pudding which involves 6½ hours' cooking, but if one offers that – and it's not a cheap dish – people say "I don't come here for that, I can do that at home!"'

Sonia agrees that the very best English cooking does not lend itself easily to the restaurant. 'How can you make a steak and kidney pudding beautifully for fifty people who might drift in between twelve and two? It just doesn't work. English cooking is often long and drawn-out – the flavours coming through over some time.'

She finds close parallels between cooking and the perform-ing arts. 'I stand up and play the violin and it's fun and then it's gone. The same with cooking. Sometimes it's a night when you fight and you struggle and nothing seems to be working – but in the end you produce a better performance than when everything goes smoothly and there's no agony. To be artistic is to be painful, I think.'

At the Horn of Plenty the Stevensons try to cater for all tastes. Their big set banquets have become famous; centred on a specific region, they offer a taste of Europe in the heart of Devon. A recent menu based on the cuisine of Savoie began with an autumnal salad of ceps, morels and other wild fungi. Then there was river trout in a little tart with herbs, cream, wine and nutmeg followed by braised partridge with noodles, cheese, onions and bacon.

In the past twenty years, every gastronomic region of note has featured in these seasonal menus but not every meal is lavish. At lunch one is offered a menu described as The Horn of Moderation, a light collation suitable for the middle of the day.

Patrick has also devised what he calls The Crumb Horn for slimmers. 'It can happen', runs the menu, 'that one's doctors, perhaps green with envy, seek to curtail the pleasures of the table on some medical pretext or other. To make life a little bit easier for those under sentence, we thought that the availability of a strict slimmers' dish, even though it cannot by its nature approach the true Horn standard, could help if it were prepared with a true interest in gastronomy!'

Now that the Horn has added rooms to its amenities the Stevensons' breakfast has become a very important part of the day. 'In the last three weeks,' says Patrick, 'we haven't repeated the menu once. You can always have a simple boiled or scrambled egg, but we like to extend people's enjoyment.' Extensions include kedgeree, fish cakes with bacon, crunchy bacon and fried haricot beans, Gloucester Old Spot ham, smoked haddock and parsley and all manner of white fish. We had fried fillet of Devon plaice because that was the fish that had just been delivered. You eat breakfast looking over the valley with Bodmin moor on the distant horizon.

The deep-freeze does not find favour at Gulworthy. 'When people come here they don't want what they had last week,' says Sonia. 'Every day should be fresh. Creating a meal is like making music. The notes are the same but each performance is different.' It is this message which Sonia transmits in her kitchen classes. She began with a course in sauces, her first love, but even more popular these days is her fish course which begins in the company of local fishmonger, Mr O'Donnell, who takes the students on a dawn raid to Plymouth's fish market.

The Stevensons' great achievement has been consistency of purpose. They have always regarded designer food as ultimately self-defeating. Gulworthy is not show business but British cooking at its best. On their twenty-first-birthday card last year they summed up their philosophy in these words: 'Our aims have not changed and neither have our standards. We have never followed fashions. Our dishes have always ranged from the refined delicacy of so-called haute cuisine to the splendid, vigorous, family and country dishes remembered from child-hood and now so seldom found properly prepared.' May they never change.

31. The Secret Sauce and
other Pleasures

Driving down to Malvern for the first day's filming this May, I overtake the real taste of Britain. The vans labelled Mr Kipling's cakes, Mother's Pride bread, Clarnico wine gums, Scrumpijell, Vandapud, Dream Topping, Tizer the appetizer and Kiddibrek. Cargoes of factory food, bound for the supermarket shelves – processed, convenient, simple to serve. The familiar packets and tins you'll find on every grocer's shelf from Lerwick to the Lizard. One day, we ought to make a programme about that: 'The Taste of Monosodium Glutamate'.

But today, it is real food: asparagus. Not air-freighted in from Kenya, or deep-frozen from New Zealand, but fresh from the declining acreage of the Vale of Evesham. There used to be 2,000 acres of asparagus ridges around Worcester; now, there are fewer than a hundred. It is a plant that takes years to mature; the season is short, every stalk has to be cut by hand – backbreaking work which young men regard scornfully.

So the Asparagus Growers' Association annual show at Badsey is something of a sad event. In the village hall, where the thick bunches of 'grass' lie in wait for the judges, it is a middle-aged occasion. The asparagus is as good this year as any, but, according to organizer Esmond Knight, as a commercial proposition it is a crop on the decline: 'This is our jubilee year as an association, but I reckon in ten or fifteen years, asparagus will be finished in these parts. Asparagus can come from Israel, Egypt, Rumania, France, but it will be nothing like the asparagus grown in the Vale of Evesham. It really is quite unequalled for flavour and quality.'

Before the judging, there is the annual lunch in the Round of Grass, a nearby pub. We have asparagus soup and plates of the noble grass, boiled with a sprig of mint and salt for twenty minutes. The landlord of the pub, Ernest Mustoe, tells me that you don't want to muck about with asparagus: 'A posh sauce interferes with the flavour. A bit of melted butter is all you want. I suck it right down to the end. I had a lady here the other day and I compared that last little bit of white at the bottom with the eye of the chicken, that little oyster bit at the tip of the wing. Delicious, isn't it? The man who used to own the Lygon Arms at Broadway refused to call it a vegetable: he said it was such a delectable article, he wouldn't demean it that way.'

Although other growers have mechanized the picking of asparagus, it won't happen in Evesham. It will just gradually die out: field after field will be turned over to more economic crops, and the distinctive flavour of Evesham asparagus will be lost for ever. I remember the words of a Worcester farmer with his thoughts on a feed of grass: 'I'll be tripping over to Evesham one of these evenings very, very shortly, when my friend, Bert Haynes, gives me a ring to say he's got some ready: you see, it's a ritual this time of the year. When asparagus comes forward, we love it.'

There are other rituals, all but gone for good: the tradition, for instance, of the small brewery which made just enough beer for the ale-house attached to it. Four only, I am told, survive in the whole of England, and one is the Three Tuns at Bishop's Castle. The beer here is unpasteurized, unassisted into the glass by CO_2: it is made by John Roberts to a formula which hasn't changed much since his grandfather bought the place in 1888: 'He'd been a tea taster up in London, but he was also fond of beer and the city life didn't agree with him. So he came home to his parents, who were farmers, and, by chance, this pub came on the market and that's how he got into the business.'

Every ten days or so, John goes into his brewhouse and, single-handed, makes between five and six hundred gallons of beer, both mild and bitter. He uses local hops from Worcester or Hereford, and the quality of the ale he produces has made him one of the patron saints of CAMRA. Anti-keg men beat a path to his bar to savour the taste of real beer.

You might think that if the beer was so popular and so good, then the big breweries would want to emulate him. Why not? 'Well, it's like one of them said to me: "It's like going up to London. You wouldn't consider going up to London now on a stagecoach: things progress and the breweries are taking advantage of technology." I've got no laboratory and I'm no chemist, but if it smells good and looks good and tastes good, then I'm happy.'

And so are the patrons of the Three Tuns, fugitives to a man from the fizziness of mass-produced keg. The only bubbles in John Roberts' brew come from a natural fermentation: 'There's a second fermentation, which occurs in the barrel, and that is where you get the nice head in the glass and the natural sparkle in the beer itself.'

Fermentation plays a great part in the manufacture of the mysterious Worcestershire sauce which, along with porcelain and apples, puts Worcester on the map. According to local legend, the recipe was brought back from India by Lord Sandys, who went into a local chemist and ordered the ingredients to make the sauce. The chemist's assistant noted the order and tried to concoct the sauce himself. This is what happened, as they still tell it in Worcester:

'This young man, Kitson, his name was, put it down in the cellar, and, after a few months, he tasted it and thought it was horrible. Well, the chemist's was taken over by Hill Evans, who were vinegar people, and then it came time to clean out the cellar, and this fellow Kitson, being a bright young chap, found this stuff he'd made nine years before, and tasted it and thought it was beautiful. And a certain Mr Perrins also tasted it, and there was another fellow in the chemist's shop called Lea, who had a lot to do with it, so they decided to go into the business.'

The original Lea and Perrins Worcestershire Sauce has had so many imitators, from here to China and Japan, that, even today, the recipe is known to only two men, and the sauce is prepared behind locked doors. The head saucemaker refused to share his closely guarded secret, not a word would he utter. There is no chance of Worcestershire Sauce disappearing, but that is not true of a delicacy from the River Severn which hasn't been on sale in fishmongers' for years now.

Few men are catching them any longer, and the most successful, Phil Gaskins, is selling most of his to scientists for research. The lampern, as they call the river lamprey here, is an eel-like fish with seven little breathing holes and a sucker instead of a mouth. 'They used to be a big delicacy round here,' says Phil. 'And there's still a lot of old families that eats lampern pie.' Despite the fact that King Henry I died of a surfeit of lamperns, or perhaps, inspired seditiously by it, the townsfolk of Gloucester used to send a lampern pie to the reigning monarch every year until the early years of the nineteenth century. We went to watch Mrs George Packwood doing lamperns the way she and her husband like them. Lamperns are fiddly things to prepare: they take much more patience than frying fish fingers.

'First, you put some hot water on them and get the slime off 'em. You don't get 'em very often; they've been using 'em for universities, for experiments. Now I'm going to cut the trumpets off, that's the head, and get rid of the insides. Give 'em a nice rinse in cold water, and then I'll put them in a saucepan with some parsley, and stew them for 'bout 'alf an hour with a bit of pepper and salt. And then I thicken them with flour and milk. Some people cook 'em in a pie-dish in the oven, but I like to do 'em in a saucepan.'

They taste not unlike elvers or eels – gelatinous, unusual. Most people, even living on the banks of the Severn, have never tasted them; nobody is likely to die of a surfeit in the years to come. Mrs Packwood enjoys her lamperns in the shadow of Tewkesbury Cathedral; there are hollyhocks in the cottage gardens, lavender round the doors. A bit of Come-to-Britain country. Those who know these parts say it is not only the heart of England, but the most ancient and lovely part. Piers Plowman had his vision of England on the Malvern Hills in the fourteenth century, and from their heights ('If you look East, the next highest bit of land is Russia') you can see the plain of Worcester, stretching away in the haze to the Cotswolds, and to the West, the rolling landscape of Herefordshire. The food from this fertile land is classically English, the plums and apples of Pershore, and vegetables and soft fruit of Evesham, cider orchards, hop fields and grazing in rich pastures – the most efficient beef-making machinery in the world, the Herefords, of which local farmers are justifiably proud.

'Nobody comes to teach us our ways,' one of them says. 'There were Hereford cattlemen years ago, and there'll be Hereford cattlemen for years to come.'

There are Hereford descendants from China to the Urals, from Alaska to the Rockies: breeders come from fifty countries to choose their stock, and, likely as not, they will wind up for lunch or dinner in Tony Morrison's low, rambling farmhouse. He runs the Hereford Society, and he takes pride in the sirloin he serves at table: 'A lot of the meat you buy in a butcher's is slaughtered far too young; it hasn't been hung properly. It's probably off an animal that isn't going to eat tenderly, anyway. This meat has been hung for at least two weeks and, as you can see, it's so tender you can almost eat it with a spoon.' Tony Morrison points out the marbling in my slice: 'You can go into a butcher's in Paris and you'll see a very lean joint, with a bit of pork fat tied hopefully on the top. But good Hereford beef has fat interspersed with the lean; that is what gives it the flavour.'

Champion bulls fetch up to £3,000 each, and sales of Herefords are booming. These placid animals, grazing under oak and elm in the green fields of England, are part of picture-book England. But how long before economics change all that? There are food engineers who predict that, in quite a short time, sheep and cattle will no longer safely graze outdoors: they will follow the sad procession of calves and chickens and turkeys into the artificially lit, computer-controlled sheds, and be vitaminized and hormoned and programmed into bland portions for the freezer.

Not a day I want to see.

32. A Strong Streak of Irreverence

Dr Alan Long is one of the funniest and gentlest men I know; he bubbles with enthusiasm and mischief. It was his strong streak of irreverence that impelled him in 1933 'as an eight-year-old' towards what was then a ridiculed movement associated with sandals, nut cutlets, hiking and Higher Thought.

'My mother thought I should be exposed to various religious experiences and I used to attend a Sunday school where we always ended up with the 23rd Psalm, the Lord is my shepherd. One day, quite innocently, I asked the teacher did Jesus want to castrate us little boys because that's what the shepherd did to little male lambs? Well, that didn't go down too well! And I went on to ask whether Jesus in his role of shepherd wanted to send us to the butcher to be slaughtered. I got chucked out at that stage and my mother said, "If you don't want to eat lamb we won't have it." That was when I decided I'd rather see lambs in the field than fried and grilled on my plate.'

Alan remembers loving things like steak and kidney pie but by the end of the year, and just turned eight, he gave up eating meat and within months his parents had joined him.

'None of us knew a calorie from a protein at that time. It was more difficult for my father who was a civil servant. He was very daring and used to take wholemeal sandwiches to work; eating brown bread in those days was the equivalent today of coming out of the closet.'

Neighbours and relatives viewed the small boy's refusal to eat animals as almost subversive, certainly dangerous. 'There were people who said "That boy won't live!" If ever I got a cold it was put down to not eating meat. They couldn't understand why I wasn't anaemic. I had an aunt and when we went there my mother used to go in the kitchen and say, "Don't cook meat for him, he'll just have the vegetables." But it didn't work; she'd come in and say, "Look what auntie's cooked for you." I'd go a nasty shade of green and my mother would take some of the meat off my plate and I left the rest. There were all these pressures on vegetarians.'

After these forays into enemy country the Longs would retire home for a wholesome meal. 'I must say when I was a lad I used to enjoy nut cutlets. There were some dreadful tinned things which we tried to keep away from, mock sausage like rubber. But looking back we were really living on a Mediterranean diet. When the war broke out the one thing we had a lot of was brosemeal; it was really our equivalent of a curry. The Scots would normally put meat in it but we put lentils and beans. I often say to cookery writers why don't you write about brose, great stuff!'

After the war Alan took a degree in science, went to Cambridge to do a PhD on the germination of plants and became interested in the relationship between man and animals.

'By this time my mother, a pharmacist, had moved into making cruelty-free cosmetics. She hadn't very much time for the vegetarian movement which was very religious and airy-fairy. They attracted a lot of virtuous and ineffectual people and this irked us. Over the years I decided to look more closely at the food chain. Being a chemist I could comprehend the science of it. I spent the odd week working on farms and finding out more about the way in which our food was produced. When I ultimately got involved with the Vegetarian Society it was as a research adviser.'

In the 1960s Alan was instrumental in setting up the Vegetarian Nutritional Research Centre composed of vegetarians with a scientific and medical background. 'In London I organized a publicity and campaigning group. My theory was that it was no use collecting facts like stamps or butterflies and admiring them every now and again – facts should be able to explain things. Because we had no resources we did it mainly by putting out press releases and journalists came to trust us; they felt we knew what we were talking about and that we were objective. It wasn't just a flood of emotion.'

In 1976 Alan brought out a Green Plan for farming, food, health and the land which anticipated many of the ecology blueprints of the last few years. It laid out the alternatives facing the food and farming industry. This was unpaid work done in his spare time. 'We had a good group and we were doing some useful work, a lot of it centring on dietary health. We have a twelve-year study with Oxford university involving 6,000 vegetarians which is being done in conjunction with the NHS. That will tell us what vegetarians die of, how often they go to hospitals and what ailments they have.'

Already, halfway through this study, some interesting results are being thrown up. 'Generally vegetarians suffer from degenerative diseases a decade later than meat eaters and they spend much less time off work.' But Alan is keenly aware of the care you need to exercise in interpreting statistics. 'Although vegetarians might not visit their GP so often they might well be the sort of people who go to alternative or complementary practitioners. They wouldn't smoke or drink as much as ordinary people and would be more moderate in their habits; probably they take more outdoor exercise than other people and therefore they have a healthier style of life.'

I asked Alan about all these press releases which seek to prove that vegetarianism is a tidal wave engulfing the British Isles. I quoted a statistic released in May which claimed, improbably, that during 1990 28,000 people a week were converted to vegetarianism.

'I think that's very dodgy. What the figures ignore, if they are accurate, is the number of people *lapsing back* – there could have been 28,001 of those. I've seen a Ministry figure suggesting that one in three people was eating less meat. Supposing the other two were eating *more* meat? That wasn't mentioned.'

Probably one in a hundred vegetarians has moved to the logical end of the herbivore line and eschewed all forms of animal products. Alan is one, a self-professed vegan. 'I could do nothing else. I kept saying to my friends, if you just eat more eggs, butter and cheese instead of meat you're doing no good at all. Animals still suffer. We did surveys which established that vegetarians were eating as much animal fat as meat eaters. People don't seem to realize that dairying is just as intensive as poultry-rearing and pigkeeping and that it's less unkind to eat Aberdeen Angus beef from the Highlands where the calves run with their mums than take burgers from some unfortunate culled cow whose calf has been taken away in the interests of providing unwanted milk for the EC surplus of butter and cheese.'

Alan takes the view that vegetarians should campaign to decrease the consumption of animal products. 'I feel it's much better to reduce the eating of animal products by half than double the number of vegetarians.' He believes there's often just as much cruelty involved in producing a pound of cheese or a dozen battery eggs as in a pound of pork chops.

'Factory farming has been a great catalyst in moving people away from meat. Vegetarians, rather like reformed smokers, become supercharged with virtue when they give up eating meat. Many vegetarians like to argue that the meat industry acts against the interests of the Third World. That's a dubious argument; it involves a lot of politics and economics.'

Alan avoids climbing on comforting bandwagons and is not given to proselytizing but he is convinced that our preoccupation with paying as little for our food as possible has created the horrors of factory farming and an industry geared to turning out highly refined and meretricious food of low nutritional value. 'In my opinion it's much more prudent, healthy and sane to spend more of your outgoings on fresh food and less on holidays abroad and on your car.'

Alan is confident that the growing distaste of consumers for dubious technologies, many of them less than caring and compassionate towards animals, will make them valueless. He sees bovine somatotropin, the artificial hormone which increases the milk yield of cows, as a development which may implode on itself.

'We're on the verge of it being introduced here, because at the end of this year the EC is due to reconsider licensing it. But who knows? Already in the US where food irradiation is allowed supermarkets have rejected it; they know their customers won't touch it. I think that what will happen with BST is that supermarkets will say that they are not going to stock dairy products produced with the aid of BST because it just won't sell.'

Although modern packaging of meat distances shoppers from the bloodiness of the slaughterhouse Alan believes that we have created a generation increasingly uneasy about the meat industry. 'The massive daily slaughter of animals, the pollution they cause, all these things are becoming of great concern particularly to young people and their parents are more sympathetic than grown-ups were when I was a child.'

Although Alan is a mild man and does not take up extreme attitudes he is outspoken. Recently he upset the committee of the Vegetarian Society and is no longer a member.

'I was expelled,' he said. 'They started selling seals of approval to firms producing foods that I as a vegetarian didn't think merited them. I wasn't standing for that and I complained. They are quite incompetent.'

As a result of his lost battle with the Society Alan and his research supporters have set up a new breakaway group called VEGA, Vegetarian Economy and Green Agriculture.

Looking back over his sixty years Alan sees today's vegan as being in roughly the same position as a vegetarian in the Thirties. 'Eating out then meant you really got very little that was attractive; for a vegan it's equally difficult today.' Added to that is the semantic confusion which surrounds those who eat no meat but accept fish and wild game, those who avoid red meat but devour poultry and those who regard themselves as vegetarians but don't come within the meaning of Alan's definition.

'I've been trying to explain to people that the word vegetarian in medical and nutritional terms really means that you ought to be a vegan. These others, these renegades, are lacto-ovos. I call them the Luvvies, they're as inconsistent as demi-veggies who eat fish. People are so illogical. When BSE was rampant you'd find people who happily ate sausages and burgers saying, "I've given up beef!" But having said that I don't like the idea of going round telling people what they should eat.'

Alan doesn't use soap made from animal products neither does he wear leather about his person. He likes beer and wine with a meal, looks radiantly healthy and has a great capacity for mirth and laughter. He soaks his muesli in ginger wine, and plays a lot of squash and no doubt in the fullness of time will wear the bottoms of his trousers rolled.

33. Recreating Babette

New Yorkers have recently been paying large sums of money to eat a real meal based on the representation of a fictional meal from a film itself based on a short story. These circles within circles revolve around a story called *Babette's Feast* by the Danish writer Karen Blixen. It takes place in the early 1880s in the small town of Berlevaag, which lies at the head of a Norwegian fjord. Here live the ageing members of a puritanical sect who have long since renounced the pleasures of this world in favour of more permanent rewards in the New Jerusalem beyond the grave.

The Dean who founded this group had married late in life, and on his demise he left behind two unmarried daughters, who spent their tiny incomes on works of charity. When Babette, a French refugee, arrived on their doorstep they took her in, taught her how to cook their frugal meals of split cod and ale-and-bread soup, and indoctrinated her in their ascetic ways.

What in life seems natural and in fiction desperately contrived, as the departed Dean's 100th anniversary approached she won the *grand prix* of 10,000 francs in a French lottery. She begged the sisters to let her cook the birthday dinner for the few remaining members of the sect. Using all her money, she imported from France the materials for the most luxurious banquet ever seen in Berlevaag, for in her Parisian days Babette had been none other than the greatest culinary genius of the age and chef at the famous Café Anglais.

Only one of the guests, a General Loewenhielm, recognized the quality of the food and wine. He had dined frequently at the Café Anglais and as one dish followed another he marvelled at their perfection. The sisters and their other guests thought it was quite a nice dinner; the wines brought a flush to their abstemious cheeks and as the evening wore on they became quite charitable and almost human.

Gabriel Axel, who wrote and directed the Oscar-winning film of the book, fleshed out the meal and its preparation with great skill and it's his extended version, rounded off with cheeses and a *Baba au Rhum*, that they've been copying in New York. Last May, Christian Delteil, chef-patron of L'Arlequin in London, attempted it too and a few days ago he did an encore for the Australian Beefsteak and Burgundy Club, who push the culinary boat out once a month.

When Christian cooked the meal last year he ran into trouble from the Foreign Office and Greenpeace with the first course, potage à la tortue. Babette imported a live turtle, which was what you did in pre-conservation days, and although M. Delteil got his farmed turtle in frozen pieces from the Cayman Isles, not everyone was happy. As he says himself it's the herbs – basil, marjoram, sage, rosemary, savory and thyme – that really make the soup, the turtle flesh is just a garnish.

With her turtle soup Babette served the finest amontillado the General had ever tasted. At L'Arlequin we drank a twenty-five-year-old reserve from Sandeman. It was the *Blinis Demidoff au Caviar Russe* that really alerted the General to the serious nature of the occasion. M. Delteil's choice of caviar was Sevruga; the briny eggs, cut with sour cream, textured with pancake, were the kind of thing which, in Babette's book, called for a really grand champagne. Her fictional glasses sparkled with 1860 Veuve Clicquot which the puritans of Berlevaag mistook for lemonade. But it was lemonade which 'agreed with their exalted state of mind and seemed to lift them off the gound into a higher and purer sphere'. We went into orbit with the 1982 Veuve Clicquot and we didn't mistake it for lemonade.

The centrepiece of Babette's feast was *Caille en Sarcophage*, quail stuffed with *foie gras* and launched on a truffle sauce. What to drink with that? Babette squandered a small fortune on a barrowload of Clos Vougeot 1846. The Aussies settled for something much younger and we committed infanticide on the Clos Vougeot 1984. But then there was Babette's fruit and Gabriel Axel's cinematic *Baba au Rhum* and a Château Rieusse 1982.

Full marks to Christian Delteil and his brigade for a bold dash at Babette's feast. What it really needed, though, was a Babette audience. I suppose the nearest equivalent in Britain these days might be a group of Seceder elders in a remote Lewis township. But such gastronomic innocence is hard to find.

34. 'Death Valley is not noted for its Food'

On the map, Stove Pipe Wells looked like a good place to stay. To get there you drive through Yosemite, which was a bonus. The desert is an extravaganza of cactus and ominous weapons ranges. Bleached assemblages of shacks sport pioneering names like Lone Pine, Furnace Creek, Skull Pass and Silverpeak. Every few miles there's a tank of radiator water in case you boil dry in the noonday burn-up. Stove Pipe Wells − a gas pump, a store majoring in ice cream and Hershey Bars, and a motel − was so here-and-gone that had we not slowed we might have entered and left in a split second, recalling it only as a mirage.

The motel had a swimming pool. Did they have a room for the night? They sure did. 'You folks Australian or sump'n?' We were used to such misunderstandings. 'If we stayed here,' I said, 'could we have an evening meal?'

'No, we don't start food till October!' In mid-September that seemed a goldarned long time to wait.

'Where you folks heading?' said Madge, the motel clerk, in much the same vein of curiosity that she might have greeted a wagon train of Forty-niners. We were going, I said, to Scotty's Castle, a mini-San Simeon built by a Chicago millionaire before the Crash.

'Well, maybe on the way back you could go by way of Beatty. Coupla places there you could have yourselves a steak.' The detour she was proposing was equivalent to booking a room in Brighton and going to Cornwall for dinner. We walked across the desert to the store. There were some tacos crisps, an orange or two and three buns. Death Valley is not noted for its food.

Nor for that matter are large tracts of the Californian hinterland. That night we holed up in Ridge Crest, a town strung out along a highway and stretched to look like a metropolis. Even the private houses seemed to be hung with neon signs. El Charro Avitia was the eating scene, the grizzled oldster at the El Rancho motel told us: 'If you folks like to eat Mexican, that is.' We hadn't eaten Mexican since lunching with César and Elizabeth Ortiz in London. Mexican would be fine.

The cocktail bar at El Charro was swinging. It was eight in the evening but the Happy Hour seemed to have started somewhere round noon. Jumbo jugs of Gold Tequila Margaritas were on every table. The enchiladas, tostadas and tacos came in many combinations, all equally awful. The components appeared to have been spun-dried, emulsified, mixed with roofing felt and then steamed for several days. Had the manufacturer stuffed his tortillas with pre-soaked Chiffon toilet rolls and then poured Polycell over them, the effect would have been the same. The food clung desperately to the roof of your mouth like Evo-stik. Nobody could have achieved that embalmed and impersonal taste in a kitchen; the stuff must have arrived frozen from some bunker in the Midwest.

Wherever we went – Nibble Nook, the Fondue Pot, Mr K's Anchorage, El Matador, the Bun & Crust – it was difficult not to be overwhelmed by the courtesy and kindness, the slightly overdone oversell: 'Have a good dinner, now . . .' 'You must *enjoy* that fish . . .' 'How are you enjoying your lunches today? . . .' 'Is everything pleasant? . . .' 'Please enjoy your soup and salad . . .' 'Have fun, you folks!'

More often than not the food didn't live up to the verbal extravagance. In a landscape of Early Bird Gourmet dinners (4–6.30pm) anything goes, even Gourmet burgers. Twenty per cent of all food is wasted in America, where big helpings are essential: salads the breadth of a tropical rain forest precede marrow-sized Idaho potatoes and jumbo tenderloins.

The junk-food scene has so blanketed the land that muffled underground cries of protest are surfacing into an extraordinary movement dedicated to all that is fresh and pure. There is an almost hysterical reaction against factory food and the increasingly suspect technology of processing. In Cambria, on the coast, a young girl dressed like a pirate was weighing out a pound of apples for a young mother got up like an Indian squaw. 'Are they organic?' the mother asked. 'Sure. *Everything* is organic. 100 per cent *safe!*'

Fear is rife. On the morning we arrived in San Francisco a new scare broke on the *Today* show. Thinking Americans have been avoiding caffeine for years now. But research has dealt them a cruel blow. Rats fed on the chemical used in the decaffeination process have been exhibiting alarming carcinomas. Within a few hours, a rival team of researchers is being rushed into the studio (presumably by the coffee lobby) to prove that the earlier reports didn't mean a goddam thing.

Fear of diverticulosis, salt, sugar, nitrates, obesity and dairy products informs all purchasing decisions among the intelligentsia; even the janitor these days has taken up yoga and yoghurt. Hardly a day passes without the nation taking a sharp intake of breath as some new food hazard is revealed. It's become almost impossible to sell breakfast foods with sugar in them or chowders containing salt.

The paradoxes of America seem inexplicable. A vast consumption of carbohydrates and a boom in the slimming industry. Truly terrible franchised rubbish alongside restaurants of international standing. Nouvelle cuisine is now as firmly established a part of the West Coast scene as sourdough bread and there are wines to go with it. The Clift Hotel in San Francisco lists in its restaurant over 160 fine Californian wines, including no fewer than 24 Chardonnays and 62 Cabernet Sauvignons.

The most expensive wines on the Clift's list are Californian not French – a 1958 Cabernet Sauvignon from Beaulieu Vineyards at £75 is matched for price only by a 62 Château Margaux. Baron Philippe de Rothschild has gone into partnership with Robert Mondavi to produce a Napa Valley Cabernet which will sell for the same price as his own famous Château Mouton-Rothschild. Moët et Chandon have bought a Napa vineyard and their *chef des caves* flies in from Epernay each year to make the *cuvée* for an expensive sparkling wine. Françoise and Francis Dewavrin, who own the great Château La Mission Haut Brion, spend a part of the year now in the Napa Valley, where they have a substantial holding in the Conn Creek Winery. It has all given California a prestige beyond price. Moët imported a pupil of Bocuse in 1977 when they opened the doors of their gourmet restaurant of Chandon on Highway 29. Some of the best French wine in the world lies in air-conditioned Californian cellars. For sheer excitement and inspired gastronomic lunacy California is unbeatable. Where else could you buy a Gourmet Sandwich?

35. Hazan at the Cipriani

Not long ago there was a conference of cookery teachers in the States. How many of you, they were asked, have taken a Marcella Hazan class? Seventy per cent of the students put up a hand. Marcella has taught the joy of Italian eating all over the world; most often in Bologna and now in Venice where her seminars are always a sell-out.

In November steam is rising from the Cipriani's heated outdoor pool. Two dozen pupils have jetted in from all over to stay at the most sybaritic hotel in Europe and take away with them some of the Hazan magic. There's Rod and Sharon from Los Angeles, a parish priest from Boston, Richard and Alice from SW3. Helen runs a restaurant called Chez Oz in Sydney and Karen has a guesthouse in Kinsale.

At the cocktail party in the Cipriani and the banquet that follows we get to know each other. Jennifer, cool and Lauren-dressed from Park Avenue who most weekends flies down to Aspen; Vincent the wise-cracking attorney from Wayne, Pennsylvania, and Charlotte from Dripping Springs: 'You English just collapse when I tell where I'm from.'

A couple have previously attended a Hazan masterclass in Bologna and will in the next few days mention this fact frequently. Others hardly know how to pod a pea. Marcella lights a filter-tipped Vantage and takes a reflective sip of her favourite Jack Daniel's on the rocks. Her voice is husky and mirth is never far away.

'Some of these people, sometimes I think they're pulling my leg. We were making this dish one day and a woman said, "How long can you keep it?" How long do you want to keep it, I say? She thinks a bit and says, "Indefinitely!" So I answer why do you make it?'

Marcella shrugs and laughs. 'And then we were having this class once and there was a woman doing nothing so I gave her a bowl and two eggs and asked her to separate them. She looked at them for a time and then carefully moved one six inches away from the other!' More laughter.

Victor and Marcella talk us through the meal and the wines. Discuss the merits of the *anti-pasti Veneziani*, the finer points of the *risotto di funghi porcini* and the *scampi griglia*.

On the first morning of the course we are due to meet Victor just beyond the Rialto bridge to be taken on a conducted tour of the fish and produce market. The private launch from the Cipriani is a bit adrift and so are we. Victor is miffed. 'This is the first time in ten years that anyone has been late for the market,' he says coldly. 'Another minute and I would have gone.' That would have been a pity for Victor is an impassioned guide. He takes us past the shining mounds of crab, shrimp, prawn, eel, octopus and molluscs dispensing culinary anecdotes, history and folklore. 'This is every bit as much a national treasure', says Victor sweeping an expansive hand over the stalls of silver lagoon fish, 'as any work of art you'll see in Venice.'

And then the meat. Americans used to sanitized pre-packs gaze numbly at viscera, tiny trotters, caul, lungs, intestines, the bleeding heads of baby lambs, the bowls of coagulated blood. 'Oh my Guard,' says Mary Jo from Mississauga, 'isn't this something other!'

At 4.30 on the dot in the Cipriani's Sala Palladio overlooking the great masterpiece of S. Giorgio Maggiore, Marcella taps her watch and begins the first of her four lessons. Dressed in a green outfit and a white apron she will cook a dinner for the twenty-four of us. She is assisted by Maria, an unsmiling and silent presence disturbingly reminiscent of Dame Edna's Madge.

As she indicates the pasta, the lamb, onions, the silvery white leaves of the cardoons and the herbs Marcella lays down the ground rules.

'I always teach a meal. We give no recipes. You want recipes, you have the books. The recipe is the starting-point for teaching. I never measure – I tell you about cooking not chemistry.'

Marcella is direct and often very funny. In the next four days she will talk and teach us about pasta, olive oil, fish, meat, soups, desserts, rice and cheese. Her approach is pragmatic and highly adaptable. 'Nothing wrong with canned tomatoes,' she says, 'they make a wonderful sauce. Don't bother clarifying butter, just add a little olive oil.' We learn how to give the kiss of life with a damp cloth to a wheel of parmesan and bestow the kiss of death on the grated stuff you buy in supermarkets: 'Better you should buy sawdust, it tastes the same. I had the president of the Kraft company in one class and I don't think he liked that.' We laugh. We laugh too, but not unkindly, when after the *agnello al ginepro* goes on to the stove Gloria from Mt Laurel asks how long it will take to cook. Marcella looks mystified: 'Until it's cooked, what else?'

At six we break for a tasting of Valpolicellas. Victor shows us how to look at wine, appraise it and enjoy it. He has produced a distinguished example made from the *corvina* grape. Then we sit down to eat the dinner which we've watched Marcella prepare: *penne* with sausage and peppers, the juniper lamb and a *torta* made with carrots and unskinned almonds. 'Eating is about taste, texture, colour, everything,' Marcella tells us. 'There is only one goal and that is that food must taste good.' We discuss the relentless pursuit of novelty which mars so much modern cooking. 'In America if they're serving the same menu this month as last it's professional suicide, but what is at the heart of Italian food is repeating the same dish for decade after decade. People are happy because there is comfort in the familiar.'

During the week we will learn about which pasta are best made at home and which are the ones it's best to buy. Always the meal must reflect the produce in the market. 'If Victor goes to the market and this or that is not there then we change the meal.' The classes are relaxed. Although we learn about the practicalities of cleaning fish and making a perfect risotto it is the Italian approach to cooking, the ethos of food, that the Hazans teach.

On Wednesday we work through *pappardelle al ragu* (home-made noodles with meat sauce), braised beef shank and a *soricciolona*, a crumbly almond cake. By Thursday everyone is thinking Italian and we're on to *teglia di cozze* (mussels, potatoes and tomatoes baked in the oven), a baby shark stew, an *insalata di finocchio* and Ricotta fritters. On the last day a *risotto* followed by chicken with red cabbage, green beens marinated with oregano and *Monte Bianco*, a chestnut and chocolate purée with whipped cream. 'Just look at that,' says the ambassadress from Dripping Springs, 'yum yummy!'

Inoculated with sound principles and a new mission to seek out the freshest produce and treat it with traditional respect we pack for home. We have seen how to achieve the most satisfying results in the simplest possible way. As Marcella reminds us, 'What you keep out is as important as what you put in.'

36. Coca-colonialism

In Colonial days in Singapore the most pervasive influence was, of course, British. There was cricket on the Padang, long curry tiffins on Sunday and a selection of old school ties in the Tanglin Club. 'A first-rate place,' noted Noël Coward unkindly, 'for third-rate people.' Then came Independence in 1959. The Union Jack was hauled down and gradually the British moved out.

'For a hundred years you exploited the place,' an old Singaporean friend of mine said, smiling, 'and then what happened?' What happened, according to him, was that the vacuum left by the British was filled by entrepreneurs who rushed in from all points of the compass. Today you see few British products on sale. The Germans are much in evidence and the Japanese are everywhere but, above all, Singapore has the feel of America. Descending in the express lift from the twenty-third floor of the Hilton, a recorded voice announces in an American accent that you will shortly plummet to the 'larby'. In the lobby you could be in Dallas or Houston. Here is the Bell Captain smiling warmly and telling you to have a good day; here is the ubiquitous Conrad Hilton coffee house and all the other manifestations of the American consumer society.

Walk down Orchard Road and you could be in California. Everywhere are shopping plazas and hotels straight out of *Dallas* – Sheraton, Holiday Inn and Hyatt. On one corner is the cut-out figure of Colonel Sanders, the fried-chicken messiah, and beyond the bougainvillaea is the plastic façade of one of the island's sixteen McDonald's franchises.

In this city of endlessly exciting local fast foods like *satay, char okay toh, roti chanai, mee hoon, poh piah* and *mah mee*, the burger is king, and it's washed down with slush drinks and shakes. Over the causeway is another outpost of the Coca-colonialists. The first American fast-food enterprise, an A&W outlet was opened in Kuala Lumpur in 1963; in 1972 Kentucky Fried Chicken came to Petaling Jaya. Malaysia was the site of Popeye's first overseas franchise and Wendy, too, chose the Malaysian capital for its commercial début in South-East Asia. They were followed by Shakeys, Orange Julius and, of course, that all-time great, McDonald's.

Robert Kwan, the young Chinese *taipan* who controls the McDonald's empire in Singapore, is already a millionaire. As in the other 9,300 outlets worldwide, you get the same bun in Singapore as you do in Paris or London. The faces behind the counter are Chinese, Malay, Indian and Eurasian but the commitment is 100 per cent American.

Kwan's marketing manager is an elegant livewire Chinese lady called Loretta Lee, a proud graduate of the $40-million Hamburger University in Illinois. 'One of the reasons for our success,' she told me as she surveyed the crowded tables and the eager young crew toiling over the chip-pans and the sizzling grills, 'is that we've imported everything from the US. It's the ambience; nice music, it's clean. It's a kind of lifestyle the young readily accept. We have a Western imported image, and the advertising and marketing programmes support all that.'

Behind Loretta, through the open door of the crew-room, I spied a notice which read: 'Hey, crews! Chant TWO ALL BEEF PATTIES, SPECIAL SAUCE, LETTUCE, CHEESE, PICKLES, ONION ON A SESAME SEED BUN in three seconds and win $5 in cash!' 'Oh yes,' said Loretta, 'that's great. We had a mammoth crew rally yesterday; we had chant rallies and things to be won. It was just a great hype for a new promotion we broke today.' Loretta demonstrated her skill and raced through the sesame bun chant in 2.9 seconds. 'It is fun, isn't it?' She laughed and clapped her hands like a child. 'And it should be. McDonald's is food, folks and fun and you don't stray away from that!' She repeated the formula as if it were a magic rune: 'Food, folks and fun all of the time.'

But doctors in this overcrowded republic are becoming increasingly worried by the popularity of imported Western foods rich in starch and sugar and low in fibre. Mrs Tan Wei Ling, a public health nutritionist, told me that in the last two decades the consumption of meat has gone up tremendously. 'Eggs and dairy produce have led to a great increase in the intake of saturated fats and cholesterol. We have a rising curve of cardiovascular disease and certain cancers. Obesity too has become a problem. People making school uniforms tell us that more and more children are ordering large sizes. Ten years ago, obesity among our five-year-olds was about 5 to 6 per cent; today we are seeing 10 to 12 per cent and it's rising.'

The Singapore government, which has already been forced to open clinics for obese schoolchildren, has set up a national advisory committee to look into food and nutrition policy, and is trying to persuade Singaporeans that the old Chinese notion that to be fat is to be happy has no place in a healthy modern community. Meanwhile the commercials on TV and radio for Western fun-foods are relentless. As I packed my bag to fly to Penang a catchy jingle singing the virtues of a curry pizza topped with beef and lamb appeared on the television screen: 'Just right for you and me at all Milano Pizza restaurants. You get more than just pizza; warm smiles too and lots of other goodies.' The medical profession is not so sure that there are any goodies in the new wave of junk food that is sweeping the island, but there is little they can do about it.

37. Memories of Other Places

In the very American Plaza Hotel dining-room in Tel Aviv the waitress who puts the bill down on the table has the purple numerals of Auschwitz on her wrist; in a moshav in the 'Arava Desert the automatic rifles (his or hers?) are stacked tidily beside the hi-fi; at Ein Gedi, where it is said David fled from Saul's wrath, there are chain-link fences, minefields, studious-looking armed guards, gun in one hand, book in the other.

Everywhere you go in Israel you are reminded of the past five wars, and there is a sad feeling of inevitability about the next. Much of our filming (for BBC Scotland's *The Food Programme*) is done on the West Bank within sight of Jordan. I am reminded of Malaya during the Emergency. Everything is absolutely normal, except, suddenly, you may be killed.

On the Wednesday morning, Mike Marshall, Israel Ben-Zeev and I take it in turns to float on the saline waters of the Dead Sea. I have found a copy of the *Financial Times* in my briefcase, and Israel, sales promotion director of Agrexco, holds the pink pages poised above the water as the sun comes up pinkly over unfriendly Jordan. It is like floating in olive oil or Polycell.

Agrexco is the non-profitmaking export association which markets the fruit and vegetables of Israel. The growth in exports is prodigious: strawberries, capsicums, avocados, onions, radishes, potatoes, celery, Chinese leaves, carrots, lettuces. Production is geared to make the most of the country's year-long sunshine. While northern Europe lies fallow, the Israeli desert is ripe with tomatoes. Air-freighted to Frankfurt, sent by sea to Marseilles, they are now, under the Carmel label, a familiar sight in every greengrocer's from Glasgow to Geneva.

If you go to Sedom, Jericho, Jerusalem, Beersheba, as we did, you can't help running into the tourists. Elderly American mummies and daddies, mainly Jewish but bolstered by Christians, walking with their cameras where He walked. At Beersheba, outside the Desert Inn, a party of oldsters from Columbus, Ohio, are embussing for Day Six. I ask a nice old party where they are off to: 'We don't know where we are going today,' she says, looking pleasantly unfazed. 'You'll have to ask Reverend Beauchamp; he's our guide.'

The P15s streak over the flat summit of Masada, last stronghold in the Jewish revolt against the Romans. 'There will never', says our driver, 'never be another Masada.' Earlier that morning, when I get in the Mercedes, I sit on a hard metallic object in Yossi Tzafrir's jacket pocket. It's a James Bond type automatic. Unused to arms, I read the name with curiosity. Beretta. The driver of the other car carrying the Israeli film crew, not to be outdone, flashes a Smith and Wesson. He unloads it before handing it over for inspection. The bullets are big and ugly, like horse suppositories.

Always the ambivalent images of war and peace: onions sprouting beside burnt-out weapon carriers; hundreds of hitch-hiking soldiers in Castro-green; barbed wire; the sudden glimpse of isolated outposts on hill-tops; the roads to Jordan that end with *Keep Out Danger* notices.

In the hotel on the salt-encrusted shores of the Dead Sea, a party from Chicago are being debriefed after a dairy dinner. 'Today,' their leader tells them in the tones of a very patient teacher addressing the hard of hearing, 'you have climbed up to wonderful Masada and seen Herod's truly wonderful fortress. You stopped at Jericho for lunch, that's where you had the fresh orange juice, remember?' They nod vigorously. The past has been unrolling like some in-flight movie for days and they all look ready for bed.

Jerusalem lives up to the expectations aroused by Hugh Burnett's gently ironic TV documentary about tourism in the Holy Land. Inside the Church of the Holy Sepulchre, my

Jewish guide and I watch in some astonishment while two Armenian priests argue about who should dowse the candles. One hits the other with his broom, an unholy scene in this Christian holy of holies. In the Church of the Nativity, a party of American Protestants with joined hands are singing a carol round the supposed site of the manger. Tears stream down the cheeks of one of the women, tears of emotion.

At the Western Wall, the devout are dressed in sepulchral black. Were it not for their long, curling ringlets descending from beneath shovel hats, and were it not for the burning sun, I might imagine myself to be in Stornoway. Indeed, when, after a long day's filming, we get back to the hotel in Tel Aviv on Friday evening, everything purchasable has been locked up. The copies of *Newsweek* and the *Washington Post* have been spirited away. I try to buy some cards. 'Everything closed, sir,' says the reception clerk. Just like Stornoway on a Saturday evening, all shuttered for *Shabbat*.

But if, at times, it reminds one of the island of Lewis, Israel makes me feel very much at home, principally because most of the people I meet seem just to have arrived from London. Beny Barjec, the assistant cameraman, talks most of the time about the girls in Belsize Park; Dov Eckstein, the sound recordist, reckons there is no place like Oxford Street.

On my arrival at the Plaza in Tel Aviv, my bag is seized by a pint-sized version of Jonathan Miller. 'Nick', his badge announces. 'Where you from, then?' he says, going up in the lift. 'Streatham?' He is from West Wickham; he loves it in Tel Aviv and talks to me for twenty minutes about London.

The following evening, David is on duty by the swing doors. 'Hi, how'd the filming go? You know we had Peter Snow here last week. Great.' He comes from Hammersmith and talks about salt beef sandwiches and all the things he misses. I ask him, and immediately wish I hadn't, why if he's so homesick he stays? 'I came out to fight in the Yom Kippur War and then my wife died. Anyway, take care, have a good time.'

There are lots of things I cannot get used to, like coming down for breakfast at 6.30 in the morning and finding everything set out for lunch. A big buffet of cucumbers, lettuce, tomatoes, yoghurt, sliced cheese, herrings, green peppers, olives, gherkins and hard-boiled eggs. And the ambulances all have commercials on them ('Donated by Heim and Ruthie Kellenberger of Brooklyn in memory of Rebecca Kellenberger') and the ethos is confusing. Is this a suburb of Los Angeles (the white concrete and bougainvillaea, the neat lawns say so) or is it a frontier outpost (the bomb shelters in the kibbutzim, the slit trenches say so). And you must learn not to talk in a British way about 'the last war'. 'Which last war?' says Yossi. 'We've had five!' And you recall that one of them was against us. The Hall of Heroism (open daily 10 a.m.–5 p.m.) still features the condemned cell and gallows set up by the British for Jewish underground fighters.

There is plenty to do in Israel. Free tours leave for the Judaean Hills every Monday and Wednesday, so that you can fulfil Leviticus ('And when you come into the land you shall plant all manner of trees') and Plant A Tree With Your Own Hands. Drive through the Negev, green with winter wheat, and you might think you were in Norfolk; lunch in Caesarea and you could be in Italy. It's a cross between a beleagured garrison and a biblical Las Vegas minus the decadence.

Visiting any country which is devoting a huge part of its income and energy to military preparedness cannot be anything other than depressing. The miracle of making the desert green turns sour when you do the arithmetic of survival: all the hundreds of thousands of tons of fruit and vegetables exported this year would only buy four jet fighters. As one Israeli put it: 'Of course, it's depressing to have to channel most of one's energy into defence. Who wouldn't have a desalination plant in preference to a squadron of jets?'

In the week of our visit, Cairo affirmed its intention to destroy Israel. Desalination plants will be a low priority for a long time to come.

38. A Scottish Heroine

There is no best book, which is why the Booker Prize never makes sense. But if I were asked to name the best book ever written about Scottish food there would be no doubt in my mind. My award would go to F. Marian McNeill for *The Scots Kitchen*. I wonder how many Scots know her name? There's certainly no memorial in her native island which may say more about the national lack of interest in food than about the great lady herself.

Florence Marian McNeill was born a daughter of the manse in Holm, Orkney, in 1885 and she spent her childhood in the islands. She studied in Paris and the Rhineland, took an MA in Glasgow, painted energetically and during the Great War was a social worker in London. In the Second World War she was a member of the government's advisory committee on Scottish rural housing and later found time to found the Clan McNeill Association.

Already a full and varied life but there were books as well: an excellent history of Iona, a novel *The Road Home* and between 1957 and 1958 the publication of her four-volume work on folklore and national festivals *The Silver Bough*. But it's *The Scots Kitchen*, never out of print, that remains her most popular work. It appeared first in 1929, an authoritative masterpiece which combined recipes, lore, literary allusion, history and social comment and created a literary form which later writers like Dorothy Hartley, Elizabeth David and Jane Grigson were to explore so profitably.

You can't help feeling that Marian McNeill wrote her classic just in time. Even then, at the end of the 1920s, she was lamenting the decline of good home cooking in Scotland: 'The old women say there is neither the variety there used to be nor the respect for quality.' In 1932 she put together her *Book of Breakfasts* and in 1956 came the companion-piece to the food book, *The Scots Cellar*, which traced the role drink has played in Scottish life through the centuries in songs and poems, oral traditions and tales of tavern life. The book is awash with a distinguished heritage of intemperance, open-handed hospitality and the genial pursuit of grape and grain.

There are separate chapters on the three great Scottish drinks, ale, whisky and claret, and offbeat accounts of libations long extinct. What, one wonders, did heather ale taste like or Ypocras the hot spiced claret which sixteenth-century Edinburgh burgesses drank on Yule day with gilded gingerbread in the form of demons and dragons? Why did country folk stop making stoorum, bee-ale, blenshaw, caudle green whey, kirn milk and soorocks? And if we did try to create *skeachan* in the way Meg Dods did with molasses, hops and fresh beer-yeast would we actually enjoy it?

In *The Scots Kitchen* Marian McNeill quotes the distinguished dietician Lord Boyd-Orr who pointed out that until the industrial revolution 'the people of Scotland were eating natural foodstuffs. With the introduction of machinery natural foodstuffs have been changed into artificial foodstuffs, with the very substances purified away that the Almighty put there to keep us in perfect health.' Sadly a lot of the recipes and traditions of the past have disappeared – now that we all eat the same things *The Scots Kitchen* is a bit of a period piece.

How nice it would be to taste some of the old Christmas fare which we've all forgotten about. In olden times preparations for 'the daft days' between Yule and Hogmanay included the baking of festive ale. Yule bread was a thin bannock of oatmeal moistened with the water poured off sowans. These cakes were baked before daybreak on Christmas morning when each member of the family was given one. The idea was to keep it intact until the evening feast – if it remained whole then unbroken prosperity was guaranteed for the rest of the year.

How nice to taste deer's pudding (a gamey version of haggis), goose blood pudding or Yule mart. This last delicacy was prepared by families who lived a long way from butcher shops. They would buy a bullock and pickle the joints in rock salt and sugar and feast off it in the dark days of winter.

And whatever happened to Het Pint, the traditional Hogmanay wassail bowl which was carried through the Edinburgh streets in copper toddy kettles and pressed on all and sundry with cries of 'a gude New Year to ane an' a'? Het Pint was a cocktail of mild ale, whisky, beaten egg and sugar served scalding hot – *and free!*

Of the long list of Hogmanay treats of the past (cheese and oat-farles, goose pie, plum porridge and sowans only a few remain. Shortbread, currant loaf, gingerbread and black bun are still with us. A proper black bun must contain big blue raisins, currants, sweet almonds, orange, lemon and citron peel, Demerara sugar, cloves, ginger, Jamaica pepper, buttermilk, eggs, brandy, flour and water – don't settle for less.

Maybe the old dishes haven't survived because tastes have changed. One favourite still with us (these days there's even a vegetarian version) is the Hogmanay haggis. There is something about the solidity, the pepperiness, the savoury goodness of haggis that puts it into the ranks of Great Dishes of the World. The finest liver I've ever tasted came from a Red Deer and I'm told that deer haggis is the ultimate experience. Marian McNeill has a recipe which comes 'from the kitchen of a Highland Chief'. You need, besides the liver, the deer's heart and suet, a teacup of coarse oatmeal, three finely chopped onions, a tablespoon of salt and a strong seasoning of black pepper. You put the ingredients into a basin, cover with paste as for a beef-steak pudding and boil for four hours. You serve it not in a skin but piping hot in its basin. And with it you should drink good Leith claret. What a dinner that would be!

The Scots Kitchen has just been issued by The Mercat Press (£9.95). Marian McNeill revised and expanded her original book in 1963 and you may be lucky enough to run one down – it appeared as a Granada paperback in 1974.

39. The Cheese and the Chine

It is hunting country, the Shires; fat land that produces Melton Mowbray pies and Stilton cheese; cheesemaking and pig-rearing have always gone hand in hand.

Jack Bailey makes up to 600 Melton Mowbray pies a day. His father opened the shop in 1905.

'In the old days, when I was a kid, everybody in the village killed a pig in about February. We always walked them down to Albert Pearce's to have them killed on a Monday. You had fatter pigs then; in those days, nobody ever dreamt of killing a pig under about twenty-two stone. These pigs used to have large layers of fat, and the fat was rendered down to make the lard for the pies. The ladies used to swap houses – go and make pork pies here, fries there, and scratchings – that's a little bit of skin with salt and vinegar on. And they'd make brawn. Maybe you'd finish up with a pantry full of pork pies and give them away to somebody else; when they killed a pig, they'd give you back a pie. The traditional pie was chopped meat, as opposed to minced, and the crust was raised by hand.

'The recipe is a family one, probably about 200 years old. We get meal-fed pigs, so that the pork always tastes the same, and it gives you a nice, light-coloured, firm pork. We slaughter our own pigs and we hang the meat so that it tenders itself. The ideal for a pork pie is a good leg of pork and back fat. We aim for two-thirds lean and one-third fat, so when the pie is cooked and cold, you've got a nice marbling of fat. When we've got it minced up, we just add pepper and salt. Some people put a flavouring in, but if you've got good pork and good pastry, you don't need anything to distract from the natural flavour.'

The real Melton Mowbray pork pie is encased in a boiled crust. 'You boil your lard with your water and then mix in the flour and a bit of salt. You get a nice nutty flavour when you've finished with it. The filling is done by hand, and you pack it as you go along. In the large factories, of course, it's all done by machine. Then you put your lid on and make a little hole in the middle and three holes round the side so that the steam can come out. We egg the tops and sides to give it a nice brown colour.'

Now and again, Jack Bailey gets a request from an old customer for a 'real' pie, one where the meat is cubed, not minced. Working on the scale they do, they normally have to mince the meat, but they like to oblige whenever they can. The jelly for the pies should be made from pig's feet: 'They've got a nice porky flavour and they make a lovely solid jelly. There's nothing better than a piece of pork pie for Christmas morning breakfast; then you can go for your Christmas walk on a nice frosty morning and come back and have your pint of beer and you feel as if you've started the day well.'

In the Shires, they like to make their cheese in the traditional way, too. They say a good Stilton deserves butter and a bad one needs it. For over 300 years, they were made in small amounts in farmhouses, and even now the making of a good Stilton needs the care of craftsmen – you can't automate Stilton. John and Peter Stockdale put seventeen gallons of milk into each of their cheeses which, when fully matured, have a mild, rich flavour and a velvety, flaky texture.

'There's a myth going about that the blue veins in the cheese are created by the introduction of copper wires, but that's all nonsense. The spores are actually in the room where the cheeses mature; the more spores you have, the more blue mould you have in the cheese. In the farmhouses, they used to leave the cheeses and hope they'd go blue. Nowadays, the cheese is pierced with stainless steel wires when it's between five and six weeks old; this allows oxygen to get in so the mould can grow.'

When the cheeses are young, they have to be turned by hand every day, even on Sundays, so that they don't acquire a barrel shape. The Stockdales react violently when misguided connoisseurs put port in the cheeses: 'Instead of finishing up with a nice blue-white flaky cheese, it goes purple and discoloured and it doesn't look like a cheese at all. We say: eat the cheese and drink the port.' And they point out that the most wasteful way to serve a Stilton is with a spoon. If you start spooning a hole in a half-Stilton, you'll probably end up by wasting more than half of it. It should be cut across the top and kept level. Stilton is now protected by a patent, and it can be made only in Derbyshire, Nottinghamshire and Leicestershire.

But it was to Lincolnshire that we went for the most unusual dish of the whole programme – something I had never heard of, let alone tasted. It comes from the Fens and, like the Melton Mowbray pie, it is based on the pig – and the bigger the better. Stuffed chine is served at harvest home suppers, at New Year parties and May Day feasts, and Jonquil and Alan Gilbert prepared one for us. 'A chine is the joint taken from between the shoulders just behind the head, and, in the old days, it used to get very dry when they had them hanging up in the kitchen, and it didn't eat particularly well, so they had this idea of stuffing it with herbs and all sorts of things, and then it just became parsley.'

You can buy stuffed chine at the butcher's, but it is very expensive. Best, if you can, to make your own. You cure the joint for three weeks in brine, and then hang it for at least three to four months. 'Round here, most people have a chine about October. You don't need any particular kind of pig, but you do really need a large one to get a decent-sized chine. This chine off one of our own pigs weighs about eleven pounds and I'll need about five pounds of parsley.'

Mrs Stockdale scores the pork in deep cuts which go right through the meat, and then she begins packing the parsley in, and nothing else. Some traditionalists use onion and herbs and a few raspberry and blackcurrant leaves, but not the Stockdales. 'How did I learn? Watching my mother, I suppose. You wouldn't think all that parsley would go in, but it chops down to nothing and, once inside the joint, it disappears and goes to nothing. The great thing is to cut right down to the bone. I've never seen it done anywhere except in Lincolnshire. There was a couple of Yorkshire people used to come here, and the man said he liked bacon all right, but he didn't like all that grass stuffed in it. A lot of housewives today wouldn't be bothered – they just want convenience foods, but I think when you live out in the country, you look for something a little bit better.'

Both sides of the chine are stuffed, and then it is sewn up in a cloth which will help to keep the parsley in. 'Years ago, it wasn't put in a cloth, it was baked in the oven in a barley paste. Now it's ready for the pot. I'm going to boil it for three and a half hours, then I'll leave it to cool all night and not touch it until the following day when it's well set.' The chine is carved in thin slices and served cold. You sprinkle it with vinegar and, ideally, you should eat it with pickled marsh samphire, the poor man's asparagus, which still grows on the desolate beaches of the east coast. And if you're eating your chine around Easter, you should drink Shrove Tuesday Ale with it: beer sweetened with sugar and honey, with sliced cooking apples floating in the bowl to give it tartness.

40. 'Gents' and Loos

I'm told British Rail is phasing out its dining cars; they will vanish valiantly defending a world which no longer exists elsewhere. On a recent journey to the West Country, I was delighted to notice that the scarlet-jacketed stewards were in fighting form. The service is still reminiscent of an army mess; for convenience, all male customers are called 'gents', as in 'You gents taking coffee?' or 'Any of you gents like an extra spud?' Women tend to be addressed by elderly attendants as 'dear', as in 'Can you move your bag, dear?' or 'More sauce, dear?'

As the train gathered speed through Reading, the bulky major-domo swayed down the car soliciting orders for aperitifs. The gents at the next table were ordering two gins-and-tonics, a lager and a Guinness when an extremely elegant woman entered the coach. She could have been a merchant banker, a UN functionary or the head of a fashion house. 'Just a minute, dear,' said the scarlet one, and finished taking the order from the four business gents; then, with the avuncularity of a lollipop man assisting a child, he said, 'Now, dear, sit over there, will you.'

By this time, we had decided to have one course, the fish. As there were two of us and as we didn't want a drink before the meal, I ordered a bottle of Waverley Vintners' rather good white Bordeaux. It didn't seem an intemperate or excessive demand. 'A FULL bottle, sir?' queried the steward in a parade-ground boom. 'Well, I don't want a half empty one,' I said to jolly him along. 'Right then! And your starter?' I said we weren't going to have a starter. He blew out a lot of air through his lips, made a note on his pad and announced our order to the rest of the restaurant car: 'Full bottle of van blonk and NO STARTERS.'

It would be nice to report that the fish was nice, but nice it was not. The frozen carrots and beans, although colourful, tasted only of the water they had been sitting in since leaving Paddington; but full marks for the Cheddar, the crisp, crunchy celery and that FULL bottle of wine. Perhaps someone should compile for visitors a manual on eating out in Britain – the pecking order, the modes of address, the put-downs, the one-upmanship. When, for instance, to cut your losses and run. Difficult to do on a train but easy enough in a restaurant when the menu turns out to be from Thawmeals Ltd and the staff gaze incuriously out of the window as they address you. Time then to announce that you suddenly feel unwell and will have to leave – offering always to pay for any napkin unrolled, any roll broken.

Experienced travellers know from the choice on the menu whether the food is going to be freshly cooked or dredged from the freezer for a quick resuscitation in the microwave. But how do you tell whether fresh is going to be good?

We were taken a few weeks ago to a restaurant in south Norfolk which had a friendly write-up in *The Good Food Guide* and the red crossed knives and forks in *Michelin* reserved for *restaurants agréables*. It was one of those places where you had to ring the front doorbell to get in; a ploy which gives promise of the bespoke. We were shown into a parlour where a couple were already sitting with sweet sherries, poring over the menu. The curtains hung in folds and every available surface held Victorian relics. There were stuffed animals in glass coffins, exotic birds under tall domes, shell-encrusted bibelots, oleographs, aspidistras, dried flowers, embroidery, knick-knackery and Hinge and Bracketry.

More people arrived. 'You must see the loo,' whispered one. 'It's a hoot!' It seemed to me that some of the patrons had come more for the fixtures and fittings than the food. With our drinks, a young woman brought some small and delicious puff-pastry things. The menu was inventive, unusual; the *Guide* talked of the chef's 'flair'.

The first courses when they came were memorable. They were served by a waiter dressed casually in a jumper, to match his casual approach. The fetching and carrying of dishes was not, one felt, really his 'thing' at all. My host, a serious amateur cook, asked about the sauce on his fish. Did he detect dill or was it something else? 'I wouldn't know,' said the Jumper. 'I don't eat here. I eat at Jack and Eileen's.' We asked who Jack and Eileen were. 'They run the fish and chip shop down the road.' It was put-down time.

The main courses, a chicken breast, some veal, a beef stew, were not worth eating. The strident sauces could not mask the tastelessness of the meat. My host explained courteously to the waiter why we were not bothering to finish the food. There was no response, no interest. The puddings were excellent and the loo really was a hoot – a cross between Miss Haversham's boudoir and Act III of *Gaslight*. The bill was £80. Perhaps it was an off night backstage, but when you can't make up your mind whether you're running an antique shop or a restaurant, where are you? In the *Good Loo Guide* certainly (three crossed legs), but not, I feel, in *The Good Food Guide*.

41. For a Few Dollars More

In Ukraine and Russia the dollar rules. It fuels the black market and dominates the economy, everyone seems to be salting bucks away as if they hold the key to eternal happiness. To get out of the airport in Kiev cost us $50 a head. Even in restaurants accepting roubles the drinks can only be bought for dollars. If you've got a film crew in tow you need a suitcase of ready money to grease your way round a country which appears to have embraced corruption at every level.

In Moscow we hear surreal stories of the gangster economy. There are alleged to be 20,000 Russians in the city who have become dollar millionaires. A young Muscovite fashion journalist told me how on a recent trip to London she had been taken to a gambling club in Mayfair. 'There were ten players at the high stake table,' she said, 'two Japanese, two Saudis and six Russians.'

In Kiev and Moscow swarthy-looking mafiosi hang round the bars doing deals in dollars – for dollars anything is possible. We hear about the TV news outfit anxious to film on board a nuclear submarine; a deal is easily fixed with $2,000 in an envelope delivered to the admiral of the base. A British TV crew in Moscow to shoot a documentary about corruption want to interview the head of the anti-corruption bureau – his fee in notes is $500.

The dollar makes life possible and as the rouble hyperinflates it is the only currency which can provide stability and for a few great luxury. Although to be honest, luxury in the former Soviet Union is little more than the ability to buy imported consumer durables, jump queues and salt a nest egg away in Switzerland.

For the majority of Ukrainians and Russians life is bleak. No one is starving, there are no hungry children but shopping is an endless round of disappointment. Everyone carries what's called a *na vsyakiy sluchay* which roughly translates as 'to be on the safe side'. The 'perhaps' bag is there because perhaps this is the day they have oranges or butter but then perhaps you have no money to pay for such things. The minimum pension is 2,500 roubles a month, this month butter is 800 roubles a kilo.

The indicators of poverty and frugality are everywhere. We ask directions of a well-dressed Muscovite who is carrying three red roses. It is his wife's birthday. He earns 20,000 roubles a month and the roses have cost 600 roubles. On the train from Kostroma to St Petersburg a plainclothes monk bearing a disturbing resemblance to Rasputin waves a small silver cross in benediction and hands over a card soliciting money to help rebuild his church. Flushed with generosity I take out a thousand-rouble note. 'Niet,' he says, 'you have dollars?' When he establishes we have only a few dollars left to get us through the trip he shuts the compartment door in disgust.

It is almost impossible for a visitor to understand the levels at which the economy works. I am told that in Moscow the average monthly salary is the equivalent of $25. In Kostroma the Intourist hotel wanted $50 a night for a room. The friends who were arranging our accommodation thought this was outrageous and we wound up in a perfectly adequate hotel – adequate that is if you don't consider a lavatory seat, bog paper, soap or hot water essential – for £1 a night.

We take a leading academic out for dinner in Moscow to a Mafia-run Georgian restaurant where dinner costs a preposterous $100. 'Have you been here before?' I ask. She tells me that neither she nor her husband has eaten out for four years.

The best meals we have on the trip are not in restaurants at all and certainly not in the Intourist hotels. On our first night in Kiev we ask our fixer where we should eat. We are staying in the Hotel Russ where the rather grand marble entrance hall is so sparsely lit you feel they might be expecting an imminent air-raid. Light bulbs are in short supply and they tend to disappear, says Liame Vitvitfka. The food is a bit dim too, she says. No, there are not many places worth eating in but maybe we should try the larger hotel up the hill which has two restaurants.

We traipse through the snow, sliding on ice, and wind up at a gaunt monolithic block which looks a bit like the Palace of People's Achievement. It too is darkened and unwelcoming. We cross acres of marble entrance hall and find the Dnieper restaurant. We sit there for fifteen minutes but nothing much happens. Five gangsters have contrived to get singing drunk at a corner table but how they got the drink is difficult to see.

After a bit we get up and go down a floor to the Polski restaurant which according to Liame specializes in Polish food. It has the same printed menus as the Dnieper and the same dishes are off. As it's Kiev we order chicken Kiev in the hope that at last we'll find out what it should taste like. The chicken is tougher than old bootskis, dry and butterless. It's served with limp chips and grated raw carrot. The bill with two cans of imported beer would keep a Ukrainian couple for a month.

On the Sunday things look up. We go on a visit to a State farm an hour south-west of Kiev. Our guide is Edinburgh livestock expert Peter Maitland who has been working at the farm as a consultant for the British Food Consortium, a body which partly through altruism and partly with commercial benefit in mind is trying to drag the old Soviet food and farming economy into the western ethos of market forces and efficiency.

As we arrive a horse and cart laden with hay catches our eye. There are tractors but not spare parts; there is machinery but quite often no petrol. The dilapidation of farms and factories is striking. We stay for lunch, a memorable occasion of herring, pickled vegetables, potato stews and good bread. Fiodor Lisovoy, director of the farm, like most Ukrainians is overwhelmingly generous and hospitable. Somebody produces a ghetto-blaster and sweeps the canteen manageress off her feet.

Energetic dancing breaks out in all directions. Outside a red orange of sun sinks below the fields of ice and the *gorilka*, the local spirit made from wheat, warms the veins.

I am amazed at the meals ordinary people conjure up in their flats. We have brought tea and chocolates but are not in a position to repay this scale of kindness. There always seems to be a guitar, singing, endless toasts to the better days to come, a spirit of optimism. 'We survived the Czars,' a university lecturer says. 'We survived the genocide of Stalin, so we shall survive this.'

It is the anomalies, the inconsistencies which stick in the memory. We visit a huge factory processing a hundred tons of meat a day. It produces six million tins of canned meat a year but then it turns out that few can afford to buy it. We go to a Moscow market selling pineapples, asparagus, plums, sucking pigs, ducks and hams. Our guide tells us that ordinary Moscow folk couldn't possibly afford to shop there. But it's full of people buying food. Who are they? Our guide shrugs: 'Just people,' she says. 'Maybe they have ways of getting money.'

But the money is fairy-tale currency. In Kiev, because the government has failed to negotiate a deal with the Americans, an economic adviser from Duke University can phone his folks in North Carolina for eight cents a minute – in Moscow an Intourist call to London costs $12 a minute. ICI ten years ago began pumping what they call 'competitive inputs, high quality agronomy and expert marketing capability' into Ukraine. With chemicals they doubled the wheat yield of the Kolkhoz they worked with but the relations have soured. They are owed millions of dollars and see no hope of getting it back. Corruption compounds a legacy of seventy years which stifled initiative, competition, enterprise and all the commercial imperatives which westerners are now trying to clip on to a clapped-out and inflexible economy.

In a soup kitchen in Moscow I meet an eighty-two-year-old engineer who in the bad old days worked for the most evil man in the Soviet Union, Beria. He comes once a day to be fed by a French charity. 'We last had soup kitchens in Moscow in 1921,' he says and you can tell that for him and millions like him perestroika has brought bewilderment and misery. For seventy years prices were stable; now the soaring price of food dominates every conversation. Food is there for the few in abundance but for the mass of people the 'perhaps bag' rules.

'You are so lucky to live where you do,' says a Kiev vet who recently spent three months in Britain. 'No queues for food, everything you want just there for the taking.' I asked him if he'd seen the youngsters sleeping rough in London, the cardboard boxes, the beggars in the Underground.

The ironies abound. While the west has at last realized the ecologically high price of agrichemicals, farmers in Ukraine and Russia are desperate to embrace all the technology they can lay their hands on. They cannot see that what the market economy has to offer in social misery may be in its way as corrupting as the doctrines of Stalin's commissars.

But try and explain that to a Russian with an empty perhaps bag.

42. My Three Childhoods

I really did have three quite separate childhoods. I grew up in a suburb of London called New Malden. I spent my summers in the Isle of Skye and had happy holidays in the cathedral town of Canterbury. Both my parents came from country stock. My mother's family were crofters in Leurbost, a straggling township on the shores of Loch Leurbost in Lewis. My father's roots were in Kent where the family had fruit fields and a brick works in Sturrey on the outskirts of Canterbury. You could say that as a family we lived off the land; had lived off the land would be more accurate. The food we ate was an eclectic mix of remembered recipes, far more fresh produce than most people eat today, bolstered by food from cans and packets and the ubiquitous sugar bowl.

As a family we got through pounds of sugar. On sunny days I would sit on the back doorstep with a plate of sugar sandwiches. White bread of course and highly refined white sugar. I was carefree but not caries-free. Now the interior of my mouth looks like the megalithic landscape of Callernish in my mother's native isle. All that's left are a few residual stumps, a shaky testimony to the destructive power of plaque and calculus.

Like most other people of my generation I received no formal training in the logic of sound nutrition. I cannot recall feeling that there was anything unnatural or untoward in the things I was given to eat and drink. Sugar? Nothing wrong with that. We sprinkled sugar over our cornflakes. We kept a biscuit barrel and a sweet tin on the sideboard. In summer raspberries and strawberries were covered with sugar. More sugar disappeared into the weekly bake: rock buns, Dundee cake, jam sponges, shortbread and treacle tart. Once a week my mother made coconut ice with condensed milk which was so sweet you could feel it eroding your teeth. No mould ever settled on my mother's homemade jam; the sugar content was so high bacteria didn't stand a chance.

Our store cupboard contained enough cans to withstand a lengthy siege – John West's middle cut salmon, Heinz baked beans, marrowfat peas dyed so generously that they were more blue than green, mandarin oranges and Bartlett pears in their viscous syrup, corned beef, oxtail soup, pilchards in tomato sauce, sardines in oil.

And yet by the standards of the time we ate very well. In our small suburban garden in Surrey my father had planted apple trees and a thicket of raspberry canes. He and my mother grew runner beans, spinach, beetroots, carrots and parsley. There were lettuces, radishes and tomatoes. When the war came we patriotically dug up the lawn and grew potatoes as well. In the long weekend between the end of the Great War and the outbreak of the Second World War we were exhorted to shop patriotically. Although I knew from geography lessons that tea came from India and Ceylon, wheat from Canada and lamb from New Zealand I had no idea of what was involved in its production. The Mercator map on the school wall seemed to be largely red and I knew that much of what we ate came from the Empire where the native peoples toiled eagerly with permanent smiles to produce the raw materials on which our wealth was founded.

In 1926, the year after I was born, the Empire Marketing Board was set up to promote Home and Empire produce. Slogans to buy British abounded. On our Shredded Wheat box there was a drawing of the factory where it was made in the garden city of Welwyn. 'Britons make it – it makes Britons'. Had I been attentive I would have noticed that the Swedish crispbread on which we spread our Velveeta cheese had been naturalized: 'How splendid! Ryvita is now British Made'. We no doubt had a flagon of Empire Burgundy in our sideboard and South African sherry to put in the trifle. Food packaging was draped with Union Jacks and engravings of Britannia ruling the waves. Ministry of Agriculture posters appealed to my mother and all the other mums to rally round in the grim days of the 1930s and help put Britain back on its feet: 'Housewives! Ask for National Mark when you shop! Food from home farms and orchards'. I never saw my mother asking if things were British but she was a great interrogator of shopkeepers. She would have had a thin time in the modern supermarket where the staff seem to know sadly little about the food which surrounds them. In the greengrocer's my mother would point to a box of limp lettuces and say: 'Are you sure these are fresh?' 'Came in this morning,' the man would lie, 'cut last night.'

In the butcher's she would look suspiciously at a bit of topside. 'That's not going to be tough, is it?' 'No, mum, that'll cook up lovely.' Why my mother asked these questions I could never fathom. When I had grown up and she was still at it – asking fishmongers if the hake was fresh when it was patently frozen – I asked her why she bothered. 'I like to know,' she said. I think I must have inherited her desire to know. I have certainly been imprinted with her taste for simple traditional food. She was a dab hand at cooking Lancashire hot pot, Irish stew, toad in the hole, bread and butter pudding. We looked forward, my brother and I, to her roast chicken before antibiotics made it possible to have chicken every day of the week and seldom enjoy it.

Liver and bacon, cottage pie, fishcakes, sausage and mash, silverside of beef with dumplings were the things she did well. Frugal is not the word I would use to describe our diet but frugality in the best sense of the word defined her housekeeping. Every summer my mother took my brother and me home to Skye; it was the second haven of my childhood. Born in the hill station of Murree in what is now Pakistan my mother and her siblings were brought up in Portree at first by her mother and then by her daunting aunt Maggie known in the village as

'Ma' Thompson. Ma was a noted Gaelic singer and a frequent guest in her house in Park Road was Hugh Roberton, founder of the Glasgow Orpheus Choir, who came as much for her cooking as her voice.

Ma was a widow with a son called Willie and a permanent lodger from Stornoway, Duncan Macaskill. On almost every night in summer Duncan and his cronies after a few drams in the Pier Hotel went out fishing. In those days Portree Bay was full of fish – haddock, saithe, flatfish, whatever took the hook. There was always fish in Ma's sink. We had it bread-crumbed and fried for tea almost every night. Herrings were plentiful too, you could buy thirteen of them threaded on wire for 6d. Every day began with porridge followed by Ayr-shire bacon and eggs. Morning rolls came fresh from the baker at the bottom of the brae. Ma bustled back and forth between the coal range in the living room and the paraffin stove in the kitchen, her hands covered with flour which she bought by the stone.

Ma was proud of her baking skills; bannocks, oatcakes, pancakes and scones appeared as if off a conveyor belt. The heavy black iron kettle was never off the boil; a steady stream of the great and good came and went. Friends arriving from Staffin or Kilmuir would bring eggs, butter and crowdie from their crofts. In his memoirs the Revd Murdo Ewen Macdonald, Professor of Practical Theology at Glasgow University, recalled the impression she made when he came in the 1930s to be Minister in Portree. 'Greatly loved by the Skye people,' wrote Murdo Ewen, 'she had the unchallenged reputation of being the best baker on the island.' He remembers the night when he was dragged somewhat unwillingly to the Drill Hall for an evening of Celtic music. 'Halfway through a woman with a harp was playing a soulful threnody. The audience was visibly shocked when Ma's stentorian whisper was heard: "and I use no cream of tartar!"'

It was on the big social occasions of the year that Aunt Maggie came into her own. On the day in July when the agricultural show was held in the nearby park the front room of her council house acted as an overflow tea tent. The house rang with Gaelic voices, the teapot was filled and refilled, the cups rattled and nobody went away hungry. My aunt had that effortless confidence and style so often found in women of the Hebrides. Title or celebrity meant little to her; she judged friends not on their pretensions but on their behaviour. In August on the day of the Skye Games Dame Flora Macleod of Dunvegan would call and Seton Gordon the naturalist and Sorley Maclean the poet. She was proud of the food she offered. 'Made with my own two hands,' she would say, 'Aren't you glad you know me.'

The Hebridean diet of my childhood – potatoes, oatmeal, fish and milk – has been seen by some nutritionists as wholesome in its way as the diet of the Hunza tribesmen locked in their Shangri-La between the Karakorams and the Hindu Kush. Perversely there were inexhaustible supplies of cockles and mussels which the islanders never ate; mackerel too were considered only fit for bait. Nobody I knew as a child would have recognized chanterelles or cepes if they saw them and they certainly wouldn't want to have eaten such things. Even so most of the food we ate was fresh; junk food didn't exist on the scale it does now. It is tempting to argue that the way youngsters ate sixty years ago in the islands gave them a healthier start than they get in this age of highly processed food.

Professor Macdonald tells how after his release from a prisoner-of-war camp in 1945 he went to stay with A. B. Wallace, the brilliant plastic surgeon who was putting him together again. Dr Wallace asked him to a lecture he was giving on muscle grafting so that his students could see at first hand what the problems were. When the class was over Wallace said, 'Murdo Ewen, you have excellent teeth, would you tell my students what your diet was when you were growing up in the Isle of Harris?'

'Certainly. Fish on Monday, Tuesday, Wednesday, Thursday, Friday and Saturday, broth and meat on Sunday.' There was no need to say more. Now and again we had salmon caught in a trammel net laid illicitly at night at the mouth of a river, but there was so much white fish to be had that salmon wasn't considered a luxury. Poaching for the pot had no stigma attached to it at all; food was there to be taken.

My third childhood was centred on my paternal grandparents' Victorian terraced house on the outskirts of Canterbury. As in Skye the living room was dominated by a black coal-fired range with an oven at the side. On winter afternoons we toasted crumpets on the end of long brass forks and put potatoes in their jackets to bake in the embers of the grate. Before the bombs blew much of it away, Canterbury had a butter market where country people sold their produce. The house was lit by gas, milk came from a big brass churn in the back of a horse-drawn float and every morning the baker sent a lad who announced his presence with a handbell. Balanced on his head was a deep tray covered with a baize cloth filled with warm white rolls which cost a ha'penny. When the grandparents died they left the house to their spinster daughter Dolly who regarded the fields and the streams as part of her domain. We picked watercress from a crystal clear stream in Thannington and walked every day down country lanes which hadn't changed much in a hundred years.

Most days we would walk up to the chalk pit owned by Dolly's cousins. Close by were fields of golden wheat punctuated with scarlet poppies. An old lady kept hens which wandered freely on the chalky, flinty soil foraging for worms and groundsel. Dolly would pop into the henhouses and pick warm new-laid eggs and pay the henwife later. Then we might set off looking for field mushrooms, coming closer and closer to the hop gardens and the orchards of plums and apples.

For these foraging expeditions my aunt armed me with a walking stick whose hooked handle was ideal for pulling down a branch laden with fruit. 'Scrumping' was not to be confused with stealing which was taking things from people who could ill afford to lose them. The farmer who owned the orchards was known to Dolly and no doubt would have given her a box of fruit whenever she wanted it but scrumping was more fun; it had a sense of adventure.

Dolly made the best steak and kidney puddings I had ever tasted. 'Nobody makes a pudding like Dolly,' she would say, mashing the potatoes with butter and milk while keeping an eye on the spring greens. We had rabbit stew with belly of pork, smoked haddock with poached egg. We went on jaunts to Whitstable where we ate brown shrimps and to Sarre to pick cherries. I lived well on my Kentish holidays and we never lacked for surprises. A neighbour would drop off a punnet of strawberries and a couple of pounds of runner beans from his allotment; the post might bring a tin of clotted cream from Devon.

In my three childhoods I recall none of the fear of eating which seems to cast a dark shadow over today's food chain. If there were food scares they never reached Malden or Skye or Kent. I never wondered why processed foods were so highly coloured nor did I question the received message that all food was nourishing, honest and wholesome. My mother bought Hovis with its added wheatgerm because she believed that there was, as the ads put it, 'strength in every slice'. Now and again she bought a jar of Horlick's malted milk to guard against dying from starvation in the darkness of the night. But as a family we were not obsessed with food. Most of what we ate was fresh and freshly cooked; that is still the way I like it to be.

Index

Index

Chernobyl 63, 89
cherries 98, 99, 334
Chevaliers de l'Olivier 12
Chewton Glen Hotel 168
Chewton, Viscount 106, 109
chicken 78
cholesterol 31, 95, 102, 121, 166, 199, 333, 384
Chorleywood process 8
Christopher, Peter 16–18
CIBA–GEIGY 153–4
cider 337
Cipriani Hotel 378
Clark, Lady of Tillypronie 102
Clift Hotel 376
Cliveden House 168, 273
Clyde Valley 108
cockles 350–1, 353
Codex Alimentarius Commission 151
Coffee–mate 76
Coleridge, Nicholas 167
comfrey 183
Committee on Medical Aspects of Food Policy (COMA) 158, 206
Common Agricultural Policy (CAP) 220
Compassion in World Farming (CIWF) 184
Compleat Herbal 22
Connemara 318
Conning, Dr David 164–5
Consumers' Association 89
Contemporary Authors 1
Cook, Elizabeth 87
Cook, Richard 87
Copenhagen 128
coracles 352
Cork 30, 304
Cornwall 97–9
Coronary Prevention Group 331
Costa, Margaret 261, 313
Cotherstone cheese 225
Covent Garden 35
Crawford, Professor Michael 158
Crayton, Lodge and Knight 46

Crieff 32
crubeens 304, 306
Cuba 85
Culpepper, Dr Nicholas 22
Cumberland hams 286
Cumbria 285–8
Cumming, Fergus and Shona 137
Currie, Edwina 183
Cyprus 256–8

Daily Telegraph 144, 185
Dairy Crest 81, 105, 225
Danish Dairy Board 79
Darjeeling 116
Darnaway 268
David, Elizabeth 234, 250, 271, 389
Davidson, Alan 83, 249–52
Davidson, Jane 249
Davies, Maurice 156
DDT 165, 174
Death Valley 375
deer's pudding 391
Denmark 80
Department of Health 182, 184
Dewsbury 298
Dictionary of Changes 230
Dinnet 137
Dionysios, Abbot 258
dock pudding 23
Dods, Meg 108, 135, 390
Dolan, Paul 308–12
Dorchester Hotel 240–8
Dow Chemical Company 161
Downey, Joan and Leon 109
drisheen 305
Dumas, Alexandre 16
Dumfriesshire 62
Dunbar, Keith 137
Duncan, Carol 79, 80, 81
Duncan, Peter 79
Dunn Clinical Nutrition Centre 331
Durrell, Lawrence 11

Earl Grey tea 118
East Anglia 26

Index

tomato 132, 146
Tomorrow's World 2
Trading Standards officers 51
trans fatty acids 159
Transnational Institute 176
tripe 265, 298
Troisgros brothers 12, 167, 305
Troston 91
trout 136
truffles 16–18, 373
Tunis 250
turkey 67–9

UHT (ultra heat treated) 210
United Nations 3
United States of America 43, 220
US Department of Agriculture 165, 338
US Food and Drug Administration 199
Utusan Konsumer 173

Vaillapol, Nitza 85
La Vallée des Baux 12
Van den Berghs 158
Vatersay 84
vegan 368
vegetables 36
vegetarian 366, 391
Vegetarian Economy and Green Agriculture (VEGA) 369
Vegetarian Nutritional Research Centre 366
Vegetarian Society 366
Venice 378
venison 64, 124–6, 134, 356
Vergé, Roger 12
Viili 80

Waitrose 132
Walker, Caroline 331–3
Walker, David 58
walnuts 42–3

Walton, Izaak 301
War on Want 2
Ward, Sarah 301–3
watercress 22–3, 410
Webber, John 273
Webbs Poultry and Meat Group 78
Wells–by–the–Sea 254
West Highland Survey 8
West of Scotland Agricultural College 108
Whealy, Diane and Kent 146
whisky 390
White, Florence 234
Whitstable 411
Whitwell, John 74
Wick 82
Wight, Isle of 25
Wilson, David 18
Wiltons 326, 330
Wiltshire 30
Windermere char 287
Wisdom of the Fields 291
Woman's Journal 292
Woman's Own 234, 235
Women's Farming Union 179
Woodall, Richard 285
Woodger, John 135
Worcester 361, 363
Worcestershire sauce 361
Wordsworth, William 287
World Bank 3, 201
World Food Conference 3, 201
World Food Day 201
World in Action 2
World Medicine 3

Yarmouth bloater 352
Yellowlees, Dr Walter 170–2
Yorkshire 297–300
Yorkshire parkin 297
Yorkshire pudding 297

Zeldin, Theodore 251

422